D1173750

# Mat Irvine's
# AUTO MODELLING
# MASTERCLASS

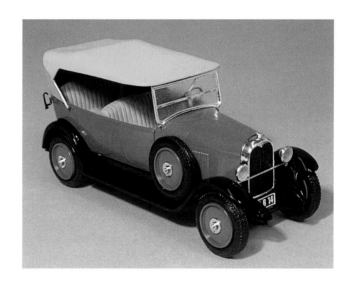

# Mat Irvine's
# AUTO MODELLING
# MASTERCLASS

Windrow & Greene

**To two fellow car modellers, from the UK and US, where it all started—Richard Coney and Dean Milano.**

This edition published in Great Britain by
Windrow & Greene Ltd,
5 Gerrard Street,
London W1V 7LJ.

© Mat Irvine 1998

Produced for Windrow & Greene
by The Shadetree Press, East Sussex.

A CIP catalogue record for this book is available from the British Library.

ISBN 1-85915-089-6

**ACKNOWLEDGMENTS**
Over the years, I have been fortunate to get to know most of the model companies and many of the people associated with them, as well as a number of individual modellers. This book could not have been written without their assistance. They are:

Accurate Miniatures—Bill Bosworth, Wes Moore
Airfix/Humbrol—Trevor Snowdon, Mike Phillips, Janet Cavill
Amaquest—Peter Chiang, Ian Irving
Nick Argento at Glencoe Models
Brian Bignell
Jean-Christophe 'J.C.' Carbonel
Tom Carter at Hobby Heaven
Richard Coney at Rabbit Models
Dennis Doty at *Model Car Journal*
John Embleton
EMA Ltd—Jim O'Reilley, Elsie O'Reilley, Norman Hands
The Ertl Company—Tom Walsh, Tom Haverland, Mary Kulper, Bridget Shine, Jeff Forret, JoAnn Kramer
Ertl (Europe) Ltd—Rob Mann, Sharon Mortimer, Bob Staff, Bill Giacci
Hannants Ltd—David Hannant, Nigel Hannant
Tony James at Comet Miniatures
Mike Jennings at Jennings Stores

Bob Johnson
KTPR—Kelli Taplin, Rea Taplin
Lindberg—Mike Perkins, Larry Perkins
Dean Milano
The Model Shop, Harrow—Arthur Cross, Alan Bedford, Simon Hoare
John O'Neill
Polar Lights—Lisa Greco, Suzi Klimek
Nik Picken at Marshall Auto Supplies
Thomas Randrup at Binney & Smith (Revell)
Revell-Monogram Inc—Ed Sexton, Bill Lastovich, Sandi Moritz
Richard Kohnstam/RIKO International—Glyn Pearson, Colin Spinner, Peter Binger
Scale Auto Parts (UK)—Derek Brown, Roy Brown
Roger Sill at SATCO
Bill Stringer
The Testor Corporation—James Mossop, Ernie Pettit, Nancy Rainwater, Dave Carlock
Toyway Ltd—Richard Morriss, John Trusell
Al Trendel at Minicraft
Tom West
Andy Yanchus

My apologies to anyone overlooked.

# CONTENTS

# INTRODUCTION

As mankind approached the twentieth century, the century of greatest technological change, there were the beginnings of two of the most significant inventions the world has seen—the motor car and the aeroplane. And this significance probably goes much of the way to explain the popularity of these two subjects in particular when it comes to model making.

If one carried out a survey of the types of models built by modellers world-wide, it would be a fairly safe bet that top of the list would be aircraft. There has always been a fascination with this mode of transport, possibly because, until recently, it tended to be beyond the grasp of most people.

The first commercial plastic kits were aircraft (the Frog Penguins), while boys of all ages—and hopefully some girls as well—have spent hours constructing devices that may or may not look like aircraft, using balsa wood and tissue paper, in the hope, however vague, that they may at least get off of the ground for a short time.

I would venture that the next most popular modelling subject in our hypothetical survey would be the automobile, surpassing both railways and ships. This should not be too surprising, as it is probably the single technological icon of the twentieth century that has changed the way in which we

all live, (more, I would suggest, than even the computer chip, which has been with us for less than half as long as the automobile). Given that the advent of the modern approach to the motor car in the latter half of this century (especially in the USA) coincided with the advent of the modern commercial construction kit, the popularity of car modelling world-wide should not come as a great surprise.

Model making itself has gone through many upheavals in recent decades. While the growing hobby became established—in the modern sense—during the fifties and sixties, the seventies saw a downturn with the oil crisis. With the basic raw materials of the kit manufacturers being by-products of the petroleum industry, price rises in the latter saw a disproportionate hike in costs for the model companies as the price of plastic soared. Many of the original companies either disappeared or were swallowed up by larger toy manufacturers. This state of affairs lasted for several years, but by the eighties, although not all companies had survived—or had survived in their original form—the situation had at least stabilized.

As we approach the millennium, the would-be model maker now has lots of other distractions to contend with, many of which are centred—like so much else in life—on

**The author with a small selection of his car models, which were on display at the 1998 International Model Show, held at Olympia in London.**

**One of the kits that started it all—a Frog Penguin. These appeared in the thirties and were the first injection moulded kits, but the material was cellulose acetate, not polystyrene.**

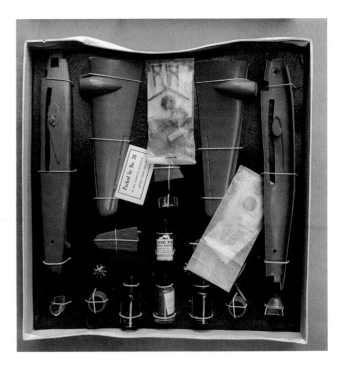

the computer. The professional model maker has to work alongside CAD-CAM and CGI (computer generated images), while the amateur must cope with the exponential growth in all aspects of video, ever sophisticated computer games and the Internet. But despite gloom-mongers who have predicted the downfall of the industry, model making has survived. Three-dimensional miniatures are still required alongside CGI for the latest blockbusting movie, while the model manufacturers have joined in the computer revolution with CD-ROMS, 'how-to' videos and Internet sites. Although greatly changed from the fifties, model making still exists thanks to those people who wish to exercise their skills in a tactile sense, instead of staring for hours at an unblinking screen.

Over the years, car modelling has seen a split in the types of model built and, consequently, in the type of modeller who builds them. This situation does not apply to other subjects, as the delineation is by scale, which will have some bearing on the reader for whom this book is intended.

When the modern model kit industry came into existence (which can be taken as around 1950—see Chapter 1 for more details), the material employed was the newly introduced polystyrene. The scales chosen for these new models were also at the 'larger' (comparatively) end of the range: 1:32 scale, where one unit of measurement on the model corresponds to 32 units on the full-size object; and 1:25 or 1:24 scales, which for convenience are usually thought of as one. And this is really where the commercial plastic car kit industry has remained. Other scales have been introduced, but they have been larger still, such as 1:20, 1:16, 1:12 and 1:8.

But there has also been a steady growth of another aspect of car modelling. A development that parallels the construction kit industry is the ready-built model car market—generally known as 'die-casts'—epitomized by Dinky and Corgi Toys in the UK, and Tootsitoys in the US. Although these ready-built model cars were introduced orig-

**Probably the two most popular modelling subjects— automobiles and aerospace—are rarely combined. However, this box art for Hubley's 1961 Rolls-Royce Silver Cloud does feature a rocket launch (a Jupiter C, which put America's first satellite—Explorer 1—into orbit) in the background.**

inally as toys, they now have a world-wide following (arguably far larger than the kit market) of collectors, and have led to the formation of a modelling offshoot that does have some bearing on this book.

Although initially die-casts were made 'to fit the box' (as indeed were many early kits from Revell, Monogram, Lindberg, Aurora and the like), eventually they became precision scale models rather than just toys, the industry settling on the somewhat arbitrary scale of 1:43. This is also O-gauge for model railways in the UK (but not everywhere else). In fact, 1:43 scale delights in the wonderfully bastardized mix of metric and imperial measurements, as its ratio is 4mm to the foot!

Many ready-built 1:43 scale cars are available, but as with other subject matter, there will never be enough variations for some collectors. Consequently, a dedicated industry has grown up to satisfy the demand for specialized model kits. However, whereas the 1:32 and larger scale kits are pre-

**Any colour as long as it's any colour... The wide range of colours that model cars can exhibit is demonstrated by this small selection from the author's collection. The only common factor is that they are all in 1:24/5 scale, as in addition to styrene kits, there are white metal and resin examples.**

The majority of 'plastic' model cars are in the 1:32 and 1:24/5 scales, but this photograph illustrates the range of scales used by Monogram. Their 1:43 Corvette Sting Ray, from the short-lived Ultimates Series, sits on the hood of the 1:8 Sting Ray.

Car modelling encompasses the sublime to... Here, Tamiya's Texaco/K-Mart Lola sizes up the LeSabretooth 5000 (from the movie *The Flintstones*). They do have some things in common, however: both are to 1:20 scale, and both have four wheels.

dominantly injection moulded in styrene, the 1:43 scale kits are normally produced in either resin or white metal.

While in the main a model kit is a model kit is a model kit (whatever the subject or scale), with cars there seems to be a definite gulf between modellers who build 1:32 scale and above, and those who build 1:43. In part, this has come about because of a variation in modelling techniques, but initially the actual subject matter probably played a major role in separating the two areas of enthusiasm. The plastic side tended to be dominated by American machinery, while the 1:43 scale featured everything but American machinery. In recent years, however, this situation has changed, with just as many non-US cars being produced in plastic, and a wide range of American cars being available in 1:43. Despite this, the separation between builders and collectors of both types has remained. (Incidentally, if you are wondering what happened with car models in the 1:33 to 1:42 scales, forget it; there aren't any—at least not enough to worry about.)

Of course, this doesn't mean that there are no modellers who build both styles of kit; there are, just as there are modellers who build kits of cars and aircraft, or cars and ships (or, in the author's case, cars and spaceships!). In general, however, and perhaps strangely, the two sets of car modelling scales do not mix.

Because the two types of car modelling are so different, this book is basically aimed at the modeller of the larger scales, which by default means injection moulded kits. But of course there are exceptions; it would be far too easy if the distinction was absolute!

Some mainstream companies have experimented with producing injection moulded plastic kits in 1:43 scale. AMT and Monogram have produced them in the past, while Heller still make a range of cars in 1:43 scale. (To add to the confusion, Renwal made a series of plastic car kits that were smaller still, in 1:48 scale.)

In addition, white metal and resin are the main materials used in the thriving market for car accessories in the larger

scales, predominantly 1:25. Resin is also widely used for specialist conversion kits and complete kits in these scales, and there are even manufacturers of white metal kits in 1:32 and 1:24 scales. Consequently, all materials receive a mention in these pages, and while the book is aimed at modellers of the larger scales, it would be nice to think that enthusiasts for the smaller scales will also find something of interest.

Of course, model making is model making, and many techniques and tips can be borrowed from one subject and applied to another. Basic assembly, painting, applying decals and building dioramas are all carried out in much the same way, whatever the subject, so hopefully other model makers will find the contents of use.

This book concentrates on the automobile first and foremost; it does not delve into trucks, commercial vehicles (with the exception of pickups and vans) or motor cycles, as they all deserve their own volumes. However, many techniques used on a car model will apply equally to a truck or bike. For example, the technique for creating authentic worn tread on a tyre is much the same whether the tyre is fitted to a car, truck or a bike—or an aircraft, for that matter.

The purpose of this book is to explain the techniques for building model cars, to provide useful tips and methods of detailing, and to show how to build dioramas and use the many accessories that are available. However, it cannot contain everything by any means; you would need several volumes for each chapter for that. What I have attempted to do is give a flavour of most aspects of the hobby, including its history, how a kit is made, and that odd aspect that infiltrates all areas of modelling—collecting. The contents are based on my own experience within the hobby over...well, let's say a good number of years, and include some of the tips I have picked up or have developed myself. I hope that these will provide you with the inspiration to find out more and experiment. There are many other publications that could also help, and these are listed in the References section.

A word is also necessary about language. The commercial kit industry was established in Great Britain and the

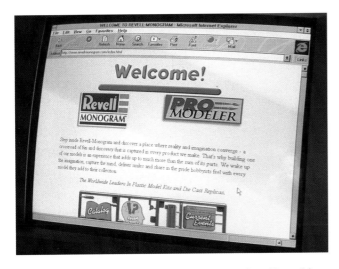

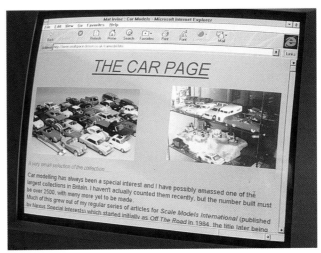

Despite rumours to the contrary, the Internet has, if anything, increased interest in model making. Many model companies—mainstream and garage—have their own web sites, among them Revell-Monogram.

The constantly widening World-Wide Web has led to many individuals setting up their own web sites. This is the Car Page from the author's site: URL www.smallspace.demon.co.uk.

United States of America, so the dominant language was English. Original instruction sheets were written entirely in English—when they actually told you to 'Cement part 1 to part 2'! However, the actual English used could be British English, where painting instructions referred to 'colour', or American English, when it was 'color'. This notion of 'two Nations separated by a common language' is perhaps most prevalent when dealing with the car. Indeed, until relatively recently, this was still commonly referred to as the 'automobile' in the US.

But the traffic can be two-way, and although the term 'panel truck' is still applied to old-style American commercial vans, in general 'van' is used for, well, a van. However, in an attempt to keep things fair, in the UK there is a tendency for trucks to be referred to as 'trucks' these days, the term 'lorry' appearing to be reserved for vehicles built prior to 1960.

Thus, the terminology used in this book will fit the car

in question. American cars are sedans or coupes, not saloons or coupés, and they do not have bonnets, boots or windscreens; they have hoods, trunks and windshields.

For many years, I have written a regular column on car modelling for the general modelling magazine *Scale Models International* (Nexus Specialist Publications). This started as 'Off The Road' in 1985, and is currently called 'Freewheelin'. Some of the material is this book is based on items that have already appeared in that column, and also in my previous book, *The Car Modeller's Handbook* (Nexus Books). After all, there is only a limited number of ways of describing how to sand a vinyl tyre... However, this book has been brought up to date with new material and new examples, and it has the advantage of being illustrated with colour photographs throughout.

However, with the fluid nature of the industry, many of the kits mentioned in the text, or included in the photographs, may no longer be obtainable. This does not make

The main split between car modellers is dictated by scale. Above 1:32 are mostly construction kits, the majority being in styrene and 1:24/5 scales (although there is a steadily growing range of ready-builts in 1:18 scale). For collectors of 1:43 scale cars, there is a mix of ready-built die-cast models and specialist kits in resin and white metal. This division is illustrated by two replicas of the transport used by a certain British secret agent, from Corgi (left) and Airfix (right).

their inclusion any less relevant, as the techniques used for a particular kit will be applicable to many others. Moreover, many such kits may be reissued in the not too distant future, either in one of the 'collectable' ranges, or as a modified reissue (see Chapter 12). There are also dealers who can supply old kits, and details of these can be found in the References section.

Please note that as a general hobby, car modelling is reasonably safe. It doesn't, for example, warrant comparison with deep sea diving or even bungy jumping. As with most activities, however, some aspects require a careful approach. One is the use of sharp objects (knives, scalpels and scissors), while another is the use of potentially dangerous substances, such as glues, fillers and paints. Always read any relevant instructions and take adequate precautions when

you are working with these items, especially when there are other people around.

All the techniques included in this book must be experimented with at the modeller's own risk, and no responsibility can be assumed by the author or publisher if something goes wrong!

Finally, many of the kits included in this book have reached the lofty heights of collectability. However, I cannot supply any of them, and can only refer you to the References section, where dealers around the world are listed.

Happy modelling!

*Mat Irvine*
*Hanslope*
*March 1998*

A wide range of types of car model—all 1:24/5—from the author's collection. They were part of a display for the 1997 International Model Show at Olympia, London. Included on the top shelf are two versions of the IMC Little Red Wagon (left back), three versions of the Revell Futura (far right) and the Testor custom Divco delivery van in resin (centre). The last is a 'slammer' kit without engine or interior. The lower shelf features a display of Revell's Ed Roth cars and after-market decals on a Monogram NASCAR T-Bird for the Hooters chain of restaurants.

A small example of the range of early kits from US manufacturers, some of whom still survive: Jo-Han (top left), AMT (centre right), Monogram (centre far right) and Revell (centre). Others do not, including Strombecker (top right) and Berkeley (lower right). Playcraft (centre left) was a name used by the original manufacturers of Corgi Toys for AMT kits sold in the UK. Two were produced, one being this 1959 Buick.

# Chapter One

# HOW IT ALL BEGAN — AND A MATTER OF SCALE

In reality, the commercial model kit industry has been around for most of the twentieth century. Model kits of sorts were available during the early decades, although mostly using wood as their main modelling material. Model kit names such as Hawk began to appear in the twenties on balsa-wood aircraft, although it was as early as November 1936 that Frog introduced the first all-plastic scale model construction kits, the type of model that started the whole plastic kit phenomenon. These were the famous Frog Penguins, the first kit most likely being a Gloster Gladiator.

At this early date, however, the moulding material for these kits was not the now common polystyrene, but an early plastic: cellulose acetate. The latter had the advantage that it could be injection moulded to produce finished (or nearly finished) parts ready for assembly. Unfortunately, cellulose acetate also had the great disadvantage that it was not particularly stable and could warp very easily — not the most desirable attribute for a scale model kit.

In fact, it wasn't until after World War 2 that a new, far more stable, plastic was introduced. This was called polystyrene, although initially it didn't perform a complete takeover, and acetate continued to find favour for some time.

Polystyrene had actually been invented far earlier in the century, but because of its stability, it was deemed to be a 'military secret' and was not made generally available. However, with the end of World War 2, and with industry in general raring to rebuild the world — particularly American industry — polystyrene was released to a wider audience. There is still some uncertainty concerning the first model manufacturer to use this 'new-fangled' plastic, although Renwal, Lindberg and Hawk are all contenders for the title with various aircraft kits. As far as model cars are concerned, we can be slightly more certain, as there are only two companies in the frame.

In 1948, one West Gallogy Sr began work on a mould for a model 1948 Ford, based (perhaps slightly oddly) on an existing Danish friction toy of the 1946 version. This was to take advantage of the growing demand for automobiles after World War 2, Gallogy's idea being to produce a scale toy version for the kids of what dad would be buying full size. This would be issued in conjunction with the full-size car, and be used by the manufacturers — especially Ford — to promote their new cars. Thus, the idea of promotional models, or 'promos', came about. The moulding material would be aluminium as, due to the scrapping of large numbers of war planes, it was readily available and cheap. Consequently, the name of Gallogy's company was chosen to reflect these factors: they used aluminium and they were model toys — Aluminum Model Toys was born. But this only lasted for a year, for by 1949, the new plastic (polystyrene) came to the attention of the company, and first the body, then all the parts were made in plastic. As a result, the name Aluminum

A range of 'promos' — promotional models — from across the years. Included are examples from X-EL, the branch of Jo-Han that deals with promos, among them the famous Chrysler Turbine Car (lower left). This is the rare white racing version, although the more usual bronze version was made as well. To the same scale as normal kits — 1:25 — promos can often provide models not found in kit form. For example, the Brookfield Chrysler Neon (top centre) is not available as a kit, nor is the Buick Regal (top right). The Ford Galaxie (centre) has an early promo feature — friction drive.

*Above* **Some of the earliest car kits in Gowland & Gowland (top left) and Revell (lower left) boxes. The Gowland box is generic and shows four models (the kit is actually the 1911 Rolls-Royce at lower left), but the Revell box is specific to that kit, the 1909 Stanley Steamer. Note that the Revell box carries a very small Gowland logo in the lower right-hand corner. Also shown is an example of the most recent incarnation of the Highway Pioneers, from the British company Dapol (right), together with an assembled version of that series' Oldsmobile. All carry the name 'Highway Pioneers'.**

*Below* **One of the kits that started it all: the 1:16 scale 1910 Maxwell. This originated with Gowland & Gowland as more or less a toy. Revell converted it into a proper kit and, although it still retained many of its toy-like features, items such as the convertible top had to be built from bent wire and a paper cut-out. In many ways, it was a precursor of the multi-material kits that would appear decades later.**

Model Toys became somewhat inappropriate, so the company became simply the AMT Corporation.

The scale chosen by AMT for their promos was 1:25, which has become *the* model car scale, especially for American machinery. Interestingly, 1:25 is really a metric scale which, in a country that is the last bastion of imperial measurements (or as most Americans still say 'English measurements'), may seem odd. However, the reason is that the clay models for the full-size cars were always created in 1:10 scale (which, of course, is metric), but as this would be somewhat large for a toy, some scaling down had to be done. Arguably, it could have been halved to 1:20, but instead a 2½ reduction was made, and the 1:25 scale was born.

These first promos were supplied ready-assembled, although they had to be built up from a number of parts (usually 15-20) in the factory. Then, around 1958, someone (history does not record exactly who) thought of supplying the parts unassembled in a box, perhaps with a few extra customizing parts, and the modern 1:25 scale customizing car kit was born. But these were not the first car kits made in injection moulded plastic.

Around the time West Gallogy was working on his '48 Ford, two Britishers (Jack Gowland and his son Kelvin) were making their way to California. The pair had varied backgrounds: Jack had been an art teacher, then an inventor of toys for his original company, Allied Toys Industries in the UK; Kelvin had also studied art, but had spent the war in the Royal Navy and had been on board a destroyer that had put into Boston for repairs. He reported to his father that this was a far better place to start a new business than war-torn England, hence the move.

Jack Gowland, the inventor and instigator of most of the

ideas, was still keen on the toy market, and some of the pair's products were purely that—toys, animals and the like, many with cable operated action features. However, one proposal that Jack came up with was for a car, a Maxwell, which was probably based on the famous car used by his namesake, Jack Benny, in a variety of movies (although this connection was never formally acknowledged). The plans for this were drawn up at 3/4in to the foot, which was a common imperial engineering scale. However, 3/4in to the foot is also 1:16 scale, and this had a significant bearing on what was to follow.

The Gowlands were first and foremost designers, and they really needed someone who knew the American market, so around this time they began looking for a salesman for their products. They found one in Lew Glaser, a Los Angeles toy salesman who ran a company called Precision Specialities.

It was also decided that the Gowland & Gowland company should branch out with a range of smaller toy cars. As some could utilize the existing 1:16 scale plans, they decided simply to half these—to 1:32 scale—and to sell them as the Highway Pioneers. Initially, these were produced only as ready-assembled toys, but they did not sell that well, and in 1951 the Gowlands decided to change direction and sell them in their unassembled form, as kits. The 1:32 scale car kit had arrived.

Meanwhile, the company that Gowland & Gowland had employed to do their selling—Precision Specialities—had decided to go into the kit manufacturing business as well. A change of name was also decided upon (presumably, Precision Specialities was a bit of a mouthful), so another name was sought, something far more snappy. Eventually, tradition has it that Lew Glaser's wife came up with the new name—Revell.

Initially, although only the distributor of the Gowland kits, Revell received equal credit on boxes and instruction sheets. Eventually, Gowland & Gowland sold their kit line to Revell in 1958. Consequently, Highway Pioneers were also available with the Revell logo alone, and in more recent years these early kits have also appeared under the Revell AG (Germany), Minicraft and Dapol names, which has to make the range some of the most travelled tooling ever.

Although Gowland & Gowland arguably came up with the first true plastic car construction kit in 1951 (AMT's were still ready-assembled promos at that time), initially they did not use styrene. The first Highway Pioneers were still moulded in cellulose acetate, mainly because it was more readily available than styrene and could be obtained in a wide range of bright colours. (The idea of actually painting a model kit was still some way off.) Eventually, however, the move was made to styrene, although early examples in acetate—invariably warped beyond recovery—still turn up from time to time.

Gowland & Gowland may not have the honour of introducing the first plastic car construction kit (especially in 1:32) completely to themselves. At around the same time, the Hudson company in America had also decided to move away from wood and metal car kits to plastic kits in 1:32 scale. Later, through the acquisition of Hudson's tooling by

*Above* **The first Airfix kit was this Ferguson tractor. It came complete with 'rubber' tyres and a tube of cement.**

*Above* **One of Airfix's first '1:32' scale cars—the 1904 Darracq—in early (right) and late (left) packaging. In reality, however, its scale is not 1:32 (as stated on the later box), but almost 1:25.**

*Below* **Although not made specifically to represent the vehicle used in the famous British movie *Genevieve*, the packaging for the Airfix 1904 Darracq always mentioned the film. Here, however, the kit has actually been built as that vehicle, one of the earliest Star Cars.**

Although most kits covered in this book are of 1:32 scale and upwards, the range of scales used for car models is actually far wider, as shown by this selection of Ferrari F40s. From left to right, they are 1:87 Monogram Exacts (ready-built), 1:43 Herpa (ready-built), 1:32 Monogram (kit), 1:24 Tamiya (kit), 1:16 Italeri (kit) and 1:12 Fujimi (kit). The Pocher 1:8 scale version could also be added!

Revell, in the late fifties, many of these were mixed in with the Gowland & Gowland originals, and were also released as Highway Pioneers.

Another famous name must also be brought into the picture at this stage, but on the other side of the Atlantic, in Great Britain. That name is Airfix.

As a company, Airfix had started in business in 1939, manufacturing rubber-based items, among them dolls and mattresses! The company's founder, Nicholas Kove, liked the idea of names ending in 'x' (they sounded modern and technical), plus he wanted to be the first listing in any company directory, hence Airfix. (Maybe the fact that the dolls and mattresses were filled with air was an additional reason.) However, World War 2 brought a demise in the supply of raw latex from the Far East, so the company turned to other polymers, and produced all types of household goods in plastic, initially using cellulose acetate. Combs were one of the company's main products.

By 1948, Airfix wanted to move away from household items (although this division continued for many years), and Kove looked at other areas of investment. In a move that, in many ways, mirrors the formation of AMT, Airfix were asked to produce a model of the then-new Ferguson tractor—the first 'small' tractor designed for the 'small' farmer. Although planned as ready-assembled models only, they were manufactured, like AMT's promos, in parts, so it was a relatively simple move to pack the parts only and sell them as construction kits. Consequently, the 1:20 scale Ferguson Tractor became the first Airfix kit.

Not counting the tractor (although it is a vehicle), Airfix actually produced their first car kit in 1955. This time, it was to 1:32 scale, which has to have been influenced by the Highway Pioneers. That first car kit was a 1911 Rolls Royce, which was quickly followed by the 1930 Bentley, 1905 Rolls-Royce, 1910 Model T Ford and 1904 Darracq. The last was actually not to 1:32 scale—it was closer to 1:25—

Some all-plastic kits continue to be issued in very small scales, among them the old ITC Precision Miniatures range, now produced by Glencoe Models. Included are a Ferrari Type 166 (left) and Jaguar XK120. Their diminutive size (about 1:72) can be gauged from AMT's largest car kit, the 1:12 scale 1937 Cord.

and although never sold as such, the fact that a similar vehicle starred in the British film *Genevieve* was always mentioned on the packaging. (This probably makes it the first Star Car to be produced as a model kit.)

The fact that the first Airfix 1:32 car kit was a 1911 Rolls-Royce is interesting, as Merit produced their first 1:32 scale car kits at around the same time, and the 1911 Rolls-Royce was among them. Gowland & Gowland's Highway Pioneers also included a 1911 Rolls-Royce, and although the kits are not absolutely identical, they are similar, and it is highly likely that the first one influenced the others. This also applied to Premier in the US, which also produced a range of Highway Pioneer-type 1:32 scale kits.

The year 1955 was significant for the model industry, as it was then that the American company Jo-Han also issued their first promos for Pontiac and Chrysler. However, Jo-Han had earlier beginnings, in 1947, and—rather like Airfix—were initially a general moulding company producing anything in plastic that could be put through an injection moulding machine. At first called Ideal Models, the company began making semi-scale flying aircraft models and scale models of kitchen equipment! (Maybe this was considered the girls' answer to the boys' promotional model cars.)

When the car promos began to appear in 1955, Ideal Models were approached by the non-connected Ideal Toy Company (which sold kits as ITC) with the suggestion that a change of name might be a good idea, as the existing ones could be mistaken for each other. This was taken on board, and the company's founder, John Haenle, simply took his own name and shortened it: JOhn HAeNle.

Monogram also began producing car kits around the mid-fifties, although they started in 1946 with hybrid wood and plastic kits. Their first all-plastic kit was also their first car kit and, consequently, it received the number P1. This was the Midget Racer, issued in 1954. However, it was neither 1:32 nor 1:24/25 scale; it didn't actually have a scale listed, although it is around 1:16.

Many of the earliest kits retained cellulose acetate as a moulding material, even after polystyrene had been introduced. To distinguish between them, because they required different cements, Revell printed an 'S' on the boxes of styrene models and an 'A' on those of acetate versions (now rarely seen).

Other companies, no longer in production, were also part of the beginnings of the model car kit market at this time. Among them were Berkeley, an American company that mainly produced wood and cast metal car kits, although they also made a model of the General Motors Firebird show car with a vacuum formed body.

Best Products started with a series of Indianapolis racing cars in the early 1950s, the tooling for which was later acquired by Aurora. The latter also acquired the car kits of the Advance Molding Company, which gave them the beginnings of their range of 1:32 sports cars, to which they added more of their own in both 1:32 and 1:25 scales. (Although this acquisition of other companies' tooling—and names in many cases—may seem like a relatively recent phenomenon, in fact it began as soon as the industry itself was born.)

Since the inception of the modern plastic car kit, many other companies have appeared, and many have disap-

The first all-plastic kit from Monogram was a car—the Midget Racer in approximately 1:16 scale (exact scale was not the most important factor with these early kits!). Dating originally from 1954, the kit was simple in construction, but still had an engine and driver. However, the tyres were styrene, as vinyl had still to be introduced. The kit was reissued in Revell-Monogram's SSP (Selected Subjects Program) in 1995, and this is an example of that reissue.

peared. The sixties saw the growth of Revell, Monogram, Jo-Han and AMT in the US, plus the establishment of MPC (Model Products Corp.) to form the 'Big Five' of model car kit production. Companies where car kits were not such a major interest included Aurora, Lindberg, Hawk, Hubley, ITC, Palmer, Premier, Pyro, Renwal and Strombecker. Other smaller companies dealt almost entirely with cars, such as Eldon and IMC (Industro-Motive Corp.).

The dichotomy of scales was also established, as AMT, Jo-Han, MPC and Revell dominated 1:25 scale, the scale that was introduced with the promos. Monogram, however, settled on 1:24 (an imperial scale), as presumably they were not tied in to any promotional deals, and they stayed with it until the nineties.

Of the other companies, IMC also started at around this time and used 1:25, as did Aurora, while Lindberg (although they made precious few large-scale cars) chose 1:24. This slight differentiation of scales has continued to this day, for when Testors and Accurate Miniatures launched their own ranges of car kits, they went to 1:24 scale.

However, it's fair to say that, with the exception of the absolute perfectionist, most modellers will build 1:24 and 1:25 scale car kits side by side without a worry. (This has led to the scales being termed '1:24/5' for convenience.) If you do compare kits of the same car in the two scales, there should be a perceptible difference. In theory, a 1:24 scale car will be around 1/24in longer than a 1:25 scale version of the same vehicle, but this assumes that the companies have scaled the subjects accurately in the first place.

The scale problem was exacerbated when other manufacturers around the world entered the model car field. When existing and new companies in Europe and Japan started manufacturing car kits—invariably of anything and everything except American subjects—they all chose 1:24 scale. Given that virtually all countries of the world use a metric system for measurement, it might seem odd that those companies chose an imperial scale, while the US remember, which prefers imperial measurements, mostly used a modified metric scale...but that is all part of what makes the hobby so interesting!

*Above* **Having moved from pure promos to construction kits proper around 1958, AMT continued with their 'annual' series, although the number of full-size cars modelled has been reduced considerably in recent years. During the early years, the company employed generic boxes for most 'annual' releases, as typified by the years 1961-63 on the left. However, from 1964 onwards (right), the cars had their own box art.**

*Below* **Some very early car kits followed the trend set by early aircraft kits and were built to fit a standard box, rather than to a specific scale. This was the case with the ITC Ford Fairlane *Dragnet* Police Car, which came in the somewhat ungainly scale of 1:19!**

*Left* **An early example of one of Revell's larger-scale car kits, the 1956 Cadillac Brougham. This featured a multi-piece body (unlike the almost universal use of one-piece bodies these days). It was based on a General Motors show car, and although not quite as detailed as we would expect today, still looks spectacular. It came with two figures, which was quite common for kits of its era. The kit was reissued in the Selected Subjects Program in 1996.**

# Chapter Two

# HOW A PLASTIC KIT IS MADE

I was once told by the product manager of a well-known model company that all they had to produce to survive as a company were kits of Spitfires and Me-109s; everything else was a bonus. This dates the quote somewhat, for these days it would be F-15s, Harriers or the latest Sukhoi, but the principle remains much the same.

The decision to produce a model kit cannot be taken lightly—especially these days with tooling and production costs soaring ever higher—and many, if not all, companies will spend time on market research to discover just what is wanted and, more importantly, what will sell in sufficient quantities to recover the costs (let alone make a profit...).

In the early days of the car model market, it was a completely open field, although it is interesting to note that a great percentage of the subject matter was from the earliest period of motoring: the veteran and vintage years. Then, with AMT especially discovering (or, in reality, inventing) the idea of 'annual' kits to reflect each year's products of the full-size car industry, a new aspect was created, which continues to this day. Now, however, it is much reduced from its heyday in the sixties, with really only Corvettes, Mustangs, Camaros and Firebirds finding favour in the 'annual' ranges.

But the motor industry world-wide has certainly produced enough full-size machinery this century to keep any model manufacturer happy. The only problem lies in deciding just what to make.

Some subjects do seem to appear in cycles, and whereas, for example, the general 'annual' kit only survives with a few sedan and sporty options, the pickup—long out of the 'annual' ranges—returned with a vengeance in the late eighties and, to date, has not disappeared.

By the sixties, no one wanted a fifties car. Now, however, many companies are issuing completely new models of fifties favourites, even though they may have had older kits of the same subjects in their lists for years.

Muscle cars of the seventies came and went, but were replaced in many instances by the earlier versions of muscle cars from the sixties. Sports cars—including many classic British examples—made their appearance alongside the only type you could guarantee that would be made, the Corvette, while the entry of the Japanese companies ensured that we would never run short of not only their home-grown products, but also a number of those from Europe, especially Ferrari, BMW, Mercedes, Porsche and even Jaguar.

The wild custom show cars of the sixties may have gone (although they reappear from time to time in the collectors' ranges), but instead there is a fascination with concept cars from the manufacturers themselves—cars that we may be

Currently, 'annual' kits tend to be restricted to sports and sporty cars, such as the Corvette. Here, the new-shape 1997 'Vette from Revell-Monogram can be compared with the 1953 original, an AMT kit, in the background.

*Left* **Almost inevitably, some marques will be the subjects of one form of kit or another, Porsche being one. These are two recent examples from Tamiya: the GT-1 (rear) and Boxster (front).**

*Facing page, top* **Although no one wanted fifties cars in the sixties, some did creep through, including AMT's 1955 Chevy Nomad (right). However, it took until the nineties before anyone—Revell-Monogram—made the 1956 equivalent (left).**

*Above* **Currently, one of the most expensive car construction kits is Tamiya's 1:12 scale Caterham (ex-Lotus) Super Seven.**

*Below* **Tamiya's 1:24 scale Minis were tooled by the simple expedient of dismantling a full-size example!**

driving in the future. However, this is really no more than a continuation of Revell's idea when they produced the Lincoln Futura and Pontiac Club de Mer from the mid-fifties.

So the choice is wide open for the model companies, although one factor has changed since the inception of the hobby. In the beginning, at least nine out of every ten kits sold were bought as toys: they would be built, broken and, to keep the cycle going, thrown away. But they paid for the tenth kit, which was built as intended and, you never know, may even have survived to this day. (And it is probably true that many modellers who started in this casual manner returned to the hobby after many years, and now want to find all the kits that they built in their youth—and didn't keep. This is probably what started the collectors' market...)

These days, I would suggest that the ratio is significantly different. In the sixties, the cost of kits was spread over a relatively narrow band. Admittedly, in the UK, the Airfix range ran from the pre-decimal two shillings (10p), which was just about pocket money for most of us, to a massive ten shillings and six pence (52.5p), which was birthday and Christmas present time. At the time of writing (late 1997), the cheapest kits are at the £3 mark, most at £10 or more, and the most expensive...well, the Tamiya 1:12 scale Caterham Super Seven is around £250, and there are others that are more expensive still. Add to this the specialized kits in resin and white metal from the massive garage industry, which can start retailing at £50, and it is clear that there is a different balance. Consequently, the ratio has to be moving away from those that are bought as 'expendable' toys towards those that will be built as properly constructed scale replicas.

New modellers are still vital, however; without them, there won't be a hobby, and these days there are far more distractions than there were in the sixties. Then, the choice was probably only whether one went out and played football (Association or American...) or stayed in with the latest kit. Now, attention must be divided between a multitude of distractions, both outside and inside the home. Chief among these is the lure of the television, video and computer.

Model car manufacturers do have one slight advantage over, say, model ship manufacturers. It is somewhat impractical to dismantle a battleship to ensure that all the details are absolutely correct, but this kind of task is regularly performed by companies such as Tamiya, who will dismantle a full-size car and make patterns almost directly from the parts. (Anyone who doubts this should take a look at their 1:24 scale Mini; if you've ever spent hours carrying out repairs beneath the car itself, you'll see how close it is!)

Full-size examples of potential model subjects will always be sought out, photographed from every angle and drawn up in detail. For example, when Monogram wanted to produce a kit of the Buick Grand National (recently reissued), they learned that one of their employees drove the real thing, so they borrowed it. In a similar vein, Ertl discovered a pristine 1966 Chevy Nova conveniently cruising the streets of Dyersville, and it became the raw material for the design of one of their kits.

With the decision to manufacture a particular car made, the next stage will be to produce the original master pattern or die model. Even today, with the growing use of CAD-CAM (computer aided design and manufacture) allowing tooling to be produced directly from the computer program, a three-dimensional pattern is made. This is usually to the scale of the patterns for all the original full-size cars—1:10. Moreover, many are still made in that oldest and most traditional of all modelling materials, wood, although resin is used increasingly these days.

Most of the main chore of cutting the steel tool is done by an automatic pantagraph process, although individual details—panel lines, emblems and the like—still tend to be hand cut by a specialist.

High-grade tool steel is used these days, but previously tools were made from beryllium, a gold-coloured metal that began life relatively soft, but which hardened under continual use. (It is because of this use of beryllium that much older tooling no longer exists. The metal was expensive, and when a kit was deemed to have reached the end of its life and

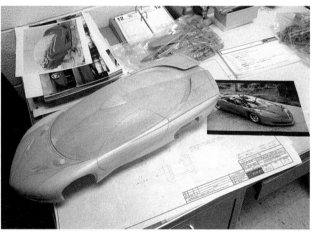

*Above* **Old meets new—the 1:10 scale wooden pattern for the Revell Pontiac Banshee show car.**

*Below* **A newer approach to pattern making, still 1:10 scale, but this time in resin—the pattern for the Lindberg 1953 Ford Victoria.**

*Left* **An injection moulding shop: in this case, Ertl's factory in the late 1980s. Prominent on the machine is the hopper for the styrene beads (centre right).**

*Below left* **The parts as they come out of the injection moulding machine. This is a test shot of AMT's 1950 Cameo pickup. The parts are all on one runner and will be cut up to fit into the box.**

*Bottom left* **The interior of a typical model kit tool. The mould cavities can be clearly seen, as can the channels that connect them.**

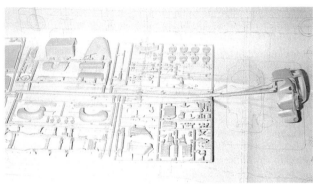

was no longer selling, the beryllium would be reused to make a new kit.)

Older tools also tended to be made as one piece, the cavities being cut directly into the steel. When a section was damaged, or it was decided that a part was to be altered, that area of the tool had to be ground out and an insert fitted. Most modern tooling is made with built-in inserts as standard, so if a section becomes damaged—or more likely the kit needs to be changed to a different version to maximize the use of the tool—the appropriate insert can be removed and a new one slotted into place. Consequently, a stock version of a car can be converted into a show car, and converted back if necessary. This occurred when the stock Monogram 1958 Ford Thunderbird became the customized Macabremobile of Elvira, Mistress of the Dark, reverted to stock form for the Rockin' Rods series, then was converted again for the Macabremobile reissue.

Besides the cavities for the parts, a tool also incorporates channels along which the plastic flows into the cavities; the point where the plastic passes into each cavity is known as the gate. The plastic left in these channels remains with the kit as what is still commonly, although wrongly, called the 'sprue'. In fact, it is the 'runner' (or possibly 'tree'). The sprue does exist in the system, but it's the main inlet of plastic into the whole tool and is part of the material that is recycled back into the system.

Most tooling consists of two halves that fit very tightly together, and which are held together under immense pressure. Where undercuts are unavoidable, movable sections can be incorporated that automatically slide into place for the injection process, then slide back to release the part. This strong steel tooling is necessary for the injection moulding process, since the moulding machine is really no more than a large press that will push liquid plastic into the mould cavities, usually under several hundred tons of pressure.

The polystyrene is heated to a temperature of around 400°F (204°C) and injected at this high pressure—300 tons on average—into the mould cavities. Here, it is cooled

**Two problems than can occur with plastic parts. Flash is caused where the mould halves have not fitted tightly enough together, or because the mould is worn. It can be seen around the engine halves (centre left) and also towards the top. Although irritating, flash is easily cured with a sharp knife. Ejector pin marks often show up, but usually on inner—hidden—surfaces. They can be seen on the back of the grille (bottom) and the panel just above. If they will be concealed on the finished model, they can be ignored. Alternatively, cut them off.**

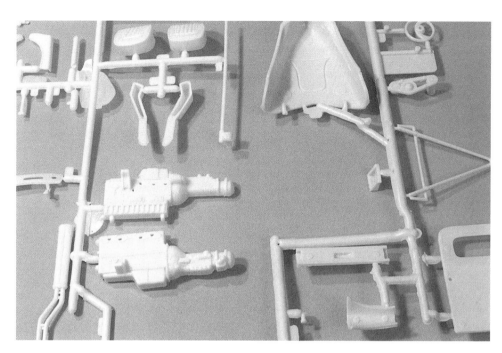

rapidly; the tooling has built-in chambers for this, like a car engine block. The tool is pulled apart and the newly mould-ed plastic parts are ejected by pins. Then the process starts again. This cycling can be extremely fast: modern machines can recycle in 30 seconds. It is not difficult to understand that these tools come under extremes of temperature and pressure throughout their life—and many run on a 24-hour timetable for popular kits. Consequently, they have a limit-ed life, although a properly made tool can go through mil-lions of cycles before it requires major attention. It also means that if a tool has to be stored this must be done cor-rectly, otherwise surfaces rust—the usual problem—and ejector pins can jam and snap off when it is next used. With the increasing reuse of old tools to cater for the collectors' market, correct storage has become even more important.

Even with the immense stresses experienced by the tool-ing during a single cycle, faults with the plastic parts are few and far between. If they are present, they tend to be flash, ejector pin marks, short runs or surface pitting due to rust.

Flash tends to be the most common problem and occurs where the mould hasn't fitted together quite well enough, allowing a thin 'flash' of plastic to flow between the sur-faces. This usually occurs with older tools that have become worn, but it must be said that flash can also be found on some of the most modern kits, perhaps where the pressure to hold the two halves together hasn't been quite high enough. Unfortunately, if it is being caused because of an old worn mould, there is nothing really that can be done about it, apart from totally retooling the section, which is usually prohibit-ed by cost. Fortunately, although irritating, flash is easily cured with a sharp knife.

Older tools can also produce ejector-pin marks. This may be because the pins that push out the moulded plastic have not been adjusted correctly or, frankly, have simply worn and are either proud of the main cavity (where they will leave slight depressions in the parts), or are slightly too short (where they will leave bumps). Ejector pins are usual-ly designed to push on the back of a part or on the runner, so

slight misalignments will not be a problem. On occasion, however, they may leave marks that will be visible in the fin-ished model, in which case, they will need sanding or filling.

Short runs occur where the plastic hasn't reached the end of its cavity. This can be due to the temperature or injec-tion pressure not being high enough, but is most likely to be caused by the mould design and should be picked up during the test-shot stage, when the new tool is being tried out. Short runs are usually cured by adding an extra cavity beyond the main cavity, allowing the plastic to flow com-pletely through the main section.

Surface pitting is only associated with old tooling that has been stored incorrectly, allowing the inner surfaces to rust. Some cleaning up can be done, but there comes a point where the tool cannot be cleaned any more and the decision must be taken either to issue the kit 'as is', or not at all. Although it is irritating and requires some work with wet-or-dry abrasive paper to clean the surfaces, it is rare.

In its raw state, polystyrene is a clear brittle substance, but when used in kits, it is mixed with other materials. Most polystyrene found in model kits is described as 'high-impact', which means that it incorporates a certain amount of rubber, plus an appropriate colour—around 1% by weight. Also, a lubricant may be added to help the flow, especially in old worn tooling. Sometimes, this can remain on the surface of the plastic and must be removed with min-eral spirits or warm soapy water before painting.

Some items in most kits make use of the styrene in its raw state (i.e. clear), for the glass, headlamps and the like. Simply sawing through clear and opaque parts can illustrate the main differences between raw and high-impact poly-styrene. Invariably, the clear will be far more difficult to cut cleanly at the edges, and may craze or even shatter.

Because even this raw material is steadily increasing in price, a certain percentage of the plastic used in any kit is recycled, 15% being the average. Some recycled material can lead to problems. In the very early days, when Airfix produced their first kit (the Ferguson tractor), plastic was in

such short supply after World War 2 that the company used broken down ball-point pen cases as the raw material, giving some kits an interesting—and very colourful—texture! In more recent years, Jo-Han tended to use bulk supplies of some very lurid colours, including turquoise and orange. (These were difficult to change if you wanted a different colour as a finish.) These days, thankfully, most companies settle on either white (R-M and Lindberg) or pale grey (AMT-Ertl), or choose an appropriate colour for the body and leave the chassis grey or black (most of the European and Japanese manufacturers).

Besides the standard opaque and clear parts, most car kits will contain 'chrome' parts to represent the brightwork found on many cars. Even in these days of black plastic trim, most kits still contain their chromed runner, if only for the wheels and the 'glass' for the rear-view mirrors.

Chromium plating on full-size cars is applied by electrolysis, as both the metals (the chrome itself and the underlying steel) are electrically conductive. Plastic, of course, isn't conductive, so another method had to be found. This doesn't even involve chromium, but another metal—aluminium—which is applied by a vacuum process.

The parts to be plated, which will have been cast on their own separate runner, are covered with a lacquer. This gives them the required amount of gloss (so satin or matt plating can be achieved with different types of lacquer). The lacquer is hardened, then the parts are placed in a vacuum chamber. Alongside the parts are blocks of aluminium called 'canes'. The chamber is evacuated of air and the aluminium is heated so that it vaporizes. The gaseous aluminium spreads all over the inside of the chamber, including the plastic runners. Here, it literally sticks in a very thin coating—around 0.01in (0.25mm). The process takes around two hours, although the final plating itself only about two minutes. If the required finish is 'brass' or 'gold', additional lacquers can be sprayed on to the plated parts.

Besides the plastic parts in the average car kit, there is usually a set of 'rubber' tyres. These are rarely genuine rubber, however, being moulded from vinyl instead. This is another form of plastic, but with a PVC (poly vinyl chloride) base. It cannot be glued like normal styrene, but since the tyres are invariably sandwiched between wheel halves, this doesn't matter. Vinyl is used because it has a softer more rubber-like appearance than standard styrene.

However, the use of vinyl for tyres can present a problem in that occasionally (admittedly, very occasionally) the

*Above left* **The appeal of car subjects tends to go in cycles, but they may be decades apart. For example, the zany creations of Ed 'Big Daddy' Roth, which were popular in the sixties, reappeared in the nineties, Revell-Monogram also issuing one of his latest creations, the Beatnik Bandit II. Here, Roth greets visitors to the 1996 Chicago Model Show with the actual car.**

*Left* **The appearance of the box art has a great effect on the appeal of a kit. Sixties-style artwork tended to be bolder than that used in more recent years. These Revell examples—all of Ed Roth cars—were used again when they were reissued as part of the Selected Subjects Program in the nineties.**

The old-style instruction sheets, however, have all but disappeared. In the sixties, customizer George Barris took great delight in his contributions to the instructions for AMT kits, including many hints and tips. One of these was to cut the tips from two spotlamps and glue them together to make bongo drums for the trunk of the 1962 Corvette!

vinyl will react with the styrene and start to melt the wheel. It should be emphasized that this does not happen that often, and if it does occur, it can take many years to have an effect.

This problem actually caused many manufacturers to move away from vinyl to other materials for a time. Some moulded tyres in styrene, so that there would not be any compatibility problems. Others used real rubber, which did not affect the styrene (but it was expensive), or even other polymers, which produced even more difficulties when it came to cementing than vinyl. Currently, however, the vinyl used in kits appears to have been reformulated, and most manufacturers have moved back to this material for tyres.

With all model kits from the mainstream companies, several other items have to go into the product besides the plastic itself. One major item is the box, which will have suitable artwork on the lid. The latter is an important factor in any kit, often determining whether or not it will catch the eye of the casual purchaser. It is also a critical aspect in the collectors' market where, ironically, the original box and box art are deemed to be almost more important than the plastic in the kit itself! Kits have always been issued and reissued, but when Revell-Monogram took the step of reissuing classic kits with original artwork (although not always original-style boxes), under their Selected Subjects Program, followed by Ertl with Buyer's Choice, these became a great hit with both builders and collectors.

Box art has tended to follow certain trends over the years. Car kits that were released in the sixties almost exclusively employed artwork for the main box-top illustration, not photographs. Both AMT and Jo-Han employed generic artwork for most of their 'annual' ranges until the early sixties. These featured a common piece of artwork for the main illustration, the particular kit being identified only by the end-panel or an insert in one corner.

Revell and Monogram tended to go for a good individ-ual painting of the subject as their main box illustration, with perhaps an alternative scheme for the side panels. As customizing was popular at the time, great emphasis was usually put on the various options the kit offered. Stock, custom or competition were the classic '3-in-1' choice, although variations on 'full custom', 'stylized', 'service vehicle' or even 'rally' were often alternatives. These could be illustrated on the sides, or shown as larger inserts to the main picture. Monogram especially made great play of this type of illustration, invariably showing one particular option as a main artwork and others sometimes as photographs.

The instruction sheets also signify the era of a kit and follow the pattern set by the style of box. With the construction kit industry starting jointly in Britain and the United States, where English was the (more or less) common tongue, original instruction sheets from both sides of the Atlantic were in English. Because only one language was involved, it meant that the instructions could actually tell you what to do ('Cement Part 1 to Part 2') and could also be deemed educational, for the parts were actually named. So you knew that the object at the bottom of the engine block was a sump or, if you were looking at an American sheet, an oil pan, and that the engine at the front was attached to the axle at the back by a propshaft, or drive shaft.

With English only being used, hints and tips could also be included, AMT being especially enthusiastic about this aspect. Many customizers of full-size cars were associated with most of the companies from time to time, and AMT utilized these experts more than others. Among them were George Barris—'King of the Kustomizers', Gene Winfield, the Alexander Brothers—Larry and Mike, Bill Cushenbury, Dean Jeffries and, for a time, the late Bud 'The Kat' Anderson. Gene Winfield even ran AMT's own Speed and Custom Division, which built full-size cars, making AMT the only model kit company that built 1:1 scale cars, if only

*Above* **When companies decide on the subject for a model, a connection with the latest blockbusting movie is—usually—a safe bet. Revell-Monogram took this step with *The Lost World—Jurassic Park II*, and in addition to the vehicles, they also produced kits of some of the other stars.**

*Left* **When it comes to kits, humour is not normally high on the agenda. Sometimes, however, it breaks through. Revell made three models connected with the popular *M\*A\*S\*H* TV series, including a scene of The Swamp with a Jeep. To the signpost outside, contemplated here by Hawkeye, they added the name Morton Grove, which is the home of Monogram—now Revell-Monogram—in Illinois.**

for a short time. (AMT's *Man from UNCLE* car and its drag version—the Piranha—were both built full-size by the Speed and Custom Division.)

Revell called on the talents of Ed 'Big Daddy' Roth, a partnership that was revived recently with the issuing of the new Beatnik Bandit II in the nineties. Meanwhile, Monogram had Darryl Starbird and Tom Daniel on board: Starbird for his radical custom road cars, and Daniel for zany show rods. When MPC started in 1964, they too employed George Barris, Dean Jeffries and Budd Anderson.

Most of the time, the consultants were involved when their existing full-size creations were chosen as the subjects of model kits. However, George Barris, Ed Roth and Budd Anderson also wrote columns in early car modelling magazines in the States—*Car Model* especially. Budd Anderson even went on to IMC (Industro-Motive Corp.), writing a series of promotional columns in the magazine.

Tom Daniel took a somewhat different approach and specialized in designing scale models for Monogram, some of which were only built full size later. His most famous creation, the Red Baron, was made in two scales by Monogram—1:24 and 1:12—both powered by miniature renditions of a six-cylinder Mercedes aircraft engine. However, when it came to building the car full-size, Mercedes aircraft engines were in somewhat short supply, so a six-cylinder overhead-cam Pontiac engine was used instead!

AMT especially used their consultants in all stages of a kit's development: from designing the customizing parts to adding additional tips in the instruction sheets. Most, if not all, AMT instructions from the early sixties feature a back page with ideas for swapping parts from one of the latest kits to another. I personally recall the 1962 Corvette—unique at

the time, as it had an opening trunk lid as well as hood—because George Barris had suggested modifying the two spotlamps (included with virtually all of that period's US car kits) by gluing them together, cutting the tips off and making a pair of bongo drums for the trunk! This I did, and I still have them, sitting in the trunk of the 'Vette.

Over the years, however, the internationalizing of everything has led to a diminishing of the information given in instruction sheets. First the British kits went to three languages (English, French and German), while the American kits used English, French and Spanish. Even more recently, a plethora of languages has appeared, reaching the somewhat over indulgent and, to my mind, ludicrous situation of the European issued kits having to be in all the languages of the EC and more. Airfix regularly supply basic instructions in 12 languages, while the current record is held by Revell AG kits at 18—including Russian! This, of course, has led to the actual worded instructions ('Cement Part 1 to Part 2') being discontinued. Instead, guidance is reduced to a series of annotated diagrams with odd multi-lingual captions pointing to specific areas to indicate 'Glue', 'Don't glue' or 'Apply decals'. I don't mean to imply that non-English speaking countries should not be given equal rights when it comes to building model kits, but one does feel occasionally that the whole business has been taken too far. Perhaps this view has led to AMT and Revell-Monogram kits for the US market returning to the (virtually) all-English layout, and although they haven't actually reverted to saying 'Cement Part 1 to Part 2', at least all the parts are named.

(As a footnote to the language business, a very old French friend maintains that he learned his excellent English by studying Airfix instruction sheets!)

# Chapter Three

# WHO DOES WHAT?

Over the years, many companies around the world have specialized in manufacturing model cars. The following gives a brief run-down of the major car kit producers, from their inception, indicating their major output and their current status—assuming they are still around. This list is not intended to include absolutely every kit company that has had some car kits in a catalogue at some point in the past, rather it details the major players, and some of the minor ones where their contribution is—or was—important.

(*Note* Following each name will be the code 'c/p' for 'currently in production', or 'n/p' for 'no longer in production'—sometimes followed by an additional explanation. However, some of the models may still be available under a different name.)

This listing includes only companies that are deemed to be mainstream companies. Relevant garage and after-market accessory companies can be found in the References section. Full details of the companies that are still in operation can also be found there, together with their addresses, phone numbers, e-mail and Internet sites.

## EUROPE

### France

#### HELLER (c/p)

Heller originated many of their own car kits in 1:24, plus they also introduced—and still make—a range in 1:43 scale. In fact, Heller are the only company that still make a range of injection styrene construction kits in the 'die-cast' scale of 1:43 (although both AMT and Monogram have attempted this in the past). In addition, the company have produced some in 1:16 scale and one (a classic Citroën Traction Avant) in 1:8 scale. Invariably known as the 'French Airfix', Heller joined with the British company when Airfix were taken over by Humbrol in 1986. Heller had already been acquired by Humbrol from Jouef in 1979-80, although still operated very much as they had before. Many kits, including

*Above right* **Heller have a reasonable range of car kits, both in 1:24 and 1:43 scales, plus 1:16 and even 1:8. Many of the 1:24 scale range especially are of interesting classic examples, such as this Citroën B-14 Torpedo Phaeton.**

*Right* **Much of the car output from Revell's European subsidiary, Revell AG, tends to centre on modern German machinery from Mercedes, Porsche and BMW. However, there are some older examples, too, such as this exceptional BMW 507 Cabrio.**

some of Airfix's 1:24 scale Japanese originated sports cars, appeared under the Heller name, although not the 1:32 scale range. Since 1996, when Humbrol were sold by their parent company, Borden, to the Irish holding company Alan McGuire and Partners, Heller have been effectively split from the Humbrol-Airfix set-up, although kits continue to be exchanged between the two names.

### Germany

#### MONOGRAM-EUROPE (n/p as such)

A short-lived offshoot of Revell AG to sell Monogram kits into Europe, including a number of car kits.

#### REVELL AG (c/p)

Revell in Germany currently run as a virtually separate organization to Revell-Monogram Inc. in the USA, with their own catalogue and list of kits. Although Revell GB

were formed first and, for a time, were one of the largest kit producers in Europe, because of the Jouef take-over in 1981, the Revell European HQ was established at the German base in (then) West Germany. Currently, although Revell AG come under the auspices of the new owners—The Hallmark Corporation—they still operate independently of the American organization (although some kits are shared). For the car market, Revell-Europe (as they are generally known) tend to specialize in European based machinery—Porsche, Mercedes and BMW—and work with both Italeri in Italy and Dragon in Hong Kong.

## Italy

### ESCI (c/p, but with no cars left in the list)

Esci did not start car kit production until 1978, but then they issued a range of racing and off-road machinery. They are still the only company to produce a Land Rover in LWB form in 1:24/5 scale, plus a number of other off-road/utility vehicles from Jeep, Toyota and Mercedes. The company also made the only 1:24 scale kit of the original rear-wheel-drive Ford Escort, including a version with a completely clear body. Esci were acquired by the Ertl Corporation in 1987 and, for a time, their catalogue and list remained virtually unchanged. Then, having acquired AMT in 1982, Ertl put several AMT originals into the Esci lists (although it is doubtful that all of those included were actually released). Most recently, all the car kits have been removed from the Esci lists, and they continue with military vehicles and figures only.

### ITALERI (c/p)

Italeri, which started as Aliplast, and then went through the somewhat ungainly original version of the current name, Italaerei, began manufacturing car kits in 1980. The initial output concentrated on classic cars of the thirties: cars at the very expensive end of the market, from Rolls-Royce, Cadillac, Chrysler, Bugatti and Mercedes. This is a field that

**Italeri offer a range of kits of both modern and vintage machinery. Some are produced in more than one scale, such as the classic Mercedes 300 convertible, in both 1:24 and 1:16. This is the smaller of the two.**

has never been fully exploited in 1:24/5 scale, Monogram, MPC and Jo-Han being the only other producers, and even then the numbers were small.

Italeri have also moved into more modern machinery in recent years, with various Ferraris and Porsches, an intriguing Volvo 760 saloon and, in 1:16 scale, a magnificent Mercedes 300 Gullwing. They have also collaborated with Revell AG, jointly producing kits for the European market, and with Testors for the US. Even some Heller kits were Italeri for a time. Ironically, the most recent issue of the 'Heller' 1:24 scale Gullwing Mercedes is the Italeri kit, odder still when you consider that Heller originally made one of their own!

### POCHER (c/p)

Pocher specialize in giant 1:8 scale multi-material kits (metal and cloth, besides injection styrene), mostly of classic cars of the thirties. There are a few modern examples, however, such as the Ferrari Testarossa and F-40, while their Volvo tractor unit can probably lay claim to being the largest static model vehicle kit ever produced.

### PROTAR (c/p)

Protar concentrate on racing machinery, both four- and two-wheeled, the former mostly Ferraris. In recent years, they have worked with Revell AG, and some kits have been jointly produced and released. In addition, Protar's existing Alfa Romeo Guilietta kit has been issued under the Revell-Europe label.

## UK

### AIRFIX (c/p)

From the early beginnings with their veteran car series, Airfix continued the 1:32 scale car output, adding a 'modern' (for the sixties, that is) car range, plus more veteran and vintage cars. Figures were added to some of the existing kits, while some retooling was carried out on others. Airfix added a number of MPC car kits to their own range in the sixties (this was long before both companies were taken over by the General Mills conglomerate). The company also tooled their own 1:24 scale kits in the form of the James Bond Aston Martin DB5 and Toyota 2000GT, then added stock versions of the DB6 and Toyota Coupé. These were the only 1:24 scale car kits Airfix ever actually originated. The later series of somewhat simplified sports car kits was acquired from a Japanese source in 1981, while others were Heller and Gunze Sangyo originals.

Airfix made one inroad into large-scale car kits with the 1:12 1930 Bentley 4-Litre. Originally issued motorized, it reappeared later without this option. It remains one of Airfix's best and most comprehensive models.

Airfix were taken over by the General Mills conglomerate in 1982 and, as GM had also bought MPC, the outputs of the two names were combined for some time: Airfix kits were added to the MPC catalogue for the US, and MPC to the Airfix catalogue for Europe. However, General Mills sold on their hobby side in 1986, and Airfix were acquired by Humbrol, back in the UK, where they remain to this

**Airfix make a number of kits in 1:32 scale, but few of their own in 1:24. However, there is the sole example in 1:12, the magnificent Bentley 4.5 litre.**

day—Humbrol themselves were sold by Borden to Alan McGuire and Partners in 1995. The car range has not been increased in the intervening years, although some of the 1:32 series continue to be reissued.

## DAPOL (c/p)
A recently established company that mainly specialize in toys and, through their acquisition of the Airfix ranges, railway rolling stock and trackside accessories. However, they also own the tooling for the original Gowland & Gowland Highway Pioneers, which they have reissued recently.

## FROG (n/p, although the name has recently been acquired by Amaquest)
Although a major manufacturer of aircraft kits, Frog entered the car kit market in the sixties with their own range of motorized 1:16 scale cars and the Dennis Ambulance. Like Airfix, they also reboxed some American originals. Frog, however, dealt with AMT, issuing many kits under a joint name. There were also plans for more AMT reissues, although they never arrived, plus the intriguing notion of a new range of home-grown car kits in 1:25 scale, including a Volvo 1800 and a caravan. Frog ceased operation in 1976, much of the tooling being acquired by the Anglo-Soviet set-up Novo. Some of the car kits were issued in the old Soviet Union, but have not generally appeared in the West.

## MATCHBOX KITS (c/p, under Revell AG)
The trade-name of the Lesney Corporation, Matchbox, has long been associated with cars through its die-cast models. However, the company went into the model kit business in 1974 and launched a range of car models in 1976. These must have been influenced by the Airfix range, as they were to the same scale (1:32) and to the same quality. The subject matter was similar, too, although Matchbox tended to concentrate on historical cars—both road and track, with a smattering of modern racing machinery.

The Lesney Corporation took over the AMT Corporation in 1979, and this situation lasted until 1982 (when AMT were acquired by Ertl). In that time, AMT and

Matchbox kits were combined into one catalogue, and although the British catalogues tended to give equal prominence to both manufacturers' names, in US operations AMT was retained as the prominent name on all the kits. After the split, Matchbox returned to their previous range of models, including the 1:32 scale cars, but in 1991 Lesney leased the 'Matchbox Kits' name to Revell AG in Germany. After this, some of the 1:32 scale Matchbox car kits were included in the Revell lists and, in addition, the Matchbox name appeared on six 1:24/5 scale kits from various sources, including Revell themselves.

## MERIT (n/p)
Merit issued a famous range of racing cars in 1:24 scale, and veteran vehicles in 1:32 scale, although most production had ceased by the late fifties. The 1:32 range was comparable to the Airfix and Highway Pioneer ranges, while the cars in the 1:24 range have never, in the main, been duplicated by anyone else. Two, however—the 1949 Talbot and 1950 Alfa Romeo—plus some of the 1:32 scale kits, have been reissued in recent years by the Czech company, SMER.

## REVELL GB (n/p)
The second of the original subsidiary companies of Revell, following on from Revell Canada in the late fifties, Revell GB originated many kits of their own. These included the 1:25 scale E-Type Jaguar, the range of 1:32 scale British sports cars and the variously scaled Cadet series of European cars. After much reorganization in the eighties, Revell GB ended up as part of Revell AG in Germany. After the whole company were taken over by the Hallmark Corporation, Revell GB ceased to exist.

## SOUTH-EASTERN FINECAST (c/p)
One of the few specialist white metal kit companies that produce 1:24/5 scale cars. (The majority only make 1:43 scale.) SEF took over the original Wills Finecast metal kits and added them to their own line.

**Combining their own kits with the original Wills Finecast and Autokits, South-Eastern Finecast are the UK's major producers of large-scale all-metal car kits. These include the remarkable Morgan three-wheeler.**

## ASIA

### Hong Kong

### DRAGON MODELS/SHANGHAI DRAGON (c/p)

Primarily an aircraft and AFV kit company, Dragon have recently entered the car kit field, currently with a range of BMW vehicles only. The company works in conjunction with Italeri, Hasegawa and (especially with these car kits) Revell AG. They are known as DML in the USA. With Hong Kong's reacquisition by China, Dragon established a base in Shanghai and introduced a separate logo.

### Japan

As with most commercial products, when the Japanese discover the market, they take it by storm. Initially, their model kits were somewhat basic and almost always motorized—the companies had yet to make the distinction between a toy car and scale model car. But then they realized that there was a substantial market crying out for the sort of detail they could provide and, since the seventies, have produced a wealth of finely detailed kits of cars from around the world.

### AOSHIMA (c/p)

Although an old company, Aoshima have only turned to car kits in relatively recent times. They tend to have several ranges running at any one time, with minimal differences, of very specific Japanese machinery. However, among the various Japanese saloons are vehicles of more international interest, particularly a range of off-road vehicles, including the Mitsubishi Pajero, Nissan Terrano, Toyota Hilux and even the Range Rover. Aoshima also make the MGB in 1:24 scale and have links with both Revell AG (the Range Rover and MG were released in Revell boxes in Europe) and SATCO, a small company in the US that make left-hand-drive instrument panels and other necessary mods for the US market. In addition, Aoshima produced the series of *Back to the Future* time-travelling DeLorean sports cars, issued by Halcyon for the European market and AMT for the US.

### DOYUSHA (c/p)

Producer of a varying range of car kits, mainly in 1:24 and 1:12 scales. Most of the 1:24 range are of Japanese cars, although there is a 1973 Ford Capri and 1976 Mustang Mach 1. Doyusha also recently released a new 1:24 scale kit of the James Bond Aston Martin DB5, with figures, that was neither the Airfix nor Aurora kit. Doyusha reissued five out of the six Eldon show cars in 1987.

### FUJIMI (c/p)

Fujimi did not really enter the model car business until the mid-eighties. The company had previously dabbled with a variety of odd scaled, invariably motorized, kits, including the occasional radio controlled set-up, but they did not have a coherent listing. However, by the eighties, they had settled on 1:24 and 1:16 scales and began to produce a range of kits with details that, frankly, have never been surpassed. This was the Enthusiast Model range, where even a disc brake could consist of four parts! The company also introduced many other ranges—arguably too many—where differences could be purely a set of wheels or the inclusion of a boot mounted spoiler. These diverse ranges continued for the intervening years, although most recently, the catalogue has been rationalized to a great extent.

### GUNZE SANGYO (c/p)

Gunze Sangyo is, first and foremost, a chemical company that produces paints for the model market, rather like Humbrol in the UK, and Testors in the US. However, like their contemporaries in the West, the company branched out into the model kit business itself, manufacturing kits, or arranging with companies such as Airfix and Heller to rebox those companies' products for the Japanese market. Although Gunze have never produced that many car kits, in both their 1:32 and 1:24 ranges are specific examples not found anywhere else. In 1:32, there are two American cars—'59 Cadillac and '55 Chevy Nomad—not made by even any US company, while the 1:24 range specializes in European sports cars and saloons. This features the only models in 1:24/5 of the Lotus Elan, Austin-Healey Sprite MkI (the 'frog-eyed' version) and the Messerschmitt Bubble Car! Gunze also issued their own super-detailed car kits—the High Tech range—and here the company were really the first to use the multi-material approach in a big way, providing the kits not only with styrene parts, but also white metal and photo-etched components.

Most classic British sports cars in 1:24 scale come from Gunze Sangyo. Some are produced as high-tech multi-material kits, others in styrene only. Some are available in racing guise, others, like this Triumph TR3A, in stock form.

Specializing originally in aircraft, Hasegawa entered the car scene relatively recently. They have concentrated on sports, race and rally cars, and besides more well-known types, have made some unusual machines, like this Mazda Cosmo Sport.

## HASEGAWA (c/p)

Hasegawa began car kit manufacture fairly recently in their history. Having specialized in aircraft, ships and armour for many years, the company introduced five 1:24 scale American sedans in 1987. For a Japanese company to issue US vehicles as their first car kits was unusual, but what was stranger was the fact that they had generic interiors. It eventually transpired that they had been developed from slot-car racing bodies which, of course, did not have interiors. At the same time, however, Hasegawa introduced their own range of 1:24 scale kits, beginning with the Jaguar XJS. This has led to more sports cars of the world, plus a wide range of track and rally cars of Japanese and European origin.

## IMAI (c/p)

One of the smaller Japanese companies, offering a limited range of car kits. However, they are still the only company to make a 1:24 scale kit of the classic London black cab (also reissued for a time by Revell AG).

## TAMIYA (c/p)

Tamiya is arguably the best-known Japanese kit company,

*Facing page, left* **Increasing their output of cars, Aoshima have moved from purely Japanese products to those with a more international appeal, like the MGB and Range Rover.**

*Facing page, right* **Fujimi's car output has varied considerably, from their exacting Enthusiast Models range to a wide selection of home-grown Japanese machines. Some of these are more intriguing than others, such as this early Datsun sports car—the Fairlady 2000—which bears a passing resemblance to the MGB.**

*Right* **Tamiya's car scales range from 1:12 downwards, although now most are in 1:24. The selection is varied, including stock saloons, sports cars and off-road machinery. There are also many racers, such as this HKS Nissan Skyline.**

and they first went into the model car market with large-scale, highly detailed kits, notably their acclaimed 1:12 scale Formula 1 series. The beginnings of the 1:24 scale range did not appear until 1978, and initially these were motorized. However, as the range grew, the motors began to disappear and the fully detailed kits that we expect began to arrive. The range continues with some that contain engine details, and others that are curbside (no engine—destined forever to sit by the curb...), but motorization has not returned. The 1:24 scale range—called Sports Cars of the World—includes a varied range of machinery from around the globe. The categories are mixed into the one range, so you will find track cars and Group II racers, besides stock saloons, off-roaders and even a Toyota delivery van and a set of figures (the Campus Friends). Some early kits also included a range of motor scooters, which became very useful for dioramas. There are some classic cars in this range, such as the original (external door hinge) Mini, Fiat 500, VW Beetle and the Jaguar MkII. Although the range is dominated by Japanese and European machinery, US vehicles have begun to creep in, among them the Jeep Wrangler and Cherokee, and even the Ford Mustang.

## Korea

### ACADEMY
The best-known name working out of Korea, Academy have issued some car kits, although the majority have been from acquired tooling. The company also worked with Minicraft in the USA, but this official relationship ceased in 1997. Also in 1997, Academy produced their first, and probably sole, 1:20 Formula 1 kit.

## USA

### ACCURATE MINIATURES (c/p)
One of the USA's latest companies to produce newly tooled kits, most of Accurate Miniatures output has been aircraft, although the company have issued classic racers—the Corvette Grand Sport and McLaren Can-Am—to a very exacting standard. They use 1:24 scale for the car kits.

### AMT (c/p)
Formed in 1948 as Aluminum Model Toys to make promotional model cars from aluminium, for many years the AMT Corporation made nothing but 1:25 vehicles, and their products typify the American car kit in that scale. The company introduced the '3-in-1' kit, which offered the modeller a choice of three different ways of building a model.

AMT produced all types of vehicle: 'annuals', customs, show cars, NASCAR racers, dragsters, CART racers, vans, pickups, classics, off-roaders, construction equipment and Star Cars. Mostly, they have used 1:25 scale, although they have also issued cars in 1:32 and 1:16. A sole excursion into 1:12 scale was represented by the 1937 Cord 812. AMT are also one of the few companies to make styrene kits in 1:43 scale. In the sixties, the company had a tie-in with Frog in the UK, with an exchange of kits. For a short time, they also issued some Aoshima originated kits in 1:24 scale.

AMT were acquired by the Lesney Corporation (Matchbox) in 1978 and issued many of the Matchbox 1:32 scale range in AMT packaging. This lasted until 1982, when they were bought by the Ertl Company. Although Ertl continued to use the AMT name alongside MPC (acquired by Ertl in 1986), the latter's kits were gradually absorbed into the AMT line until only the former remained.

AMT's car kits have ranged from customs to racers, and Star Cars to NASCAR. However, they began with 'annuals', and from time to time some of these are reissued, such as the 1965 Lincoln Continental, shown in custom station wagon form.

### AURORA (n/p)
One of the best-known modelling names, Aurora never particularly specialized in cars, but over the years they issued a reasonable range in both 1:32 and 1:25 scales. (Confusingly, most catalogues did not differentiate between the two ranges, there being no indication as to which was which!)

Aurora acquired a series of 1:32 scale sports cars from Advance, together with the oddly scaled (1:30) racers from Best in the early sixties. They also offered some kits in 1:16 scale, both veteran and a series of seventies garage scenes, being one of the few companies to produce anything like complete dioramas as kits.

Monogram acquired all the surviving Aurora tooling in 1977 and have reissued a number of the 1:25 scale cars, including the E-Type Jaguar, Maserati 3500GT, Aston Martin DB4 and Ford GT.

### ELDON (n/p)
A short-lived company that only issued six 1:25 scale custom show cars in the sixties, among them the Pink Panther-mobile. Five of these were reissued by Doyusha in 1987.

### ERTL (c/p, but not as a producer of plastic kits)
Originally the manufacturers of die-cast farm machinery

models (which continue under their name), Ertl also produced a range of plastic kits, mostly trucks and construction equipment. The company acquired AMT in 1982, MPC in 1986 and Esci in 1987. Ertl had introduced a magazine, *The Blueprinter*, in 1975, but purely covering their own truck kits. The publication was relaunched in 1987 to deal with all the products, and several Blueprinter Exclusive kits have been issued.

Most recently, Ertl introduced the Buyer's Choice range of reissues, (following Revell-Monogram's example with the Selected Subjects Program). This comprises classic kits in almost original packaging. Ertl's own name has not been used on kits for some time, and any they did produce have been combined into one of the other ranges. However, the original Ertl logo will appear on any kits reissued in the Buyer's Choice range.

## GOWLAND & GOWLAND (n/p)

The pioneers of the modern model construction kit, the company being started by two Britishers—Jack and Kelvin Gowland—in California in 1947. Their Highway Pioneers models were probably the first all-plastic car kits in 1:32 scale. They may also have been responsible for the creation of Revell, as they employed Lew Glaser and his Precision Specialities company for marketing. Precision Specialities were to become Revell.

## GLENCOE MODELS (c/p)

One of the newest names in kit manufacturing in the USA, Glencoe mostly reissues old kits from companies that are no longer in production, under their own name. Glencoe have access to the ITC moulds and have reissued a few of the small-scale Precision Miniatures cars. At present, none of the larger scales has been reintroduced, but this is likely in the future.

## HAWK (n/p)

One of America's original model kit companies, Hawk's car output was mostly 1:32 scale sports cars, some motorized. The Hawk name and tooling were acquired by Testors in the early seventies, and although many Hawk kits have been reissued under the Testors and Glencoe Models names, they have not included any of the cars.

*Facing page, left* **Accurate Miniatures offer a small range of car kits. However, they are to an extremely high standard. The first pair represent two of the five Corvette Grand Sports, including the metallic blue number 2.**

*Facing page, right* **While Aurora no longer make kits, much of their tooling survives with Revell-Monogram. In addition, Polar Lights are retooling Aurora-style kits. Aurora made a number of sports cars, including the Aston Martin DB4.**

*Right* **Although a short-lived company, IMC (Industro-Motive Corp.) issued a number of special car kits. Some tooling went to Union in Japan, but the rest survived with Testors, and the kits have been reissued by Lindberg. IMC made several factory experimental cars, including the Mustang II.**

**Best known for metal car kits (many of which survive under the Scale Models name), Hubley also made styrene kits in 1:24 scale. Besides the Triumph TR3A and 1961 Rolls-Royce (both reissued by Minicraft), there was the Metropolitan.**

## HUBLEY (n/p)

Most famous for their range of 1:20 scale metal and plastic kits of classic American vehicles, Hubley also issued a range of 1:24 scale car kits, all in styrene. These included the 1961 Rolls Royce Silver Cloud, Austin-Nash Metropolitan and Renault Dauphin. Hubley ceased trading in the late sixties, and most of the metal kit tooling went to Gabriel (n/p), but is currently owned and issued by Scale Models. The plastic kit tooling has been through various owners, but some now resides at Minicraft

## IMC (n/p)

The Industro-Motive Corporation was formed in 1966 and lasted until 1977. Most kits were in 1:25 scale, although there were some NASCAR racers in 1:32 scale. Included in the 1:25 range were highly detailed racing cars such as the Ford GT, GT-40, Ford J-Car and Indianapolis Lotus Ford, together with show cars such as the Ford Cougar II and Mustang II, the VW Beetle and 1948 Ford. There was also a Dodge A100 pickup as both The Little Red Wagon and Touch Tone Terror. Union in Japan issued some IMC kits, including the Ford GT, although that tooling now appears to be missing. Testors acquired IMC in 1977, and—as a result of their original RPM connection with Lindberg—some of

One of the original 'annual' car kit producers, Jo-Han also branched out into the classics. Among these was the excellently detailed 1935 Mercedes Roadster Limousine.

In recent years, Lindberg have established themselves in the car field with an ever growing range, dominated by cars from the sixties. They have created new tooling for well-known racing machinery, such as the Ramchargers Dodge.

the surviving kits, including the Little Red Wagon, have been reissued.

## ITC (n/p)
The Ideal Toy Company had a number of 1:25 car kits in their catalogue, but ceased production in 1962. Glencoe Models have access to the ITC tooling, although no cars (with the exception of some of the smaller Precision Miniatures) have been reissued to date.

## JO-HAN (c/p)
One of the oldest model car companies in the USA, beginning life in 1947 as Ideal Models. The name was changed to Jo-Han in 1955 when their first promotional models appeared. Jo-Han paralleled AMT's development for many years, producing a similar range of cars to a similar quality. The company also made some classic cars, based on Mercedes and Cadillac chassis, plus the only kit of the Chrysler Turbine Car. By the eighties, however, the company had fallen well behind AMT, and the name and tooling were leased to Seville Enterprises. A few kits appeared, while the promos continued under the X-EL name. Although production had slowed to a virtual halt by the mid-nineties—and, in 1996, Testors had started to issue some of the Jo-Han kits under their own name—by 1998, the Jo-Han name had begun to reappear.

## LINDBERG (c/p)
One of the oldest American kit company names, Lindberg began trading as O-Lin in the late forties. They continued as a family owned business until 1989, when they were purchased by the Crafthouse Corporation.

Until very recently, Lindberg were never really known as model car producers, although they have made various ranges of car kits over the years (even a 1:8 scale Model T Ford Hot Rod to rival the Monogram kit) and acquired the Pyro 1:32 scale range. However, they did make two excellent classics: a Mercedes SSK and Bugatti Royale Victoria in 1:24 scale (both issued by Revell AG for a period).

By the nineties, however, Lindberg had begun to introduce a new range of modern cars and trucks in 1:20 scale, then by the mid-nineties, a series of classic reissues from IMC (through the ownership of Crafthouse and Testors by RPM). Most recently, a brand-new series of 1:25 scale car kits has been introduced on the company's own instigation, the range of which continues to grow.

In 1997, RPM sold Crafthouse to the Brynwood Partners III company.

## MINICRAFT (c/p)
Originally a packager of other companies' kits, Minicraft also enjoyed a long-established tie-in with Academy in Korea. However, this direct connection was abandoned in 1997, and Minicraft continues as an independent company. They offer several Gakken originated 1:16 scale kits, some of which they have modified. The company also own some Premier/Hubley tooling and have issued a modified version of the Triumph TR3A.

## MONOGRAM (c/p as Revell-Monogram)
Monogram began in 1946, at first making kits in wood. The company then developed hybrid models in wood and plastic: the Speede Bilt and Super-Kits aircraft models. The first all-plastic kit, the Midget Racer, appeared in 1954. Since then, Monogram have produced car models across the range, including hot rods, dragsters, NASCAR racers, early Fords, sports and high-performance cars, plus an excellent series of classic luxury cars.

The company have also offered the widest selection of all-plastic car kits in 1:8 scale, (the Pocher kits are multi-material). These include the Big T hot rod, the E-Type Jaguar, Corvette Stingray, Camaro and Pontiac Firebird.

For many years, Monogram used 1:24 as its main model car scale, although there have also been cars in 1:12, 1:20 and 1:32 scales. They started to make a series in 1:43 scale—the Ultimates—to take on the specialized resin and white metal kits, but ceased production of the series after only two releases.

Over the years, Monogram have produced a very wide range of car related kits: sedans, sports cars, racers, customs and dragsters. The ultimate dragster, though, has to be their S'Cool Bus.

MPC produced a similar line of kits to AMT: 'annuals', sports cars, NASCARs, dragsters and customs, plus a number of Star Cars. Of the last, the Raiders' Coach, for Paul Revere and the Raiders, was one of the most exotic.

Monogram were acquired by the Mattel company in 1970, but by the mid-seventies the company had regained their independence. In 1986, Monogram were bought by the Odyssey Partnership in New York, which had also bought Revell. Much swapping of catalogue items was done, and Monogram moved all their new domestic car kits—with the exception of NASCAR racers—from 1:24 scale to 1:25. In 1992, Monogram and Revell introduced the Selected Subjects Program of kits in original-style packaging, including many cars.

In 1995, both names were sold to the Hallmark Corporation. In October 1996, both names were combined as Revell-Monogram for all future kits.

Currently, the Revell-Monogram car list features classics from the thirties, forties and fifties, show cars, customs, pickups, funny cars and dragsters.

## MPC (n/p as such)

Formed in 1964 as a rival to AMT, MPC (Model Products Corp.) produced a very similar range of kits. (Surprisingly, although rivals, there was a certain amount of tool sharing between the two companies.)

MPC produced a wide range of kits: 'annuals', NASCAR racers, dragsters, show cars, off-roaders, vans, pickups, customs and Star Cars. They were acquired by General Mills in 1982, along with Airfix, and the two companies shared kits, MPC including many of the Airfix 1:32 scale car kits in their own catalogue. MPC were acquired by Ertl in 1986, joining their original rivals, AMT. Although the MPC name continued to be used for many years, by the mid-nineties it had been all but dropped by Ertl, only to appear on relevant Buyer's Choice reissues.

## PALMER (n/p)

During the sixties and early seventies, Palmer made car kits in 1:32 and 1:24 scale, plus promotional models and slot-car bodies. Some of the 1:32 scale range were also issued by Pyro. Lindberg now own most of the Pyro tooling, plus a few of the larger-scale range direct from Palmer.

## POLAR LIGHTS (c/p)

The plastic construction kit arm of the Playing Mantis company, Polar Lights issue retooled kits from the Aurora catalogue, kits for which the original tooling no longer exists. These include various vehicle-based monster kits, such as the Mummy's Chariot, plus Carl Casper's show dragster, The Undertaker.

## PREMIER (n/p)

Producer of 1:32 and 1:24 scale car kits in the sixties. Some of the 1:32 scale range were issued by Revell as part of their Highway Pioneers range.

## PROMODELER (c/p)

Formed as an offshoot of Monogram in 1995, ProModeler make exacting kits to a high standard. At first, only aircraft were made; now cars have been introduced, among them the 1969 Dodge Charger R/T and the 1948 Ford.

## PYRO (n/p)

Pyro produced a wide range of 1:32, and a few 1:24 scale, car kits in the sixties and mid-seventies (the larger scale including the only 1:24 kit of the Triumph GT6). Life-Like (n/p) took over virtually all of Pyro's catalogue, although this company only lasted until the late seventies. Lindberg currently own most of the Pyro car kit tooling and have reissued much of the 1:32 scale range.

## RENWAL [n/p]

Best-known as the manufacturers of the 'visible' range of anatomical models, Renwal also made a 'visible' V-8 automobile engine and chassis. (The latter had to be the largest automotive associated plastic kit ever.) In addition, Renwal made a series of 1:25 scale Renwal Revivals—updated thirties-style cars, such as Duesenberg, Bugatti and Packard—in 1965, plus some 1:12 scale cars and a range of cars in 1:48 scale. Revell acquired the Renwal tooling in 1976 and have reissued many of the kits, including the 1:12 and 1:48 car ranges, but not the 1:25 Revivals. (Some Renwal tooling has since been sold on to Skilcraft, the educational division of Crafthouse.)

## REVELL (c/p as Revell-Monogram)

Following their beginnings as Precision Specialities and their dealings with Gowland & Gowland, Revell became the largest model kit company in the world, and the best-known, with divisions in Canada, Britain, Japan and (West) Germany, and subsidiaries in many other countries. They were one of the major players in the model car market, offering kits in scales ranging from 1:32 through 1:25 and 1:20 to 1:16. These included a wide variety of vehicles: dragsters, funny cars, show rods, custom cars, stock machinery, a short season of 'annual' cars, sports cars, classics, Star Cars, pickups, vans and off-roaders.

Revell managed to acquire the Renwal tooling in 1976 and, although they have reissued the 1:48 and 1:12 scale car kits, to date, they have never released the 1:25 scale range of Renwal Revivals.

The eighties was a time of turmoil for Revell, as they were sold to the French organization Jouef, which saw the logo 'Ceji' appearing alongside that of Revell for some time. This led to Revell's German division becoming the company's headquarters, and the establishment of Revell GmbH (now Revell AG) as, in effect, a separate company. However, in 1986 Revell had been acquired by the holding company Odyssey Partners in New York, which had already bought Revell's original rivals, Monogram. As a result, the overall headquarters was moved back to the USA, to Monogram's factory in Morton Grove, Illinois. Many kits, including cars, were also swapped between the two names.

In 1992, Revell and Monogram introduced the Selected Subjects Program of kits in original-style packaging, which has included many cars.

Odyssey Partners sold both companies to the Hallmark Corporation in 1995, and in 1996 the two names were combined as Revell-Monogram.

Currently, Revell-Monogram's car list features classics

**Revell have produced many car kits over the years, so trying to typify the company's output with a single picture is difficult. However, the 1932 Ford Speedwagon incorporates both stock and custom features.**

from the thirties, forties and fifties, show cars, customs, pickups, funny cars and dragsters.

## SCALE MODELS (c/p)

JLE Scale Models still produce many of the original Hubley metal and plastic 1;20 scale cars and trucks.

## SMP (n/p)

Although apparently an offshoot of the original AMT company, SMP (Scale Model Products) were a separate business set up in 1956 to provide General Motors' promotional models. The fact that their logo mimicked AMT's white lower-case lettering in a red box, and that AMT's address was included in the instructions, probably added to the confusion (although it is fair to say that there were financial connections between the two companies). SMP remained separate until 1961, when AMT bought the company outright.

## STROMBECKER (n/p)

The trade-name of the Strombeck-Becker Manufacturing Company, one of the earliest US model companies. Strombecker actually ceased all kit production in the early sixties, although they continue to produce Tootsitoys.

Strombecker issued a range of 1:24 scale cars kits, mostly sports car orientated. Glencoe Models have been reissuing many Strombecker kits in the nineties, although to date none of the cars has reappeared.

## TESTORS (c/p)

Testors are the largest model paint producer in the USA (and world-wide, probably rivalled only by Humbrol). Over the years, they have acquired tooling from such companies as Hawk and IMC, while very recently they have begun to use their own name on kits, including cars. The name has also appeared on Fujimi and Italeri kits, Jo-Han reissues and on resin 'slammer' kits from Jimmy Flintstone Productions. Testors also issue a Boyd Coddington range of cars (in styrene) in both 'Quick Build' and 'Full Detail' versions.

**Although a major model paint and accessory manufacturer, Testors have only recently begun to offer kits under their own name. These include resin 'slammer' kits and a series of Boyd Coddington designs, the first being the Aluma Coupe.**

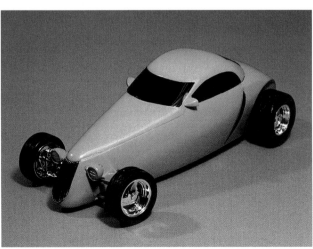

# Chapter Four

# GETTING STARTED

There has to be as many ways to build a model car kit as there are full-size versions, but as a very general rule, the majority of car construction kits will present the same sort of appearance when the box is opened. The colour of the plastic may vary, the number of parts may differ, the way in which they are packed may alter, but overall the majority of kits can be approached in much the same way.

## WHAT YOU GET

By far and away the majority of car models use the one-piece body approach—that is the main body shape is moulded in one piece—which makes assembly and painting quite straightforward. There are exceptions, of course. When Revell started making car kits, they opted for a multi-piece body, whereby the overall body shape was built up from several parts: sides, top of boot (trunk), top of bonnet (hood), roof and so on. This is fine as long as you are confident that you can assemble the whole body 'as one' before you have to start doing any other work, particularly spray painting, otherwise it can make life difficult. Frankly, this really only applies to the very earliest of kits, which may enjoy a resurgence of life in the various 'collectable reissues' ranges. Most, if not all, modern kits employ one-piece bodies, although admittedly items such as front and rear pans may still be separate, while trunk mounted spoilers and fender/door mirrors (the last of which are the bane of car modellers) will certainly be separate.

Of course, multi-piece bodies do still have a place when it comes to classics, where separate fenders (wings) are normal on the full-size car. In this case, the fender assembly is usually a separate part, which may even be supplied in left and right halves. However, as many of these cars tended to have their fenders painted a different colour to the main body, this separation does in fact help, so it's not all bad news. This approach usually means that the rest of the body-work will be multi-piece, too, although it is often possible to semi-assemble the parts to allow a spray finish to be applied 'as one', then disassemble them prior to actual construction.

Car kits used to be made in a variety of colours (some more lurid than others). Now, with the general acceptance that modellers like to paint their models, they are normally supplied in white or light grey plastic. The exceptions tend to be cars in the smaller scales and the snap-together kits. With these, it is assumed (rightly or wrongly) that the builders will be inexperienced, so the bodies are more likely to be pre-coloured.

Besides the major parts, you will also find a clear plastic runner for the window glass and light lenses, and—if the kit is American—transparent red and maybe orange for the stop lamps, turn signals and the like. Emergency vehicles may also feature transparent blue for the flashers. Non-American originated kits tend to supply all these parts in clear, leaving the builder to tint them the appropriate shade with transparent colours.

**A typical layout for the parts of a 1:25 scale car—or, in this case, pickup—kit. The majority of the kit will normally be in a neutral colour of styrene, such as light grey. There will also be chrome plated and clear runners (right), vinyl tyres, decals and possibly a metal axle. The last is a throwback to the kits of the sixties, but is still the strongest method of attaching wheels.**

35

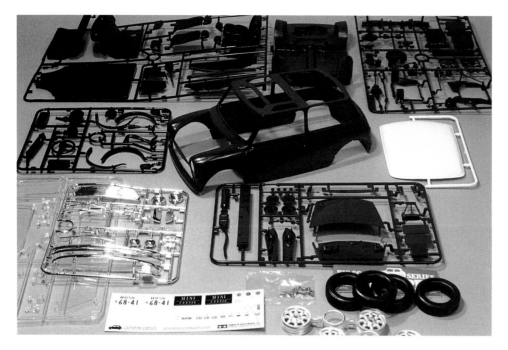

Scales other than 1:24/5 do not differ greatly in their approach. This the 1:12 scale Tamiya Mini, which has the majority of its parts moulded in British Racing Green, with a white roof, chrome and satin plated parts, clear parts, vinyl tyres and decals. There are also small machine screws for some of the construction.

In addition, a chrome plated runner will usually be found in the kit, and possibly a separate satin plated runner for those parts that are not 'bright chrome'. The latter is becoming increasingly common.

Axles—always a weak point with car models—can vary from the old-style metal type found in many American kits to more modern plastic versions, or prototypical stub axles utilizing nylon bushes, into which the wheels must be pushed carefully.

A sheet of water-slide decals will also be found in most kits, although this can range from the complex sheet of the sixties—with flames, stripes, sponsor decals and names for any dragster versions—to the nineties style that simply offers a licence plate. Racing machinery will still tend to have complex decal sheets, while others may have the increasingly common feature of tiny decals for the instrument dials. Another growing trend, especially with Japanese kits, are metalized decals, which are used for badges and logos and represent the full-size versions slightly better than the water-slide type. Recently, many kits have begun to include other materials: for example, nylon mesh to represent the mesh of a grille, which is far closer to scale than a pure plastic moulding. Photo-etched components are also becoming common, as indeed are multi-material kits, such as those produced by Gunze Sangyo, that supply white metal parts as well as styrene. In a few kits, there has even been a return to the US practice of supplying pre-cut self-adhesive carpeting and seat material. This does have the slight disadvantage that it hides any detail in the plastic, but it can be very effective if the kit just has a flat floor. Decals may also be used to represent special seat materials where it would be impractical to paint in every single detail.

## THE WORK BENCH

Where you choose to build a kit is purely a personal decision and, obviously, everyone's situation will be different. There are modellers who travel for most of the time and take a sort of portable work area that can be set up in a hotel room, but most of us will rely on something at home. This can range from a tray arrangement, which can be used on the dining-room table and stored on top of a cupboard when not in use, to a purpose-built modelling bench in a spare room, attic conversion, garage or even—as is quite common these days—an office-type structure in the garden. With more and more people choosing to work at home and, consequently, space having to be made available, perhaps adding a small area for the modelling bench may not be beyond the realms of feasibility. For the model maker, a work bench next to the computer, scanner and printer might become as natural as having an e-mail address!

It is beyond the scope of this book to actually detail the building of such an area, although it's fair to say that the car modeller, in general, has a slightly easier time that someone

Work benches, by their very nature, take on a personal appearance. This is the author's, in a reasonable state of tidiness, with space for tools to be stored at the back, paints on the left and direct lighting above. The bench is also in front of a window to take advantage of natural lighting during the day. The TV and radio (right) are optional extras.

A feature of some of the earliest car kits, which reappears when any are reissued in one of the collectors' series, is the multi-piece body. This is the Revell Austin-Healey 100-Six, which was reissued in 1996 in the Selected Subjects Program. However, the multi-piece body can be assembled, as shown in the background, then treated in the conventional manner.

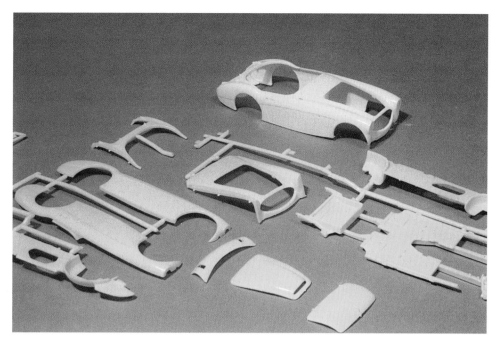

who wants to build a 4ft (1.2m) long model of an aircraft carrier. The main work area will probably need to cover no more than 2.5 x 3.5ft (say 750 x 1000mm if you've gone metric) and can be constructed from any suitable wood. Blockboard, plywood or MDF would all serve this purpose, although you will probably need to seal both sides to prevent warping, or even cover the work surface with melamine. Even easier would be to buy a melamine-faced panel from a DIY store. A lip around the edge would be advisable to prevent small parts from rolling off, especially if the work area is on the small side. If the board is to be moved a great deal — out of the way of the most inquisitive members of the family (children and cats), especially when paint is drying — handles would be a useful addition, and maybe even a cover. Tools of the trade (paints, knives, glue and the like) will also need storing, and DIY stores sell a wide variety of cabinets that can be adapted.

Experienced modellers will need no advice as to the types of tools that will be required to build a model kit. However, if you are new to the hobby, or perhaps only intend to build one or two models, some guidance may be useful. Although the need for some special tools will be obvious, many others can be adapted from existing household items, and overall the total number required need not be that great.

## ADHESIVES

Assuming that the kit isn't a snap-together type (and an increasing number of car kits are based on this type of construction), you will need to glue it together. (Even if the kit is a snap-together type, you may want to glue it together anyway.) Styrene plastic is joined with a glue that melts the edges to weld the parts together. This, in theory, produces a seamless joint.

Originally, the glue — polystyrene cement — came in a tube, and it can still be bought in this form. These days, however, the normal plastic cement is of the liquid variety. The older tubed cement consisted of a solvent (acetone- or

methyl-based) with some styrene already dissolved in it. The liquid variety is just the solvent.

Liquid cement is far preferable to the tubed type, as unless the latter is used in extremely small quantities, it can leave behind a solid residue. At best, this will need to be removed when dry, involving extra work in filing and sanding; at worst, it will remain 'active' inside parts that otherwise appear dry, sometimes for many years. This can lead to the outer surfaces caving in under some apparently mysterious influence. It isn't — it's tubed cement! (The tubed type of cement also has the unfortunate habit of invariably being under your elbow when you lean down hard, and it is not the easiest of substances to remove from a carpet.)

Liquid cement is far more controllable than the tubed type. It can be applied with a small brush dedicated to the task (this will tend to rot after a while) or a small pipette. However, even liquid cement is not totally immune to accidents, and the bottle is easily knocked over. (That said, if you take the *Hitchhiker's Guide to the Galaxy* view and 'Don't panic', it usually evaporates and leaves the surface untarnished — usually.)

Of course, there is a third type of glue in common use these days: cyano-acrylate or, as it is more commonly called, superglue (or just CA). Although not actually designed for use on plastic, it is normally employed with the multi-material kits. It is invaluable for joining metal to metal (white metal or photo-etched brass) or simply applying very small plastic parts to a plastic body. In the latter case, the joint will be mechanical rather than a weld, but this is usually sufficient. As with any superglue, less is better, and the tiniest of drops are all that will be required. Accelerator (also called 'kicker') is available for superglues and does have its uses, speeding up the curing of the adhesive, which means that it gets very hot. The accelerator can affect painted surfaces if you spray it on. It weakens the joint as well, although this is not usually critical for a static model kit. Superglue can be useful for cementing items such as fender and door mirrors, as these items are most likely to be knocked off. Since the superglue does not actually dissolve the surfaces (although it produces a strong mechanical joint), it can be subjected to sheer effects. These can occur if you accidentally brush the side of a model and hit the mirror. The result is that the part tends to snap off at the joint. (However, you will then have the problem of finding the mirror, which is bound to have fallen in some inaccessible spot on the floor—better not to knock it off in the first place...)

Superglue is also very useful for gluing parts that have been chrome plated. Kit instructions will invariably tell you to scrape the plating from any areas to be glued, as the glue will not stick to the plating. This is true, but sometimes the actual surface to be glued can be very difficult to reach, and you may run the risk of accidentally scraping the plating of an area that will be in view. However, superglue sticks very well to plated surfaces and, if kicker is carefully applied with a toothpick, can allow awkward parts to set in position where otherwise they would have to be propped or taped in place while conventional glue dried.

Cyano-acrylate is available in several grades, or thicknesses, from extremely thin (like water) to relatively thick. The grade that is one up from 'thin' appears best for most model work.

Gluing clear parts, especially headlights, has never been that straightforward, as ordinary polystyrene cement (tube and liquid) gives off fumes that tend to cloud the clear surface. Even superglue does this. You might get away with it if a headlamp lens is a good fit and a very tiny amount of liquid cement is run around the edge by capillary action. Even if the surround is chromed, which means that the joint will be mechanical and not a weld, the parts are so small that this is usually sufficient. However, it is safer to use a water-based glue instead. With this, there will be no danger of clouding, as there are no damaging fumes. Ordinary PVA wood glue— thinned with water if necessary—is very useful in this respect. It goes on white, but dries clear. These days, many of the model adhesive manufacturers can also supply a spe-

cial type of glue made specifically for the task of gluing clear parts.

*Note* Suitable precautions must be taken and ventilation provided when using adhesives, some of which can be inflammable. Always follow the manufacturers' recommendations for use. This applies particularly to superglue, the fumes of which, together with those of the kicker, are not pleasant and can be toxic. Superglue must also be handled carefully. Remember, cyano-acrylate is very good at gluing skin together. After all, that is what it was invented for— emergency surgery during the Vietnam War.

## TOOL KIT

In reality, only a minimum of tools will be necessary to build a basic kit, although many others will become useful if you delve deeper into the hobby.

A modelling knife is the most useful of the basic tools needed. It can be used to cut and trim parts, remove dried glue residue and any flash, and even (if you haven't got a pair of scissors!) cut up decals. Two sizes should be obtained: a small scalpel type and a larger craft knife.

The parts from any kit should be cut away from the runner, not twisted off, although this is the usual approach for the novice (and even many experienced modellers!). However, this will usually leave a large section of the part still attached to the runner, while an inevitable gluing, recutting and sanding saga will follow. It is far safer to carefully remove parts with a modelling knife, although a small pair of side cutters will be more effective, and an old pair of nail clippers even better still—and probably cheaper.

Parts can be trimmed with the knife, but needle files are an asset in this respect. A selection of basic shapes will allow flat filing, the removal of mould lines and the easing out of holes. Similarly, several grades of glass paper will be useful: if you buy a standard sheet of each grade and cut it into smaller, more manageable, sections, it will last for ages.

A selection of modelling tools and cements (including both superglue and liquid cement) plus body putty. The knife in the foreground is designed for scribing and cutting plastic sheet, while behind it are two scalpels and a larger craft knife. In the centre are several sizes of tweezers, and behind them two sizes of razor saw. Behind these is an assortment of clothes pegs (pins), some cut into specific shapes for ease of use. To the left are needle files and two small pairs of side cutters. Also useful are toothpicks, a tape dispenser and kitchen roll, which usually sits under the bench in a dispenser.

For small-scale drilling, pin-vices (foreground) tend to be best and are available in several sizes. Sets of small drill bits can be bought in various sizes, those shown (centre) being both 'numbered' and metric. An electric drill is also very useful, especially with a mains speed controller (on which the drill is sitting in a purpose-built cradle). A set of larger numbered (1-60) drill bits is also worth having for this drill (left), as are various cutters and sanding attachments (right).

A good pair of scissors will always be handy—if only for opening the many polythene packs in which the runners now arrive, and for cutting up the decals.

A razor saw is very useful, too. This has very thin blades and fine closely spaced teeth. Several sizes and blade depths are available. A razor saw will even cut metal if you are building a multi-material kit, although it is advisable to keep separate saws for this task and for cutting plastic.

If you intend drilling holes, a pin-vice will be invaluable, and if you expect to drill a lot of holes, an electric drill more so. A pin-vice (which has a tiny chuck and can be spun between your fingers) is useful even if you have an electric drill, as it will be far more controllable for very small holes.

Electric drills for modelling come in a variety of sizes and specifications, although one with a proper chuck will be easier to use than one that holds the tools by means of a collet. Some drills are battery powered, while others require mains transformers or are even run directly from the mains. The last will have the power for really tough jobs. In addition, some sort of speed controller will prove invaluable.

A wide range of accessories is available, and many of the drills can also be used as pillar drills, small lathes and miniature jigsaws. In addition, a variety of rotary tools is available, making a drill very useful for cutting, grinding and polishing tasks.

One aspect of building a model that is often overlooked is the need to hold parts together while the cement dries. A standard adhesive tape dispenser will be of use for a wide variety of tasks, and can be obtained very cheaply from a stationery supplier. (In some cases, a dispenser will come free with a reel of tape.) Small G- or C-cramps can be bought from model shops in several sizes and, again, are very handy, although the most useful modelling clamps have to be clothes pegs (US—clothes pins), which are the cheapest source of clamps around. Perhaps ironically, the wooden types are better than the plastic variety: they seem to be stronger, and can be sawn and filed into various shapes to suit different jobs. However, some of the larger plastic pegs incorporate holes, which are a help when it comes to hanging them up to allow the parts to dry (see also Chapter 7).

Another effective means of holding parts—especially small parts—is to use modelling clay, although be warned that the old favourite, Plasticine, has the disadvantage that paint will not dry on its surface. As a result, removing the part will probably lead to semi-dried paint becoming mixed with a bit of dissolved Plasticine around the attachment point. A better material is Blu-Tack, as paint will dry on its surface, although this does not stop it being rolled into a ball ready for reuse.

Larger pieces to be painted—particularly sprayed—can be supported by lengths of bent wire, held in place by small pieces of double-sided foam tape (also available from stationers). The metal-wire technique is the favourite method of holding car bodies for spraying, and old coat hangers are an excellent source. The wire can be bent to shape with enough 'spring' to hold it against the sides of the body, perhaps with tape acting as a reinforcement.

Many early plastic kit car bodies—especially those from AMT and Jo-Han—actually had convenient holes in the underside (to allow the original promo-based bodies to be held to the chassis by self-tapping screws). These made very useful sockets for the wire ends, but unfortunately this option has all but disappeared, only being found in the odd reissue. (See Chapter 7 for more tips.)

## PERFECT FINISH

When model plastic kits were first introduced, the idea of painting them was never really entertained. A few odd details may have been touched in, but that was about it. Consequently, many kits were moulded in (supposedly) appropriate colours. Thus, you would get—as far as model cars were concerned—the body in one colour, the chassis in another, while the whole of the engine assembly could very well have been chromed. Add to this the clear window parts and red taillights, and the whole kit presented a pretty colourful spectacle when the box lid was removed.

In fact, Jack Gowland, of Gowland & Gowland, initially kept to cellulose acetate as a moulding material for the original Highway Pioneers range, and didn't move straight to styrene, as at the time the acetate could be obtained in a

Good brushes are vital for model making, although the largest shown is kept purely for dusting purposes and never goes near a tin of paint. Specific model paints are generally split between enamels (left) and the newer acrylics (right). The major manufacturers around the world—Humbrol, Testors, Gunze Sangyo, Tamiya— make both types.

brighter range of colours than styrene. These made far more of an impact with the builder. This theory was also subscribed to by Monogram who, by then well into styrene, presented kits in a multitude of colours well into the sixties. In many cases, there was no need to think about painting the bodies of these kits, as at the time they had probably the highest gloss finish of any of their kits. For a short while, Monogram also made some cars that were plated entirely in a chrome and brass finish, which did not need painting at all.

Although many companies moved to more muted shades for the plastic parts, the idea of pre-coloured components is still with us. AMT's SnapFastPlus range (which, in reality, are unassembled promos) and Revell-Monogram's snap kits in both 1:32 and 1:25 are usually moulded in relevant colours.

**Some kits still come pre-coloured, the intention being that you need not necessarily paint them. Lindberg have adopted this approach with their 1:20 car and truck range. Here, their Chevy Blazer has been finished without painting the main body colour. It has been simply polished, although the black trims had to be added as usual.**

Although one of the oldest kit company names, Lindberg have only recently become movers and shakers in the model car industry. They use pre-coloured styrene for their 1:20 scale series, which is moulded to a very high finish. This means that, if necessary, the modeller need only polish it.

When Lesney introduced their Matchbox Kits ranges, they made a point of moulding their models (cars, aircraft, the lot) in three shades of plastic so that novice modellers would not necessarily have to be bothered with paint: the kits could be assembled 'as was'. This led to some interesting colour combinations, especially among the aircraft.

In addition, some manufacturers have played around with supplying pre-painted bodies. Fujimi did this for a time, and Revell AG have introduced them again—even down to painting on some of the markings that normally would be provided as decals.

Despite all this, by far and away the majority of model car kits are designed to be painted, and to this end a whole industry of model paint manufacturers has grown up alongside the kit companies themselves.

Most car builders will be concerned with two types of painting, with the possible addition of a third. The main two are brushing and aerosol spraying, while the third is airbrushing. As a very general rule, large areas are best sprayed, and small areas painted by hand, although naturally there are many exceptions.

Until recently, the paint you would buy for hand painting a model, whether in a tin or a bottle, would be enamel-based. This flowed on to the plastic surface well, dried reasonably quickly and could be recoated. (It also did not affect the styrene surface, whereas other mainstays of the paint industry—especially cellulose and some lacquers—did.) Enamels were available in a wide range of colours and finishes: gloss and matt (or flat), and finishes in between that invariably were termed satin or semi-gloss (or semi-matt for that matter...).

**Matchbox experimented with moulding their kits in three colours, plus chrome and clear. This simplified the task for the beginner when it came to building.**

However, in recent years, there has been a move away from enamels to acrylics. There appear to be two reasons for this. One is environmental, as the spirit-based acrylics are supposed to be less harmful than the oil-based enamels (although exactly how is difficult to rationalize, as they both have to be manufactured). The other is that many modellers found that acrylics went on to their models better, although it must be said that many others still preferred enamels. Much of this disagreement was actually due to the introduction of moulded vinyl kits, which does not really affect the model car industry, but came about especially with the growth of science-fiction and fantasy figures. Enamel paints will not dry if applied directly to vinyl, while acrylics will. That said, enamels work perfectly well if applied over a suitable primer.

Consequently, and currently, all major model paint companies make both types of paint, with many (although by no means all) colours, shades and finishes being duplicated in both ranges.

Enamels and acrylics do not mix (literally that is), but can be used in conjunction with one another, which is useful. If a surface has been painted with, say, an enamel paint and you want to add details, occasionally you will find that the enamel (especially if it isn't quite dry—and we are all in a hurry sometimes...) will start to run or bleed through if another layer of enamel paint is applied. However, if acrylic is used instead, the different chemical bases will prevent one dissolving the other. Enamel can also be applied over acrylic without causing problems and, in theory, you could proceed through several alternating applications in this way. This is particularly useful when painting figures, which becomes relevant to car models when figures are required for a diorama (see Chapter 10).

For hand painting, of course, you will need that vital tool, the paint brush. For model purposes, paint brushes come in a wide range of sizes and qualities, and you should always buy the best you can afford.

A range of sizes will be necessary for most tasks, and four is the minimum you will need. As any artist will tell you, brushes must be treated with respect, so after each use, they should be cleaned immediately in good quality white spirit (or similar), dried and stored upright in a convenient container. For acrylics, you will need something like methylated spirits for cleaning. Plain water does work with some acrylic formulas (Humbrol for example), but not all.

Needless to say—I trust—both white spirit and meths are extremely flammable, so do not indulge in smoking while modelling. Apart from the irritation of ash falling on drying paint, sparks in the direction of the brush cleaners could affect your heath far more than the nicotine and tar ever will!

It does seem obvious, but *never* leave brushes standing in the cleaner: the structure of the bristles will be wrecked. However, no matter how good a brush may be initially, it

**Older-style cars and trucks still tend to come with the body and fender assemblies moulded separately, such as this Revell-Monogram 1937 Ford. This makes it much easier to paint the two assemblies different colours.**

will not last forever, and when its life of applying fine detail is through, it can be used to apply 'cruder' paint finishes or liquid cement. Until you have assembled a collection of 'old' brushes, you can use some of the cheaper brushes for applying liquid cement. A large reasonably expensive brush is also a useful addition to the tool kit: this can be used for brushing dust from the surfaces of models and should never be used for paint.

Incidentally, the most convenient source of cleaning rags for modelling is a roll of paper kitchen towels. This can be held in a standard dispenser fitted to your work bench. Besides being used for drying brushes and the like, the towels will always be immediately to hand when the cleaner is knocked over (and it will be...).

Currently, the major specialist model paint manufacturers in the world are Humbrol, Testors and Gunze Sangyo, while Tamiya and Revell AG also make their own ranges. All offer a wide variety of colours, both in enamel and acrylic. These include standard gloss and matt (or flat), satin/semi-gloss and metallic shades. Some even supply marker pens in many of the colours. Most also include transparent colours in their acrylic ranges, which are very useful for taillights, indicators, emergency beacons and anodized fittings on engines. Other companies produce specific ranges: Tru-Match in the USA, for example, specialize in the colours used in NASCAR racing, and can supply both bottles and sprays. Revell-Monogram have introduced a range of bottled acrylics for their ProModeler subsidiary, initially for aircraft, but increasingly with car colours. Revell AG now make a reduced range of paints, but this includes the excellent Basic Color white primer.

## SPRAY IT AGAIN...

One painting device that, while not exclusively the prerogative of the car modeller, is certainly the most usefully employed by this side of the hobby, is the aerosol spray can. Attempting to duplicate the factory paint finish of a full-size car, if not impossible, is highly impractical by hand painting

(although there *are* modellers who swear by this method). Consequently, the first modellers' aerosol sprays were introduced especially for model cars at around the beginning of the sixties. At that time, the market for aerosols was dominated by American companies, with AMT producing their own range, which was extended by others from Belmont, Testors and Pactra (then, the last two were independent, but now Testors own Pactra). These provided the modeller with a wide range of automotive finishes, from solid gloss and metallics to the mainstays of the custom car market: metalflakes and candy colours (or, as AMT had it, Kandy Kolors...). In full-size metalflake finishes, actual metal particles are combined with the paint to give an over-the-top type of metallic finish. Candy colours are slightly different in that they are not based on pigments, but dyes. They give a progressively darker and deeper appearance as each layer is applied.

Model car aerosols are not all enamel-based: they are split equally between enamels and lacquers, the latter being more usually associated with full-size car paint, although model lacquer is specially formulated so that it will not craze the plastic surface.

Currently, the model aerosol industry has settled down, there being several major, and a few minor, players around the world. Legislation, however, could affect the market. World-wide concern about depletion of the ozone layer led to aerosols being held partly to blame—ironically, not because of the substances being sprayed, but the propellant used to spray them—and the contents of many aerosols were reformulated. At present, the situation seems to have stabilized, although it is quite possible that more changes will be made in the future. Some have predicted the complete demise of the aerosol, which would take the car modellers' spray paint with it. Acrylics do not spray as well as enamels or lacquers, and at the moment there are no commercial acrylic sprays, although they can be air-brushed. This brings us to the third method of applying paint to model cars. However, for details of this technique, see Chapter 7.

New approaches to kit materials mean that some items, such as badges and logos, are produced in photo-etched metal instead of as the more traditional water-slide decals. This AMT release of the Aoshima Lexus has metal 'LEXUS' and 'L' logos, although the licence plate remains the traditional water-slide type.

# Chapter Five

# BUILDING A BASIC KIT

If you take a standard car construction kit, normally you will be faced with four sub-assemblies: the body, the chassis, the interior and the engine. Of course, there will be exceptions to this. There may not be a separate engine, and some modern sports car kits have the chassis and bodywork so inextricably intertwined that it is difficult to deal with them separately, but in most cases you will find that this rule is a convenient one.

The instructions—however basic and non-language based—will take you through the assembly in the order deemed most appropriate by the manufacturer. Experienced modellers invariably take perverse pride in ignoring these plans and working to their own agenda, but even the best of us have come unstuck, for example when a small hose that should have been installed in Stage 1 has been missed because Stage 6 has been carried out first!

In addition—besides actually reading the plans—it is always wise to check that all the parts are present before starting. Quality control for kits has always been good, and these days, when most are packed in polythene bags and shrink wrapped, it is even better. But it is not unknown for a small part to have fallen off the runner before it was put into the bag, or for small sections of the kit—metal axles or red taillights—to have been overlooked completely. If parts are missing, the place of purchase is supposed to be your first point of call, although most companies also run a help line or even, these days, an Internet site, where details of replacements can be found. However, this is unlikely to apply to the second-hand or collectable market, so you may come across the situation when an odd part must be made from scratch (see Chapter 11).

Check also that the kit parts are free of defects. Flash is still the most common fault, but although irritating, it can be removed with a sharp knife, or filed or sanded if necessary. On older reissued kits, you may find ejector pin marks, which can be filled or sanded flat. Short runs or misshapen parts are very rare, and here the only action is to return the kit and hope that it was an isolated example.

## THINK BEFORE YOU CUT...

Never remove parts from the runners until you require them. Although the purpose and position of some parts may be obvious (it is difficult to mistake the chassis pan for anything else...), other items may be handed left or right, and if not in their position on the runner (hopefully with a number as well), it can be difficult to identify them. Leaving parts on the runners is also advantageous when you come to painting. It is usual to paint all parts before assembly, but often there will be many sub-assemblies that can be put together first. The classic example is the engine, which normally will arrive as the block in two halves, the sump/oil pan, the heads, the cam/rocker covers, the inlet manifold, water pump, etc. These are usually painted one colour in any case, whether it be the stock Ford Engine Blue or something more custom orientated. Consequently, these can be assembled as one before starting any painting

**Most, although not all, car kits tend to break down into interior, chassis and engine, and body, as in this case— Lindberg's Maverick Dodge.**

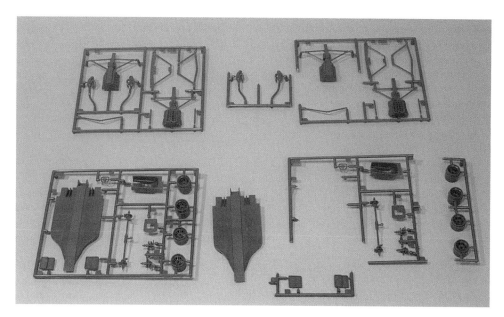

*Left* **Sort out the parts on their runners, deciding which can remain and which need to be removed for painting a different colour. Here, two sets of runners for Revell AG's Williams F1 car show how they arrive (left) and how they look after the initial sorting (right).**

*Below* **Use snips, scissors or a knife when removing parts from the runners. Don't twist them off, no matter how impatient you feel!**

There are likely to be several other similar sub-assemblies that can be glued together before painting. Older-style rear axles usually come in two halves, possibly with a separate differential cover. You may be able to attach the suspension and steering systems to the chassis before painting, while inside the car, the seat backs may be separate from the rest of the seat. These are general ideas though; each kit will have its own idiosyncrasies, which is another reason to read through the instructions thoroughly first.

However, do not take this sub-assembly business too far. The instrument panel may be the same overall colour as the interior, but you may find that pedals have to be added, or that the instrument faces are supplied as an insert or decals, which makes application far more difficult if the panel has been glued in place already. Similarly, installing separate seats first will make painting the door panels far more difficult. So although some sub-assembly work is usual prior to painting, each example must be taken on its own merit.

## ONE PIECE—WITH BITS

As pointed out previously, virtually all bodies come as one

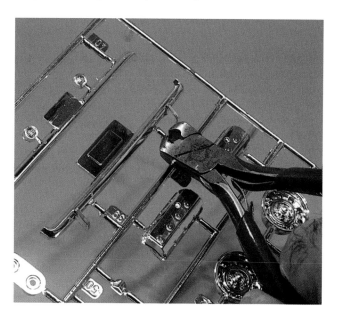

piece these days. Even so, there are exceptions, and the usual separate parts will comprise the pans that sit under the front and rear bumpers (assuming it *has* separate front and rear bumpers, which is not normally the case with modern cars). The pans are usually moulded separately to make the car body easy to remove from the mould. However, they could also be separate to allow the body to fit over the finished chassis. Consequently, if you *do* intend attaching the pans first, it is vital to make sure that the body will still fit over the chassis without straining anything too much. Usually, the instructions will indicate this, and a quick check is advisable to determine if the pans should be installed before, or during, final assembly. Even if the instructions specify that this should be done during final assembly, it doesn't necessarily mean that you can't fit them beforehand, but you will have to check very carefully as you go.

The idea of fitting the pans first, of course, is so that you can spray paint the body in one go to ensure that the finish matches all over. However, modern spray paints are actually very good—and forgiving—in this respect, so even if you do have to spray parts separately and fit them together later, usually this will not show. Items such as wing/door mirrors (increasingly painted the body colour) and trunk or roof mounted spoilers are best left off anyway at this stage, to allow the paint to cover the area beneath them completely.

Leaving small parts on their runners is also useful when it comes to painting. Individually, they will be difficult to hold, but the runner will be easy to grasp. Large parts can be snipped off—still attached to a piece of runner—held in the ever useful clothes peg and painted separately. However, parts that will all be the same colour can be assembled on one runner and spray painted collectively. This may mean rearranging the parts—not everything on the same runner will necessarily be the same colour, so sort out the runner with the majority of the parts you want to paint, and snip off the rest with their sections of runner. (The latter may be attached to another runner for painting a different colour.) Add the other parts by gluing their sections of runner to the main length. Spray painting this lot in one go will be easier and quicker than hand painting each item individually.

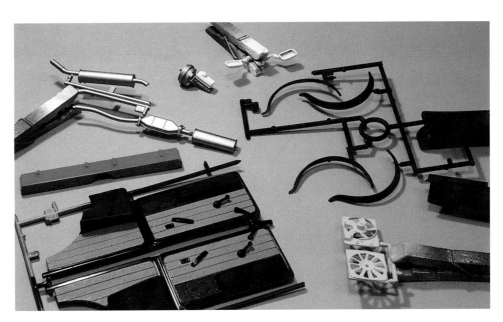

*Right* **Clothes pegs (pins) are a great help when holding smaller parts for painting.**

*Below left* **A length of bent wire is the best way to support the body for painting. Old coat hangers are the cheapest source and can be held in place by double-sided foam tape.**

*Below right* **Small parts can be held by shorter lengths of wire, clothes pegs or wooden skewers pushed into convenient holes in the parts.**

If, for example, you are painting the parts black, and several different shades are required, you can then be very sneaky. First paint everything matt black. Then remove those parts that require a matt finish, and spray those remaining satin black. Remove those that will remain satin black, and spray the remainder gloss black if required. As gloss, and even satin, finishes benefit from an undercoat, or primer, the matt black will have done this job.

## 'COLOR ME GONE'

Aircraft modellers have hard and fast rules about paint schemes and individual colours, and invariably deviations from the norm are viewed with disdain. However, car modellers are the opposite, and virtually every shade and finish of every colour imaginable (and probably some that aren't) can be employed.

To begin, however, some generalizations must be made, and car modellers do have one great advantage over modellers in other subjects: if all else fails, there will usually be a full-size example of the car being modelled relatively close that can be examined. (Aircraft modellers tend not to have

this luxury, unless there is an airfield at the bottom of the garden, or they are on the flightpath to Heathrow!) In addition, most instruction sheets do give some indication of colours, and many are common sense.

Paint applied to full-size cars serves two purposes. Its secondary purpose is to become part of the design and aesthetics, but its primary purpose is to protect the metal underneath. (And when Henry Ford realized that the Model T Ford would have to be painted, he did not specify 'Any color, as long as it's black' because he had a thing about black cars — it was because, at the time, black paint dried quicker than other colours, and he had to keep the assembly line going!)

Engine blocks also have to be protected and usually start life painted a single overall colour. Many manufacturers have their own individual shades, such as Chevrolet Red (which is more orange), Ford Blue and Chrysler Red. British cars of the post-war period tended to have dark green or maroon engines, while reconditioned units could be a distinctive gold. Modern high-specification blocks manufactured in aluminium tend to stay that shade, as aluminium

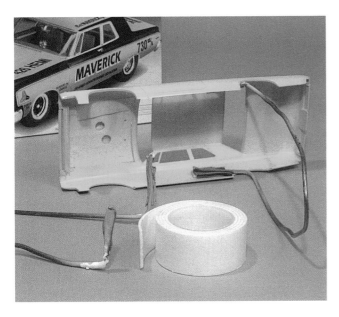

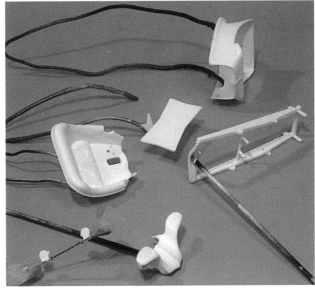

does not rust (well it does in the sense of oxidization, but not in the same way as iron and steel).

Engine details—such as hoses, alternator and the like—also have their own schemes. Hoses are usually black, although they are not necessarily 'pure' black (they could be a very dark grey), and they will have clips and fittings that are different colours. Fan belts are black as well, although again, shades can vary considerably. Old-style generators were usually black, but modern alternators can be orange, silver, black, or a mix. Starter bodies are usually black, but the solenoid section can be silver. Check a full-size example for more details.

Distributors can be black, but the caps may also be dark rust red, tan or blue. The base is usually aluminium, although it could be the same colour as the engine block. Batteries, although traditionally black, are now white, red, blue, yellow, probably green as well, or even translucent, often with bodies and tops that differ in colour.

Traditionally, radiators are black, but the header tanks on older cars are more likely to be bronze, while race car radiators will probably be aluminium. Washer bottles and overflow tanks may be clear, translucent or solid. Wiper motors, if visible, can be black or silver, while the many control boxes that litter the inside of a modern engine bay can take on a wide range of hues.

## METALWORK

Many kits supply engine and running gear parts with a chrome finish. Often, except perhaps in the case of a full custom, this is inappropriate, as the real parts would be painted. However, although the plating can simply be painted over (or, if you are really fussy, removed and repainted), over-painting with various other finishes can be effective. 'Metallized' finishes, made by both Humbrol and Testors, can be brushed on to chrome to make a more authentic finish, while if you use transparent acrylics over chrome, you can obtain an anodized effect. Tamiya make six transparent acrylics, including transparent blue, which is particularly effective on parts such as hose fittings—as seen on race cars—or mufflers on hot rods. Transparent yellow will give that 'goldish' hue often seen on chromed exhaust systems as a result of being heated. A metallized finish will improve a chromed carburettor no end, while transparent smoke grey tones down garish chrome plating to a more authentic look.

Air cleaners also tend to suffer from over-chroming and are more authentically gloss black, blue or another primary colour. The air filter element—if visible—is usually white or buff in colour.

Wiring abounds in engine bays, although much will be moulded into the firewall and wheel arches. Although the wiring harness itself will be multi-coloured (otherwise it would be impossible to trace an individual wire from one end to the other), it will also be covered in a black shrink-wrapped tape, so at least the overall colour is straightforward. However, you will need a fine brush and a sharp eye to paint it. Remember also that the harness is usually held in place by clips, which can be moulded into the detail, but which will be the body colour.

Engines and associated equipment are areas where it is becoming increasingly common to supply decals for the various labels, so you may find that the kit provides these for the battery, air cleaner, alternator and the like, and there may be lots more. Many after-market companies also make suitable decals.

These days, engine bays are becoming full up with engine management systems, air conditioning, fuel injection, and more pipes and hoses than you ever thought possible. This makes it all the more important to check out full-size examples.

## GETTING IN GEAR

Moving back from the engine bay, gearboxes used to be

*Right* Clothes pegs are also very useful for clamping parts, as illustrated by this AMT Kraco transporter trailer, which has long flat sides that need cementing together. As the pegs tend to be painted along the way, be careful where they touch already painted parts. It may be necessary to place small pieces of clean plastic or paper between the pegs and parts.

*Below right* Chromed parts can be tinted with various shades of transparent or metallic paint, or simply painted another colour. You can remove the plating beforehand, oven cleaner being one recommendation, but try it on unwanted parts first!

painted the same colour as the block, although modern boxes can be mostly aluminium or composite, so they will be a silvery colour. Propshafts—assuming the vehicle has a front-engine/rear-drive set-up—are usually deemed to be black, although aluminium and metallic finishes do crop up. Custom cars can use any colour you like, and there is at least one example (AMT's Orange Blossom Special puller) that has its propshaft painted in an orange spiral! Stock rear axles can be black, or maybe a red primer colour. If the car is a custom, though, anything goes, either to complement or contrast with the rest of the scheme.

Front axles and steering assemblies are usually given the overall chassis colour, but chrome or a bright colour would be quite suitable for a custom or hot rod. Shock absorbers, as standard, invariably were black, but replacement uprated examples are all colours of the rainbow—blue, yellow, red, even white.

Leaf springs on an older style of car would usually be chassis colour or just plain rusty. For a pristine appearance, paint them black, perhaps adding bolts and shackles in silver. Coil springs may be incorporated with the shock absorbers, and many of these springs are finished in bright primary colours to start, such as yellow. If the shock runs through the centre of the spring, but the assembly is mould-

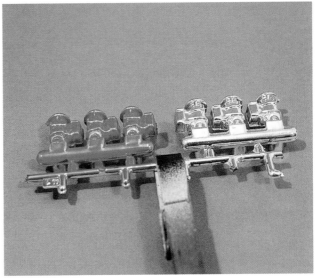

*Facing page* **Sub-assemblies are usually built up separately, only coming together in the final stages of construction. Some kits will have more separate parts than others at this point, such as this 1:20 scale Honda Formula 1 car from Tamiya.**

*Right* **Transparent paint—made by most of the model paint companies—is vital for achieving the correct look on tinted light assemblies such as taillights and indicators. It works well on both clear and chromed parts, and is far more effective in this situation than normal opaque paint.**

A wide variety of special colours is available for kits these days, even down to specific engine colours, such as this example from the ProModeler range of acrylics.

British car engines tend to be painted less brightly than their American counterparts. Dark maroon, dark green—in this case for the Tamiya Morgan—and even black are common.

ed in one piece, paint the shock first, then paint the spring around the outside. This can be achieved by loading a fairly large brush with paint and carefully applying its side along the edge of the spring, so that none flows into the gaps to reach the shock.

Exhaust systems begin life with a steel or aluminium colour, but by the time they have been in use for even a short time, they take on shades of dark red, brown or just rust. Modern catalytic converters involve yet more shades, as usually they have a more gold-like colour. Exhaust headers of race cars are usually dark metallic or white VHT (very-high-temperature) paint. The latter is best duplicated by applying straight matt white or matt white primer, which tends to be 'denser'.

## CLASSY CHASSIS
The chassis—or rather floorpans—of modern monocoque cars are first painted the body colour, but then the whole underside usually ends up coated in black underseal (which

has an advantage for the modeller—paint the whole underside black). However, many modern sports cars have their main under-body panels in the body colour, so you can end up with the bizarre situation of a white floorpan. Race and rally car chassis are often white, too, but in these cases it is because damage and/or leaks will show up immediately.

Fuel tanks are usually built into the chassis moulding and can be left the chassis colour. However, there can be merit in picking them out in a different shade, especially if the vehicle is a custom. Pipes and wiring may also be moulded into the underside. Again, they can be left covered with 'underseal' or carefully emphasized by picking them out with different colours.

Although most modern car kits have a fully detailed chassis—with individually moulded parts for suspension, axles, drive shafts, fuel tanks and the like—some older kits (especially AMT and Jo-Han) provide a one-piece chassis with all this detail moulded in. This situation was inherited from the promos.

Chassis details can vary enormously. This recent kit of the 1967 Chevy Impala, from AMT, features separate chassis rails and floorpan, which is unusual for this type of kit. However, they make it much easier to paint the pan and chassis itself different shades of black.

Even the old-style one-piece chassis, as found in the early 'annual' kits (and consequently any reissues), can be made to look very effective with the addition of only paint. Here, AMT's 1965 Lincoln Continental chassis is shown unpainted and finished. Note that although it is in one piece, even the brake pipes have been included in the moulding. Of course, it could be argued that normally the whole lot would be covered in black underseal, so you could simply paint it all black instead.

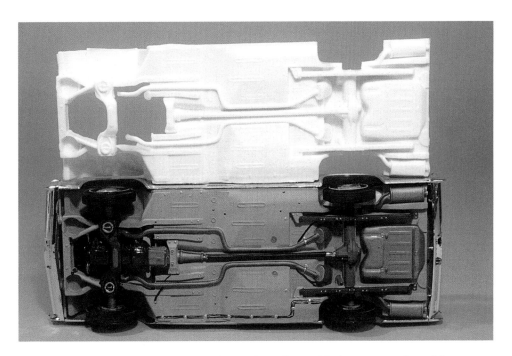

The same can also apply with some modern kits, notably the snap-together ranges (many of which are also unassembled promos). For speed and convenience, the usual recommendation is to paint the lot black, but for a change, the individual components can be picked out with paint. Even if you have to compromise somewhat—the axle, propshaft, exhausts and the like will not be completely round, as they will all be moulded in—the final effect can be quite convincing.

If engine, chassis and running gear are hidden to a great extent on a model car, two areas certainly are not—the body and interior.

## BACK SEAT OF MY CAR...
The interior of most early kits was a one-piece 'tub'. The classic case had the rear seats moulded in, while the front seats would be separate, as would the instrument panel, steering wheel, and possibly a centre console and gear-shift. Although this 'tub' style can still be found, many manufac-

turers have adopted a multi-piece approach—with separate floor, side panels and all the seats—or a hybrid arrangement in which the side panels, at the very least, are separate mouldings. This makes painting far easier, as you can reach all the fiddly details (like interior door handles and window winders) without straining to manoeuvre the smallest brush you can find around the back of a seat, with the accompanying risk of applying silver paint everywhere but the place it is required.

The interior is one area where examination of a full-size example will be most beneficial, since colours can vary considerably, especially as the materials used can differ widely. An American car with fifties-style vinyl seating in bright red will look somewhat different to a Jaguar with red leather seats, or a VW Golf with red cloth covers. Even in the same interior, what is supposedly the same colour on carpets, seats and dash will take on different sheens. Good reference is vital here, and investment in one or many of the various books on cars will be extremely useful.

Revell's GMC Syclone—the world's fastest production pickup—comes in any colour as long as it's black, so it makes a change to paint the running gear in a contrasting colour.

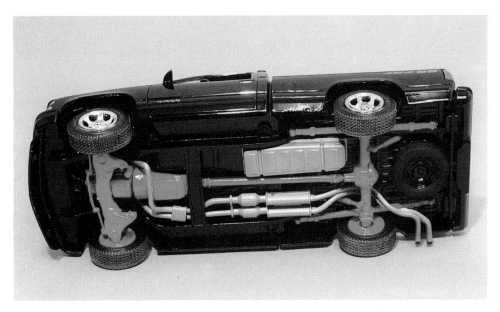

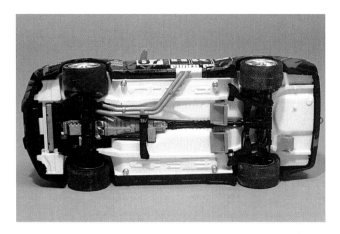

*Above* **It may seem odd, but many race cars have white chassis pans, the reason being that this makes spotting oil leaks and damage far easier. This is Tamiya's Nissan Skyline GT-R GrA in HKS colours.**

*Above* **Even with no further detailing, engine bays can be made to look good by the careful application of paint. On this AMT/MPC Chevy Silverado, the moulded-in wiring harness has also been picked out on the firewall.**

**Although the drive shaft is probably one of the least interesting aspects of a car—when it comes to colour—with one kit, the AMT Orange Blossom Special puller, you were instructed to paint it in an orange and black spiral!**

The best overall reference, especially for American cars, is the periodical *Collectible Automobile*—the bible of such cars—each issue of which examines several automobiles in great detail. Even if the exact car you are modelling hasn't been covered to date, you can be sure that it will be in the future, or there may be something similar already in print (see References).

A colour that effectively demonstrates how different surfaces, ostensibly in the same colour, can vary in appearance is black—the favourite interior finish of many a sports car. In this case, 'black' is certainly not the same 'black' all round. You will find different textures on seating, side panels, inserts, the steering wheel and gear-shift, and the instrument panel—even though they may all be described in the instructions as 'black'. However, the careful use of various forms of pure black—matt, gloss and everything in between—will immediately show the differences. You can also experiment with 'near' shades as well, such as very dark grey or perhaps a metallic black.

## CONTROL FREAK

The instrument panel is an important part of any vehicle, and the model companies vary in the way that they present its details. Most panels come in one piece with the instrument faces moulded in, along with the radio, heater controls, etc. Increasingly these days, companies are supplying either a single decal for all the dials, or even—as in many Japanese kits—individual dials. There may also be additional decals for the radio and heater control panel, and maybe even for the whole surround. Some cars at the luxury end of the market still use a lot of wood trim, which can be found as separate decals in many kits. In these cases, a decal softener is vital to get these types of transfer to seat properly, but more information on advanced decal placement techniques can be found in Chapter 7.

Seats, too, have gone from one- or two-piece mouldings to styles with moulded-in head rests, asymmetrical design left to right and, in some cases, suitable name tags for the seat backs. However, items that are rarely found today are seat belts.

In American 'annual' kits of the sixties, you would always find moulded lap belts to place on the seats. These days, most seat belts world-wide are of the automatic retractable type, which disappear out of sight when not in use. However, they can still be seen in many race and rally cars where full racing harnesses are used. These may be already moulded into the seat, or be supplied as decals, possibly individual moulded parts, or increasingly separate seat belt material with photo-etched buckles and fittings. This is where the after-market suppliers can help (see Chapter 10.

## BODY WORK

The main feature of any car model will be the body. The actual methods of painting and applying decals (if any) are described in Chapter 7, but there may be several areas that require attention before any painting can be carried out.

As Chapter 7 will describe in detail, although most car bodies are moulded in one piece these days, it may be advisable to paint other parts at the same time. These may include

These days, more and more interior details are being supplied straight from the box. With specialist racers, such as this Tamiya Alfa Romeo, there are individual decals for all the electronic boxes seen sitting in the position normally occupied by the passenger. Decals are also provided to represent the seat belts.

Careful use of paint can enhance any interior. Here, red and white has been added to the grey floor of the Jo-Han Cadillac ambulance. Chrome strips (from Metalskin) have been added to separate the colours.

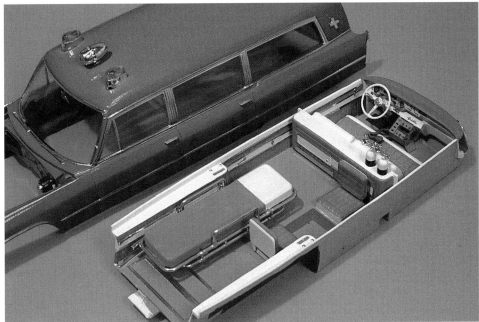

the front and rear pans (under the bumper positions), the bonnet or hood, and possibly any opening trunk and doors.

Check also that no holes need opening out for any reason. Some race cars—especially from the Japanese manufacturers—share their main body parts with several other kits, and may need holes cut out for filler caps, scoops, etc. This is best done before painting, as you will be sure to scratch the new finish if you leave it until later. (These kits usually have 'flashed over' recesses beneath the car's body, so cut from the inside.)

## CONSIDER YOUR OPTIONS

Although the old concept of the 3-in-1 kit only really appears these days with reissues, these are classic examples of kits that offer many options. Besides whole custom treatments for front and rear, even the simplest versions may provide optional aerials and spotlamps. The holes for these accessories should also be drilled out at this stage, before any painting is started.

Hood scoops are favourites, too, being used for racing or maybe the hottest street version of a car, which may have carburettors or a supercharger protruding through the hood. Again, appropriate holes must be provided. Some body parts, such as rear deck spoilers, may also come in several parts that need pre-assembly, although in this case, they are usually best left off the bodywork until the paintwork has been completed.

Race cars, especially those that use drag slicks, may need their rear wheel arches opening out to accommodate the bigger tyres. Again, this only really applies to the older-style 3-in-1 kits, where the bodywork has to cover all versions, but a number of relevant kits are still to be found in the catalogues.

When the body has been painted, there will still be some work to do, but avoid touching the painted bodywork too much until the paint has dried completely. Paint formulated for models is softer than general automotive paint and will pick up fingermarks very easily. At this stage, it may be best

*Left* **Even where much of an interior is in one colour—in this case black—the use of other colours can improve the overall look. Grey for the roll cage, and red and silver for the electronic boxes are just some additions.**

*Below* **Trends in car design change over the years, most notably when applied to the exterior. Here, a '67 Chevy Impala (AMT) contrasts with a nineties Toyota RAV-4 (Aoshima). In addition to the different body styles, the lack of chrome on the RAV-4 is particularly noticeable.**

to leave the body still attached to whatever holding device you used when spraying it.

## GILDING THE GREENHOUSE

One area of the body that will need attention now—with virtually no exceptions—is that of the window surrounds, which will not be the body colour. There is a distinction here between 'older' cars and 'newer' cars: the former have chromed window surrounds, and the latter black. The exact change-over point is difficult to pin-point—it varied from car to car, and country to country for that matter—but the bright chrome effect, so common to American cars of the fifties and sixties, has now been replaced by matt black surrounds and plastic 'bumpers'. This has helped reduce weight, of course (plastic is somewhat lighter than chromed steel), and also reflections, which is why wiper arms have gone the same route. Although old-style chromed surrounds can be suggested with paint—a new tin of silver paint can produce a pretty shiny result—most modellers tend to use foil for the chrome areas of cars (see Chapter 6 for more details on its use). However, some areas may still need the

gentle touch of a brush laden with silver paint, but be very careful not to overload the brush, as attempting to remove runs of silver from your newly painted car body is not to be recommended!

If the model requires black window surrounds, it is likely that the window glass will also need black adding around the inside of the surround. Many modern car kits have this line etched into the glass, and a steady hand will usually be able to follow it without additional masking. If you use acrylic satin black for this, instead of enamel, it will allow any slight errors to be wiped away without damage to the clear parts. Some kits also supply masking for the windows, but it is vital that this is firmly stuck down to the glass, otherwise the paint will creep underneath; it is probably best not to use this type of masking at all if you have any doubts on this score.

You may also find that the body's side 'bump' strips must be black, so these will need careful painting, too, unless you use one of the black foils described in the following chapter. However, if you do use paint, choose an acrylic satin black. With this, assuming that the body has

*Right* **Some kits may be more complex than others, but they need not be any more difficult to assemble if the instructions are followed. AMT's most recent Big Foot kit duplicated the vehicle's space frame. Although daunting, this went together in a straightforward manner.**

*Below* **Car and van kits come in a variety of styles, even if the basic vehicle is ostensibly the same. Compare Revell AG's VW Bus, in UN markings, with Monogram's older cousin styled for the sun and surf.**

been painted in enamel or lacquer, there will be no chance of it lifting the main body colour.

## HANDLE WITH CARE

Small items may need attaching to the body at this stage. Early kits usually have wipers, door handles and the like moulded in, and these can either be painted silver or finished with foil. Modern kits—even of older subjects—tend have these items moulded separately, which gives them a more authentic appearance, but has the slight disadvantage that they are more easily knocked off! Attaching these small items is not always easy, and a small drop of superglue, instead of styrene cement, could be the best way. This applies particularly to door/wing mirrors, which are the bane of any car modeller's life and are always being knocked off. If they are attached with superglue, there is a better chance that the break will occur at the glued joint and not half-way along the part. (Superglue, although structurally very strong, does not withstand sheering effects all that well.)

Head- and taillights will also need fitting at this stage, and unless the rear lights are moulded in transparent red,

they will need the appropriate tint of red and amber. You may also find that black edges need applying around these light clusters. The inner surface of the light lenses can be painted silver or, better still, the recesses of the body: the slight gaps between the lenses and the silver surfaces always seem to create a better appearance. When attaching the light clusters, try to avoid standard styrene cement, as there is a danger of clouding the parts, or of the glue running down the back of the parts, which will produce much the same effect. Use one of the specially formulated modelling products for clear parts, or water-based PVA wood glue.

The same applies to headlamp lenses, and in the case of side indicators, it is even more important to use a glue that will not dissolve the paint on the edges of the lights or body. Because the parts are so small, fit them with the aid of a small piece of Blu-Tack, or similar, on the tip of a cocktail stick. Apply the cement to the point on the body, very lightly pick up the part on the end of the stick, and transfer it to its position. If you've picked up the part as lightly as possible, the surface tension between it and the glue should be enough to break the hold of the Blu-Tack. If not, try again.

# Chapter Six

# SUPER-DETAILS

Although you can build perfectly acceptable models 'straight from the box', most will benefit from additional detailing. All aspects of a car model—body, interior, running gear and engine—can receive attention, and most additional details do not necessarily require a great deal of expense. This is one area where the cottage, garage or aftermarket industries come into play in a big way, as many were set up specifically to deal with this side of the hobby.

Much of the necessary material can also be salvaged from other sources. Thin wire or cable may already be in your 'spares' box, while a supply of styrene sheet (commonly referred to by its trade name, Plasticard, as made by Slaters) will always be useful, as will a selection of pre-cut styrene strips. The last can be obtained in many sizes and thicknesses, and in square, rectangular and round sections.

## ENGINES

This is one area that obviously needs additional detailing, for if you open the bonnet (or hood) of any full-size car, besides the numerous items of equipment, you will see a mass of wiring. This ranges from thin low-tension leads, which connect general items of electrical equipment, to the much thicker, high-voltage leads that provide the spark to the plugs and are usually the most prominent feature in any under-bonnet scene. Many car kits will include moulded-in wiring on the firewall and wheel arches, but few (in 1:24/5 scale) have anything else. Some kits do provide full wiring and plumbing for their engines, but invariably these are concentrated in the larger-scale ranges.

It is quite feasible to wire the engine compartment completely, from sanding off existing details and 'rewiring' them to adding absolutely everything else. However, as a start, the most obvious lack in a standard kit will be the largest and thickest wires—those supplying the spark.

Any engine can be equipped with high-voltage wiring, the general rule being that one more lead will be required than the number of cylinders, for besides the leads to the plugs, another should run from the coil to the distributor. Thus, a four-cylinder engine will need five leads, and a V8 nine leads. Even though modern engines may differ considerably from their older counterparts—computerized engine management systems have removed such niceties as contactless breakers and added ignition modules—in general, the high-voltage wiring hasn't changed at all, whether the engine is a twenties Model T Ford straight-four side-valve or a Corvette DOHC V8. (The only exceptions are diesel engines, which do not need ignition wiring—or distributors for that matter. However, although these are common in trucks, there does not appear to have ever been a diesel engine block included in any car kit at any time.)

In the 'old days' (the sixties), finding suitable material for wiring in the right scale was a problem. The logical choice would always be electrical wires: they have the correct rigidity and come in a wide range of colours (ignition leads are not always black). However, finding any that were thin enough was difficult, so other materials had to be sourced. Consequently, the main choices became nylon fishing line and cotton thread. Both could be—and were—used,

**Although it is perfectly feasible to wire and detail any engine, this is most effective on cars with exposed engines, such as dragsters and funny cars. Here, the Chrysler hemihead V8 in Revell's model of Mickey Thompson's Revelleader features ignition wiring, fuel lines and an authentic looking blower drive belt in rubber. Note also that some fittings have been tinted with red and blue transparent paint to represent anodized metal.**

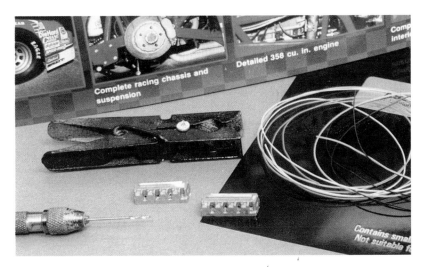

but both had disadvantages. Nylon fishing line looks right, but does not come in suitable colours—ignition leads in pale translucent green are not usual nor, for that matter, is fishing line in bright yellow (although the fish may prefer this option...). However, the line can be painted, so it is a possible option. The alternative, cotton thread, is made in all the suitable colours, but it does not have the correct look. Although there are ways of pulling the thread through wax or glue to coat it and produce a more authentic feel, this tends to be more trouble (and mess) than it is worth.

Since the sixties, the growth in communications—and the arrival of the computer industry—has led to the availability of suitably thin, cabling: offcuts of multi-core computer cable can be stripped and the inner wires salvaged. Alternatively, this is an item that the garage companies first thought of supplying, so if you are not in the mood for diving into the backs of scrap computers, packs of suitable wire, in all colours, can be bought from the specialist suppliers.

Another problem that has been solved is the method of gluing the wires in place. Originally, it had to be with globs of polystyrene cement, in the vague hope that they would hold the wires by pure friction. Now, of course, the ubiquitous superglue has come to the rescue.

*Above left* **What you need to create ignition wiring: the kit distributor (clamped in the clothes peg), the cylinder heads, a pin-vice and suitable wire for the leads. Alternatively, complete 1:25 scale distributor and wiring kits are available from such specialist suppliers as Detail Master.**

*Above right* **Ignition leads from a side-exit distributor tend to mass together in one lump. Consequently, they are somewhat easier to deal with than those from a top-exit type.**

One tool that may not be in your basic tool kit, but which is necessary for engine wiring, is the pin-vice (or a modeller's electric drill), for although often indicated on a miniature engine block, the actual holes for the plugs will not be pre-drilled.

There are many variations in the actual positions of the plugs in engines, but as a general rule, if the engine is an inline example, the plugs will be opposite the manifolds. On vee engines, they will be on the outside, usually tucked under the exhaust headers (with the exception of Chrysler hemi-head engines, where the plug leads pass down through over-size valve covers). Flat engines—technically, horizontally opposed engines (as typified by VW and Porsche)—are

**Wiring fitted to the double-blower Chrysler engine from AMT's 1953 Studebaker kit, shown mid-mounted in a Chevy Silverado. Note the loom tidies on each side and black plug extension covers where the leads pass through the valve covers. The engine also features fuel lines (to the front of the blowers) and home-made shock absorbers, the springs of which can be seen just behind the engine block. (Note that the blower scoops have been purposely fitted to face backwards, as otherwise the cab would disturb the airflow to them.)**

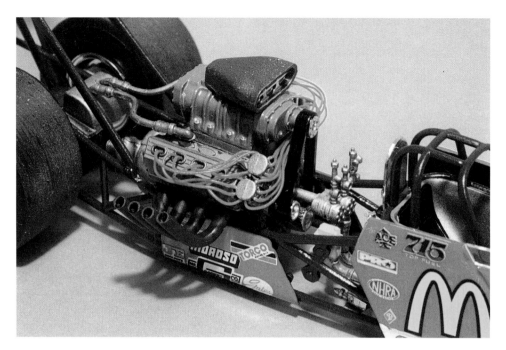

Some dragster engines have two ignition systems with dual distributors, so your V8 ends up with 16 leads to the plugs. These have been provided on this Revell McDonald's fuel dragster by an MSC wiring kit.

like inline engines, in that their plug positions are usually opposite the manifolds.

Side-valve engines (which can be of inline or vee configuration) have their plugs sitting on top of the cylinder head, and you'll normally find them moulded in place. With larger-scale kits, the wiring can be glued over these plugs in an almost authentic manner, but this is more difficult in 1:24/5 scale, although not impossible. In the latter case, a very short length of black tubing, with an inside diameter that matches the outer diameter of the plug lead, can be cut and the two carefully glued together. Then, the tubing can be glued over the plug moulding. However, this is really only worthwhile if the plug is prominent. Most plugs in modern overhead-valve and overhead-cam engines are tucked well away and can't really be seen under the manifolds, etc. Consequently, the plug (or plug position) will need drilling out, and the lead gluing directly into the hole. This even applies to the hemi head, as the plugs are actually buried well below the valve cover, so in reality all you see is the plug lead disappearing through the hole.

The other ends of the leads come together at the distrib-utor, which is slightly more difficult to deal with. Distributors either have the leads coming straight out of the top—with the wire to the coil in the centre—or bunched together at the side. The latter arrangement is somewhat easier to re-create, as these distributors do not have the very prominent top mounted sockets that make the distributor recognizable, even to the uninitiated. Because of the scale—especially when dealing with a V8, which will require nine holes in total—care must be taken when drilling the holes. It is not impossible to drill them individually, but it could be worth compromising slightly and pairing wires together so that only five holes are required. Drill the coil lead hole first, then add four slightly larger holes around it.

Most miniature distributors with top connectors have these moulded in as small 'pins'. It is not impossible to add the leads to the pins, using very thin tubing, as described above, but this is not very practical in 1:24/5 scale. Instead, saw the pins off, then carefully drill a hole in the centre and eight more around it (assuming a V8). Although needing a sharp eye and a lot of care, this task is not impossible, even on something as small as a 1:24/5 scale distributor cap!

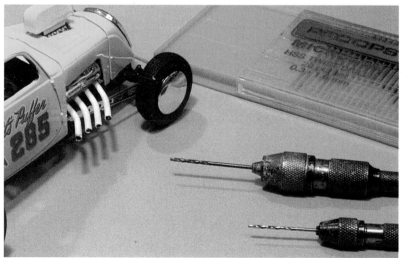

The coil lead should be the same colour as the rest and run directly to the coil. Many kits supply a separate coil as standard, although you could obtain one from a garage company. Frankly, however, a coil is simple to make from a short length of plastic rod with a conical end; the lead from the distributor fits into the centre of the cone. The coil is usually attached to either the engine block itself or the firewall. If you want to add even more detail, the metal clamp that holds the coil can be made from the thinnest Plasticard, or even extremely thin sheetmetal—the foil from wine bottle caps is ideal. Suitable decals for coils can be found on many sheets supplied with kits and by the after-market suppliers.

There is one other aspect of detailing that can be added to the ignition leads. Many engines have loom tidies in the form of perforated straight plastic mouldings, through which the plug leads are passed. This prevents them from touching one another (the high-voltage current can jump across in some cases) and makes the whole engine compartment tidier. Loom tidies can be made from thin offcuts of Plasticard, or cut from styrene strip. With the same drill bit that you used to drill out the plugs, make four holes (or as many as necessary) in a straight line. Round off the ends of the strip and paint it a suitable colour, then thread the leads through the tidy before attaching them to the block and distributor. Normally, one loom tidy on each side (assuming a V8) is all that is required, but for an extremely tidy engine, extras can be added, with correspondingly fewer holes: three, two, etc.

One point about ignition wiring is that all engines follow a specific firing pattern, which dictates the position of each plug lead in the distributor cap. For example, the plugs in a four-cylinder engine do not fire 1,2,3,4 (number 1 cylinder normally being at the front of the engine), but are more likely to fire in the order 1,3,4,2. If you really want to super-detail a model, it could be worth finding out the correct firing order of the full-size engine, allowing the plug leads to be placed in the correct positions.

Next to ignition wiring, the most prominent details in the engine compartment are the fuel lines. In the very simplest arrangement, the fuel is taken from the tank, via the pump (electrical or mechanical) to the carburettor. Long lengths of pipe, beneath the floorpan or along the chassis, are usually metal, while shorter lengths that connect these to

the tank, pump, filter and carburettor will be flexible, either black or clear hose, or braided pipe. Scale fuel pipes are available from the specialist suppliers, including the metal braided type and black hoses in a variety of sizes—some even detailed down to the lettering found on full-size hoses. Alternative sources could be standard black electrical wire and very thin coaxial cable with the outer sheath stripped off, the latter to represent braided fuel lines.

The actual position of the fuel tank can vary considerably. An ordinary road car tends to have the tank at the back if it's front engined, or the front if it's rear engined. However, a dragster or hot rod may have a small tank at the very front, while a sports racer can have a tank on each side in sponsons under the doors.

Mechanical fuel pumps can be situated on the side of the block (driven from the crankshaft), on top (driven from the camshaft) or in front (driven from the crank or an intermediate pulley). The last is a favourite position for racing V8s. There is also increasing use of professional-type fittings for fuel pipes—especially on racers. These specialist fittings can be bought in packs from the garage suppliers, and can be tinted to represent suitable anodized finishes using transparent acrylics—red and blue—over a silver base.

Multiple-carburettor set-ups require additional work with T-pieces, or even special manifolds to distribute the fuel to the individual carbs. Fuel systems on race cars may also be doubled up, with two of everything running from tank to engine. Fuel injection systems use even more pipes, the fuel being supplied first to the metering manifold, where it is distributed to the cylinders individually.

Radiator hoses are normally supplied by the model manufacturers as styrene mouldings. However, they have the disadvantage that, whereas the full-size examples are flexible, the scale versions are not, and they may not always fit properly between the radiator and block. Fortunately, the garage companies supply suitable flexible hoses—both straight and convoluted—which can be used to replace the kit versions.

The flexible hoses are easily fixed in position by drilling holes, corresponding to the inner diameter of the hose, into the radiator and engine block, then gluing short lengths of plastic rod in place. Then, the hose can simply be superglued over these pins. Extra details are the clips that hold the hoses

*Facing page, below left* **Exhaust tips can be drilled to create 'tubes'. Alternatively, use real tubing, as here, aluminium tubes having been added to the kit's exhaust headers.**

*Facing page, below right* **When drilling out the ends of exhausts, and similar hollow items, for a more authentic look, use a selection of drill bits, starting small and working up to the correct size.**

*Right* **Fuel injector stacks can be drilled out (if not already) and, as an additional touch, 'tennis balls' or similar can be placed in the openings to prevent anything from falling into them when the car is not being raced. These balls can be made from map pins (foreground) or even BB gun pellets (background). Sometimes, the balls are chained together, which can be reproduced with very fine chain (far left).**

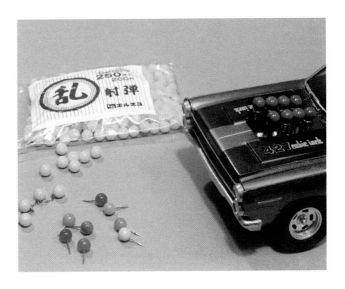

in position. The wire type can be made from two turns of thin wire, while a Jubilee clip can be represented by a thin length of Plasticard, or foil cut from a wine bottle cap.

T-pieces for water hoses can be made by gluing together lengths of styrene rod, or by soldering together brass tubes. Alternatively, they are obtainable from the garage suppliers. Heater hoses can be approached in the same way, although they are usually of thinner diameter than the radiator hoses. The overflow pipe from the radiator—or more commonly these days, the separate header tank—can be formed from even thinner black or clear tube.

Favourite for sixties-style American V8s were fuel injector stacks. These are long tubes that act as intakes for the simplest of fuel injection systems and, as one tube is needed for each cylinder, for a V8 you need a bank of eight of them. In reality, they are only suitable for racing engines, but they often found their way on to show cars—most of which were more 'show' than 'go'. Many older kits (and, consequently, many reissues) contain injector stacks as an engine option, and these can be improved very easily. The first task is to drill out the ends of the stacks so that they form tubes. This can be done with a pin-vice and a selection of drill bits; you do need a selection of bits, as it is always advisable to drill such holes progressively. Start with a small hole and gradually enlarge it; if you use too large a drill bit too soon, you run the risk of melting the plastic because too much force will be needed, or of cracking the wall of the part. Injector stacks are usually chromed, but obviously the inner surfaces of the drilled tubes will not be plated. However, quite often the insides of the real thing are painted, gloss red being a favourite. The plastic stacks can also be replaced with aluminium tube, which can be superglued into place. The ends can be flared with needle-nosed pliers.

There is another detailing trick that can be used with injector stacks. Because they are vulnerable to unwanted items falling inside, when not in use they are often blocked off by convenient ball-shaped objects, tennis balls topping the list of favourites. Several kits actually supplied miniature

balls for this purpose. Alternatively, the beads from a cheap necklace, the heads from small map pins, or even small ball-bearings could be used.

Another method of preventing foreign objects from dropping into the stacks is to fit mesh domes over the top. These can be represented by thin metal foil, again from the garage industries or other sources. The dome shape can be created by pushing the end of a rounded rod into the mesh.

Mesh, such as from the foil of an old electric razor, can also be useful for air cleaners, where the intake is visible. Some—of the large 'frying pan' shape—have the intake as a small opening in what would be (if it was a frying pan) the end of the handle. This can be opened out in the same way as an injector stack, first by using various sizes of drill bit, then—assuming the opening to be square rather than round—by creating the final shape with needle files. Air cleaners often carry decals, either the manufacturer's or a sponsor's, and many are included with kits. Alternatively, a variety will be found on after-market decal sheets.

Carburettors come in a wide range of shapes and sizes, and may be used singly or in multiple set-ups. If a carburettor is not covered by an air cleaner, its throat can be drilled out in the same manner as described above. However, the

*Left* **Applying a thin wash of matt or satin black paint produces an obvious effect on wire wheels (top), but a more subtle change in other cases. A 50:50 mix of paint and thinners should do, but experiment to obtain the best results. The right-hand pair of each set shown here has had the wash applied.**

*Facing page, bottom* **The same technique can be used on grilles and other parts. The rocker covers of Monogram's ZZ Top '33 Ford feature the band's symbol, picked out on one in transparent red.**

*Facing page, top* **Tyres can be sanded to create authentic looking wear. In this case, they are drag slicks with no actual tread. Coarse glass paper stuck to a rigid base makes the best sanding surface, and although it's straightforward to sand tyres by hand, special collets are available to hold them in an electric drill.**

*Right* **The whitewalls on the tyres of this Arii 1958 Cadillac have been hand painted using acrylic paint.**

first thing to be found in a genuine carburettor's throat is the butterfly, which controls the amount of air that enters. So once the throat has been hollowed, a small disc of plastic should be added to represent this valve. Working butterflies have been built in scales as small as 1:24/5, the valve pivoting on a thin rod fitted to holes drilled in the carburettor body. The carburettor is connected to the accelerator pedal by a cable and linkage of rods, which can be duplicated by thin rods and wire. Again, fully working systems have been made in this size, but it must be said that if there is an air-cleaner in the way, you will not see much of the linkage, so the accelerator cable alone will probably suffice.

Many racing engines—especially in dragsters—have another place where butterfly valves are found: on the front of an intake scoop, which sits on top of a supercharger (or 'blower'). Normally, there are three butterflies in the scoop, which can be made to work, or you can simply improve the detailing by drilling out the intake holes and fitting small-diameter discs glued to thin wire. Like injector stacks, blower intakes are often painted a bright gloss red.

Once the air and fuel mixture has entered the engine and done its work, it has to be ejected, through the exhaust system. Occasionally, the exhaust tip will be moulded as a tube, but usually it is solid, so one of the simplest tasks is to drill

out the end of the exhaust pipe to make it into a tube. This is done in precisely the same way as drilling out an injector stack or carburettor throat, starting with a small drill bit and gradually increasing the size. Alternatively, a short length of metal tubing can be glued to the end of the system to create the same effect; some kits (such as those from Fujimi) already include this option.

The technique can also work where a full exhaust system is not fitted, such as on a dragster, which will have a series of individual header pipes. In this case, there will be eight pipes to deal with (assuming a V8), but the principle is exactly the same. It is also possible to build your own exhaust systems from various sizes of rod or tube. Even where you need a convoluted system for the highly tuned exhaust of a racing car, this can be made from straight rod, carefully warmed and bent into shape. Flexible pipe or solder can also be bent into shape and held by superglue. Some racing exhausts are so complex that virtually no light can be seen between the pipes, and the use of flexible pipes works quite well, as the superglue fills the gaps between them.

As mentioned previously, batteries come a wide range of colours these days, and many kits also supply suitable decals. What they do not tend to supply are the battery leads. These are usually the thickness of the ignition leads, but they will only be black or red, depending on the polarity. Sometimes, the earth lead will be a braided flat strap instead of a round black wire. Each can be attached to the battery with a drop of superglue (which can be painted to represent the clamp). The earth lead should be taken to a position nearby on the body (assuming a metal-bodied car—on GRP-bodied cars, the earth lead will be taken down to the chassis). The live lead will run to a nearby distribution box, although a similar-diameter lead will continue to the starter motor.

Most modern batteries are sealed and no longer have separate caps for the cells, but an older battery can be represented by picking out the caps in a contrasting colour—yellow was always a favourite. Car electrical systems are almost universally 12 volt today, but older cars had 6-volt systems, with a correspondingly different shaped battery.

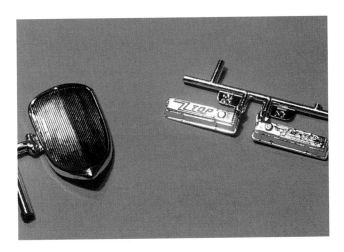

Multiple-battery set-ups are possible: two 6-volt to give 12 volts, or two 12-volt side by side and wired in parallel could be used in some heavy-duty applications, such as pickups and off-road vehicles.

## CHASSIS

The chassis is an area that is often ignored when it comes to detailing, as it is usually 'out of sight and out of mind'. This isn't helped by the older-style, one-piece chassis, which has all the details—from axles to exhausts and propshafts—moulded in. However, even here, much can be done with the careful use of paint. Most modern kits offer chassis with separate details and, in theory, you could replace every part with after-market items—from shocks and exhausts to the whole rear axle.

Shock absorbers, or dampers, are necessary on all cars: they control the bouncing motion of the springs, preventing the development of a 'switchback' ride. These days, most shocks are telescopic units, one tube inside another, the damping process being provided by hydraulic action. Most kits supply these shocks as single mouldings. With some cleaning up (these parts are notorious for displaying mould lines), and possibly the addition of suitable decals, they can be made quite presentable.

Many shocks also run through the centres of the coil springs they are damping, and if these are moulded as one, you will find even less detail in the shock itself. Occasionally, kits will supply shocks and springs separately (sometimes even real metal springs), but this is the exception rather than the rule.

Individual shock absorbers can be assembled quite simply, and can even be made to 'work' if you feel so inclined. The body of the shock absorber should be made from two diameters of aluminium or brass tubing, one just fitting inside the other. To each end, superglue a short piece of tube at right angles, which will allow tiny bolts to attach the shock to the car. If a small spring is placed inside the tubing, the shock will actually work (after a fashion). Alternatively, fit a larger spring around the outside. This will need a disc

of some sort at each end of the shock to contain the spring. Painting should be done before assembly, and if the shock is one of the usual colours—yellow, red or blue are favourites—the spring can either be left natural metal, or be painted the same or some contrasting colour. The whole assembly can be attached to the appropriate parts of the axle and chassis by small (16BA or smaller) nuts and bolts.

Leaf springs can be made from thin strips of metal or plastic, glued or pinned together at the centre. The number of leaves can vary from one to six, and multiples have bands at intervals along their length to keep them all together. A leaf spring is normally attached directly to the chassis at one end, while the other hangs on a shackle to allow for the spring's movement. These can also be built from plastic strip or, if you are feeling particularly ambitious, from metal and hinged with tiny nuts and bolts.

Most kits supply brakes in some form or other—discs or drums—but brake lines are far rarer and only found on a few large-scale kits. The brake pipes run along the chassis (although many modern cars have them inside the body-work), and in many kits they will be moulded into the chassis floor. However, on cars such as hot rods and dragsters, the pipework can be fashioned from thin metal wire and superglued, or pinned, into place. Where the pipe reaches the rear axle, there is usually a junction, which is also a pressure limiter that prevents the back wheels from locking before the front. This can be represented by a small block of plastic drilled with suitable holes.

Individual lines to the brakes themselves can take the form of very thin flexible tubes. Most modern systems are dual-line, each front disc calliper having two pipes running to it, while the back brakes are fed individually. Systems differ widely, however, so research your subject carefully.

## WHEELS AND TYRES

Besides wiring the ignition, the next favourite detailing technique is to sand the vinyl tyres to produce an authentic worn look—a tip that is even beginning to appear in some kit instructions these days. It probably began with the tyres on

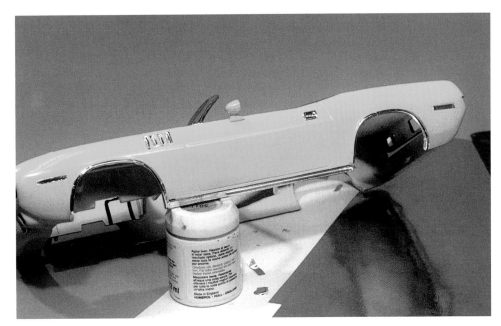

*Facing page* **The tools required for the application of Bare-Metal Foil: a steel rule or edge, a sharp scalpel and tweezers for transferring small sections.**

*Right* **Bare-Metal Foil can be used on many areas of a car, as shown by this Plymouth Hemi 'Cuda. Besides the rocker panel and wheel arches, it's used on the door handles, fender vents and the repeater turn indicators front and rear, which later will be tinted with amber transparent paint.**

dragsters, the slicks, which have a very prominent surface that contacts the strip (one cannot say 'tread', as they don't have any!), but now it applies to any model tyre. Even a new car in a showroom will have been driven, if only on and off a transporter, and the original pristine tread will become scuffed, so this tip works with any tyre in any situation.

Sanding is also vital in a practical sense if a mould line runs around the centre of the tyre and is still visible. In the past, some tyres were produced in two halves, but not in the usual vinyl, rather a polyethylene-like material, which would never glue together satisfactorily. Whatever glue you attempted to use, there would always be a line to get rid of, even with the introduction of superglue (which almost glues this material, but not quite).

Sanding model car tyres is very easy. All that is required is to hold the tyre between thumb and forefinger, and pull it across some reasonably coarse glass paper. This should be fixed to a flat surface (with spray glue or double-sided tape), otherwise you will be forever repositioning it. (The first few attempts will usually sand the tips of your thumb and finger as well, but you will soon learn to keep them out of the way!) The tyre should be rotated progressively until all of the tread has been sanded. By comparing it with an unsanded example, you will immediately see how effective the treatment is and how it makes the tyre look so much better.

This method works with the majority of tyres found in kits, although ironically the few kits that have tyres moulded in genuine rubber (some of Revell's 1:16 scale dragsters did) are the worst to deal with. They are so thin that they cannot be gripped correctly to keep them in contact with the sanding surface. Perseverance is the only answer, or filling them with a substance that will make them solid.

The amount of 'wear' a tyre receives will be directly proportional to the amount it is sanded. So if you are dealing with street tyres that have a tread, don't overdo it—unless you need a 'bald' look for a scrapyard diorama or the like.

Various devices have been invented and marketed for the mechanical sanding of tyres. For example, they can be clamped between collets fitted to a modelling drill chuck.

However, although these may make the job somewhat easier than by hand, there is the great danger of sanding unevenly or, more likely, sanding away too much and producing a far smaller diameter tyre than you intended.

Many tyres, particularly from the fifties and sixties, feature whitewalls—either the standard wide variety or thin examples, called 'thinwalls'. Plus there was a fashion for thin red walls. These are coming back into fashion, and many kits include them. Some manufacturers moulded the white tyre walls as separate inserts—Monogram started this with their classic range—and they can also be found in such as the new R-M '55 Chevy Bel Air. Some whitewalls were also supplied as peel-off/stick-on decals, so you could choose to use them or not. After-market suppliers make replacement ranges of tyres with a whole variety of colours and thicknesses—SATCO make red, white and gold thinwalls for example.

**Bare-Metal Foil is also useful for recreating the metal hold-down strips in an old-style pickup bed, such as this one belonging to the Lindberg (originally AMT) 1934 Ford.**

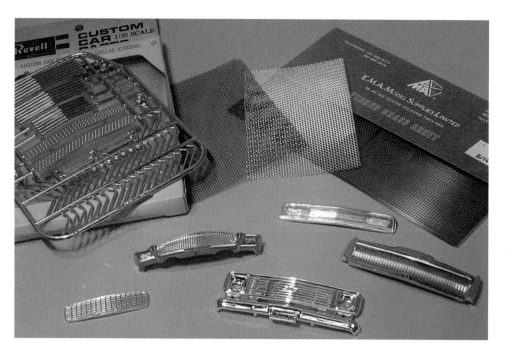

*Left* **Replacing solid grilles with custom versions (illustrated by an original Revell set on the left) or mesh (right) is another simple detailing technique.**

*Below left* **A solid grille can be ground out from the back to open up the gaps, or the whole section can be removed, as in this case.**

*Bottom left* **The grille opening has been replaced with brass mesh. Eventually, the entire grille and bumper will be sprayed one colour to match the main bodywork.**

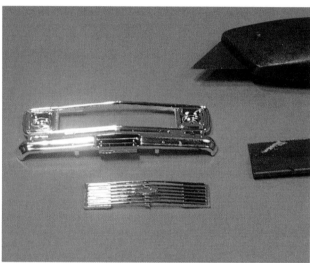

Wide whitewalls can be painted on to standard black tyres with acrylic paints. You must use acrylics, as enamel will not dry on vinyl. First, thoroughly clean the tyre surface with methylated spirits, or similar, and dry it. Then apply the paint in several coats. (Before the introduction of modelling acrylics, other paints had to be used, including poster paint.) Many tyres have a convenient moulding line that can be used as a guide for the edge of the whitewall. Thinwalls are more difficult, but if you own a modeller's lathe (or can devise a way of mounting an electric drill to achieve a similar arrangement), and can clamp the tyre somehow, a thin groove can be carefully turned out of the tyre to represent the thinwall. This groove can be filled with paint and the excess carefully wiped away.

Many racing tyres, and some others, have the manufacturer's name prominently moulded into the sidewall—Goodyear, Firestone, etc. These are often painted white, and you can achieve this effect in the same manner as painting whitewalls. In this situation, another advantage of acrylic paint is that, if you make a mistake, it is easily wiped off, and you can start all over again. The secret of painting these sorts of tiny detail is to load the brush quite full of paint and simply use the side of it just to touch the raised surface.

However, manufacturers are increasingly supplying decals for tyres, especially for NASCARs, Supertrucks and track cars. These can be supplied in two ways. US manufacturers—R-M and AMT—supply them as ordinary water-slide decals, which are applied in the usual way. Japanese manufacturers have adopted a different approach—although still water-based—whereby the decals are supplied as mirror images and, instead of being wetted themselves, are applied to a wet tyre. After burnishing down with your finger, the backing paper is carefully pulled away to leave the lettering the correct way round. Both methods work, although the Japanese technique is definitely more difficult and arguably no more effective.

Obviously, the tyres fit on to wheels, which can also be candidates for additional work. The trend with US cars particularly was to supply the wheels—or, to be accurate, the wheel covers or embellishers (generally, if somewhat incorrectly, known as the hub-caps)—with a chrome finish. However, although correct for the fifties and sixties, modern cars—if they have shiny wheels at all—will probably have satin finished aluminium wheels or embellishers. Today, many kit companies actually produce the discs with a satin plated finish, not bright chrome.

If they are chrome, they can easily be modified by spraying them with one of the aluminium finishes. (Humbrol Polished Aluminium was excellent for this, but unfortunately it is no longer available in an aerosol, although it is still available in a tinlet.)

This may not be all that you can do, either, for whether satin or chrome plated, many wheel embellishers have small indentations, actually holes, and even badges in the centre. Holes can either be cut out (pin-vice and needle files again) or filled with matt black paint.

The badges found at the centres of many discs may be supplied as decals. Otherwise, it is down to checking references and painting them on. In this case, because the paint will be applied to a chromed (or at least shiny) surface, the transparent colours work better than solid types. If embellishers are not provided, the steel wheels themselves will be seen. These were often fitted with small Moon discs on early rods and customs, which can still be found in many kits. NASCARs and similar also run without embellishers, and additional details for these could be the valve stems (very thin, short pieces of plastic rod) and balancing weights (tiny squares of plastic strip, cut extremely thinly and glued around the inside edge of the rim). These are also items that the specialist suppliers stock, in case you don't feel like chopping them up yourself.

NASCAR wheels are usually black, but with a thin red line on the outer edge. To achieve this, first paint the wheel gloss black. Next, spray some white primer on to a piece of scrap plastic and gently place the wheel on the surface so that it picks up the paint on the very edge of the rim. Then, when dry, repeat the exercise with gloss red instead of white. Some racing wheels have a similar pattern, but the red may be inside the wheel, which makes it far harder to reproduce. One way is to find a piece of scrap tube with the same outside diameter as the wheel's inside diameter. Apply the white primer to the tube and wipe it around the inside of the wheel, then repeat this with the red. There are bound to be areas that will still need touching up, but this is probably the most straightforward method.

## BODIES

With the body being the largest single part of most car kits, it will attract attention first and leave a lasting impression. Most kit car bodies are well detailed, but even the best will benefit from some extra touches.

Most car kits—especially of American origin—come with an opening hood to show off the engine. Some also have an opening trunk lid, and a few even opening doors. However, if the kit you have chosen does not supply the latter options, they can be made relatively easily. The biggest help is that the outlines for the doors and trunk—or the side

and rear doors of a van—will have their outlines already inscribed. Using one of the specialist scribing knives, or a suitable blade in a standard knife, carefully cut along these existing lines, gradually making them deeper until you cut through to the other side.

Having separated the piece, you will need to clean up the edges, but do not go too far, as you will make it rather obviously too small for the opening. Items such as trunk lids and van rear doors, which in reality do not have a great thickness, may be usable more or less as is. However, most doors are thicker than the outer shell, so they will need building up to an appropriate depth. If the model has an interior tub or separate side panels, these can be cut and utilized as the the inner surfaces of the doors, providing details such as handles, winders and the like. This will leave the edges as the only pieces that need adding. Remember, however, that the door openings will also need their sides filling in with suitable pieces of plastic sheet.

An important decision is whether the doors should operate or simply be cemented in place. Obviously, the latter will be somewhat easier, although some semblance of a scale hinge mechanism is advisable. Operating doors are somewhat more complex, as the sheer small size of scale working hinges makes them very fiddly to make, while they will not be very strong. (Some early Revell kits—for example, their 1931 Ford Woody Wagon—featured scale working hinges on the doors, although extreme care was needed, as they were very delicate.) Non-scale hinges can be adapted from those designed for flying model aircraft control surfaces, which can be quite suitable for larger pieces, such as van doors and the like. These hinges are usually made from nylon and are difficult to glue, but they can be sandwiched between two layers of styrene, while contact adhesive often works. Alternatively, hinges can be made from brass tube and U-shaped metal pins, superglued in place.

## OTHER DETAILS

With most full-size cars becoming more and more alike,

**Nothing looks quite as authentic as flexible material when duplicating seat belts. Many after-market suppliers provide seat-belt material and fittings, and some kits, like this Repsol Toyota from Hasegawa, provide both belt material and photo-etched fittings. Tiny drops of superglue hold it all together.**

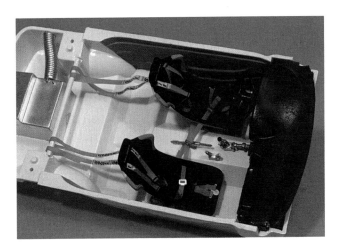

there will usually be some form of distinctive grille at the front end, which can be the starting point for a little extra detailing. As modelled, a car grille will invariably be a single solid moulding, but in reality it will have openings that allow air to flow into the radiator and engine compartment. The solid bits may be chromed, but the grille openings certainly will not be. It is possible to grind out the back of a model grille to reveal the openings, but it's a lengthy task. Alternatively, the whole grille area can be replaced with another material—mesh of some sort—which incorporates genuine holes. (Some Tamiya and Fujimi kits actually supply mesh for this purpose.) However, a very effective—and quicker—alternative is to run a wash of matt black paint into the grille area. It needs to be thinned so that it will run off the raised parts of the grille and into the recesses—an approximate 50:50 mix of paint to thinner will usually work. This approach can be used in other areas, too. Sometimes, there are rear grilles where it can used, while wheel embellishers with recesses will also benefit from the treatment.

In some kits, the headlamps are also supplied with chromed lenses as part of the grille (a favourite approach with early 'annual' kits based on promos). Although the light reflector itself is actually chromed for maximum light dispersion, the chromed lens never looks right. For super-detailing, the lens can be drilled out, a bucket formed behind and a clear lens added from the spares box. Alternatively, a 50:50 mix of silver and matt white makes the lamp 'glass' look far more realistic without any further modifications.

Grilles and bumpers may also incorporate overriders. Often, these should not be chromed either: they may be made from hard rubber, so satin black would be a more appropriate finish.

Emblems—found on the grille and other parts of the body—may not necessarily be all chrome, either. Most incorporate the manufacturer's badge, which can be a variety of colours (Chevrolet's is red, white and blue for example). Transparent colours, rather than solid, tend to work best for these types of badges.

Of course, chrome can be found on many cars, old and new, but it is typified by American cars of the fifties and six-ties. Although grilles and bumpers may be supplied chrome plated, other areas of brightwork may not be. Window surrounds and side trims are usually moulded into the body, so some method is needed to create the chrome look.

In the old days, the only way was to paint these areas silver, but this presented two problems: it never looked shiny enough and, unless you were very precise, the line would invariably wobble! Enter Bare-Metal Foil, a very thin foil supplied as an adhesive-backed sheet that can be cut to shape and buffed down over the relevant area, the excess being trimmed away. This has solved the major headache of window surrounds and trims, and although other makes of similar materials have entered the market, Bare-Metal Foil is still the best known. Today, the manufacturers make other finishes, too, including matt aluminium, gold and matt black (for those modern plastic side trim strips).

Bare-Metal Foil can also be used for all other chromed items, including make/model scripts and badges, although sometimes difficulty may be experienced with some of the tiniest lettering. In fact, some of the Japanese kit companies include 'metallized' decals in their kits, which provide this type of chromed script. These are self-adhesive decals, which do not need soaking, but rather can be peeled from the backing and applied. However, most are extremely small, so great care is needed when applying them.

Currently, this metallized-decal approach has not been adopted by the garage industries, although they have supplied photo-etched sheets of popular American chrome scripts that can be used instead of the moulded-in plastic versions. You need to make up your mind that you will use them before you start building the kit, as the relevant mouldings will need removing from the body before painting.

Materials from other sources can also be employed. For a vinyl roof, apply paper masking tape to the roof, trim it to shape and paint it satin black. Thin wood veneers, designed for marquetry and the like, can be used to create real wood inserts for the sides of model cars, or real wood pickup beds and sides. And for the chrome strips that are found on the older-style of pickup bed floor, use Bare-Metal Foil, pre-cut into thin strips.

**Real wood veneers, which can be obtained in very thin, self-adhesive form, have been used to create the wooden panel inserts on the Testors Frankenwoodiac resin 'slammer' kit.**

## Chapter Seven

# PAINT AND FINISHING

Assembling a kit is really only half the task; the final appearance of the completed model relies considerably on the final finish. Many an excellently constructed model has been ruined by a poor paint finish, although modellers are very fortunate these days, as the range of specially formulated paints has never been wider.

Faced with the finishing of any model car, really you will have only three options. If the plastic itself has a finish that is good enough, it may be possible simply to polish it. Although, these days, most model manufacturers have switched to neutral colours for the styrene, precisely to allow for spray finishes, some models are still coloured and have a finish that can be polished. Many older Monogram kits were like this, although the company have moved to white styrene for all 1:24/5 scale cars in their general catalogue. However, some older reissues—in the SSP range—should be in their original colours (otherwise they aren't SSPs!). In addition, Lindberg produce most of their 1:20 scale vehicle kits in bright colours that can be polished and that will stand alongside a completely painted version. You will still need to apply the details—windshield surround, side trims and the like—but the main colour is already in place. Pocher kits in 1:8 scale are pre-coloured, too, and many of them can be polished for an effective finish.

It is also possible to hand paint a car body, then sand it, rebrush if necessary and, finally, polish it to a shine. This is a long task, and really only for the dedicated, but it can produce excellent results. However, I suspect that most will opt for spray painting, which can be carried out with either commercial aerosols or an air-brush.

Air-brushing itself is a specialist art, and the air-brush can be a very useful tool for the experienced modeller. For the less experienced, however, there is a wide range of pre-packaged aerosol paints made specifically for plastic kits, many of which are designed purely for car models and offer specific finishes. These are manufactured by chemical companies that specialize in model products, the major names world-wide being Testors in the US, Humbrol in the UK and Gunze Sangyo in Japan. This isn't to say that there are not other manufacturers. Tamiya, for example, sell a wide range of their own paints and sprays, as do Revell AG, while Revell-Monogram (through their ProModeler subsidiary) also have a range of bottled acrylics. Specialist companies, such as Tru-Match, make a range of aerosols that duplicate colours used on the American racing circuits, and these have proved so popular that Testors have begun to distribute them. (These colours are so accurate that the owners of the full-size cars use them as touch-up paint!)

Even with this wide range of colours—and there are probably approaching 200 different shades available off the shelf for modellers—you need not feel restricted. There are other sprays designed for the lexan bodies of radio controlled model cars that may very well provide yet more shades, and there are even special ranges for model rockets that can be used—with care—over the appropriate primer.

Plus don't forget that there is a wide range of relatively cheap sprays available in the form of car touch-up sprays. Again, proper priming is necessary, but with many of them having been reformulated to remove their nastier aspects, some can even be sprayed straight on to styrene. Most touch-

A small selection of the wide range of aerosol paints available to modellers. Included are paints from the general suppliers (left to right) Revell, Humbrol, Testors and Tamiya, plus (far right) specialist suppliers Tru-Match. Don't forget the even wider selection of automotive touch-up sprays, three examples of which are also shown (back right).

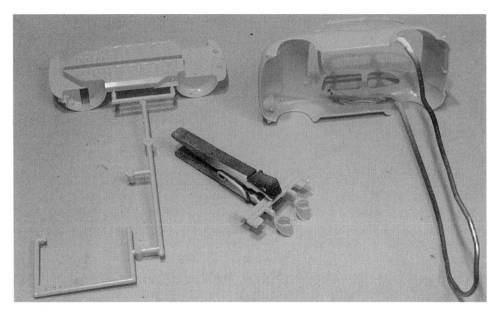

*Left* **Preparing parts for painting, using the wire coat-hanger method described previously (right); leaving a part attached to a section of the runner (left); and holding a part with a clothes peg (centre).**

*Below left* **Air-brushing is an option if the required colour is not readily available straight from a can, although many modellers prefer this method anyway. Here, it is being used to apply the special blue of the Revell AG Williams-Renault Formula 1 car. The paint is only available in a tinlet, so it must be thinned to allow it to be air-brushed. Note that several coats of the thin paint must be applied to achieve the correct depth of colour. Of the two examples shown, the finished version is on the right, while the left-hand body has only had a few layers applied.**

up sprays also have the advantage that they dry extremely fast—faster than specifically formulated model paints.

## PREPARATION

The first task when painting any model car is to prepare it properly. When spraying the main bodywork, it must be held safely in position. Over the years, two main methods seem to have been adopted.

One technique of holding a body for painting is to attach it to a suitable bottle, the top of the bottle being fixed securely to the inside of the model's roof. This provides a hand-hold (the bottle) for spraying, and it means that the body can be put down without any edge touching a surface. However, it does have the slight disadvantage that, although fine for hardtops, it is not so good for convertibles! Far better is the wire coat-hanger method mentioned previously. The wire can be bent to suit any type of car body: hardtops and convertibles, limousines and sports cars. It should be springy enough to 'snap' inside the body and stay in place, although

it can be held more securely with tape. This also has one other advantage over the bottle method, in that the body can be hung up to dry upside-down. (Why this is advantageous will be explained later.)

The paint finish, of course, will only be as good as the surface underneath. So this must be as complete as you can make it, with any necessary attachments in place and the surface as smooth as possible. This may mean filling any surface flaws with modelling putty, sanding it flat and applying more putty if necessary (see Chapter 9 for more details on puttying and sanding).

If at all possible, make sure that parts that will end up the same colour are painted at the same time. This will ensure that the parts all have the same number of paint layers, and prevent a particular area from standing out because it was painted at a different time and possibly in a different direction (that said, modelling sprays are very forgiving). However, the car will probably have an opening bonnet/hood (and possibly even a boot and doors as well), and the inner edges really need to be the same colour as the body. (Back to checking full-size examples again.) Consequently, it may be necessary to set up the body first without the hood, etc, in place so that the inner surfaces can be painted. Similarly, the individual panels should be painted around the edges. Then—having allowed them to dry thoroughly, of course—fit them into place, holding them with masking tape, and apply the main coats of paint.

## CLEANLINESS NEXT TO...

Whichever method of holding parts you decide upon, all the plastic must be cleaned thoroughly to remove any contaminants and other residue, including finger marks (another reason for using a hand-hold such as the coat-hanger). Either wash the parts in warm soapy water and allow to dry thoroughly, or use methylated spirits or a similar decontaminant, applied with a lint-free cloth or paper kitchen towel. This should ensure that any oil deposits especially are removed from the surface, and will offer the bonus of reducing the static of the plastic, which in itself can attract dust.

The bodywork will need priming first. This first stage is essential, as top-coat paint doesn't stick particularly well to plastic, no matter how clean. The primer is specially formulated to adhere well to a styrene surface. Most primers are self-etching, in that they actually 'eat' into the surface slightly—not enough to ruin the smooth finish, but enough to produce a good key. They act as a good base to the top coats. All model paint manufacturers make a primer, which usually will be white or grey. (Humbrol's is grey. Revell's is white, while Testors make both.) It is also possible to use other shades of matt paint as the undercoat, usually to good effect, but overall, proper primer will work best, although you can apply the matt coat as an intermediate stage.

Primers also help in covering surfaces of different composition. If modelling putty has been used, the primer will cover both plastic and putty to give a uniform finish in which—assuming the putty has been rubbed down properly—the dissimilar surfaces will not show.

A primer can act as a barrier to paints that otherwise would affect the plastic. The classic case is automotive touch-up sprays. These are often cellulose-, lacquer- or acrylic-based, in which form they are likely to craze the styrene. Although this can actually be used to good effect—spray cellulose directly on to, say, a model car seat and it will (or should!) give an effect that resembles leather—it is not that advisable on a car body.

However, when using any paint that is not specially formulated for plastic, always check for a reaction with the plastic first. Spray it on to an inconspicuous part—an optional accessory you do not intend using, the runners or even the inside of the car body—to make sure that it will not affect the surface. Even formulas you may have used before can alter, and it's better to check beforehand than to waste time, effort—and paint—cleaning the bodywork and reapplying a completely fresh finish.

The watchword is always check and, if necessary, experiment first—especially if you are mixing paint types, although this should be avoided whenever possible. There will be exceptions, however. You can usually apply enamel

*Above* **The author's drying cabinet, built from melamine covered chipboard and fitted with three hanging rails. At the bottom is an old airing-cupboard heater. Parts that are drying can be hung upside-down so that any dust lands on the underside rather than the tacky upper surfaces.**

*Below* **In general, different paint types do not mix and, if applied one on top of another, can produce very odd effects. Occasionally, however, this can be useful, as here, where the idea was to create the 'crazed' look of leatherette for the tonneau cover of the AMT Orange Blossom Special puller.**

Cars come in a very wide variety of colours, and trying to achieve a colour that is absolutely correct can be difficult, particularly if the car is well-known, such as Richard Petty's famous #43 in its distinct blue. However, the US company Tru-Match make a range of paints for such NASCARs (old and new), which are so accurate that the actual racing teams use them as touch-up sprays on the full-size cars!

over cellulose, but you cannot apply cellulose over enamel: it will lift the paint underneath. It is also advisable to keep to the same spray can for the whole application. It has been known (admittedly not very often) for a new can of paint—of exactly the same colour and type, from the same manufacturer—to have an effect on the first coat. This seems to occur if the first coat has been dry for some time (more than a day). However, if the paint is being applied over a surface that is still tacky, this should be fine. Consequently, unless you are absolutely sure that the paint will not affect the styrene or, for that matter, the undercoat, try it first on something expendable. Many modellers keep an old car body for this very purpose, or you can simply spray the paint on to a spare sheet of Plasticard.

If you do want to use car touch-up sprays, note that most can be misted on in such fine coats that the damaging solvents will have evaporated almost before the paint hits the surface, making any crazing or lifting far less likely.

(If, for some reason, a paint finish does go disastrously wrong, all is not necessarily lost. Wet paint can usually be removed with white spirit or a similar solvent. If it has dried, other methods can be used, as explained in Chapter 11.)

All paint aerosols work best if they are warmed before use. Place the can in a bowl of water that is *hand hot* only—if the water is too hot, the can will be in danger of explod-

ing, as the heat will increase the pressure inside. A small increase in pressure is good, as it helps the paint flow, but too much can cause the aerosol to split. Then shake the can well. All aerosols—with the exception of gloss varnish—contain an agitator in the form of a ball-bearing, which does the job of thoroughly mixing everything inside. If you've any doubt on this score, pick up a spray can that's been sitting unused for some time and, preferably, is cold. An initial shake will not produce any rattling, as the ball-bearing will be stuck in the paint that has congealed in the bottom.

Paint spraying, arguably, is an art, but it is a skill that is quite easy to learn. If you have never sprayed anything before, practise beforehand. The technique is to begin spraying off the car body at one end and to pass the spray smoothly over the surface, continuing beyond the other end—when you can stop. *Never* stop the spray on the body itself; keep the can moving all the time and as smoothly as possible.

The aim is to build up the maximum density of paint in the fewest possible coats. That said, you will usually have to apply several thin coats, and the first may not be dense enough to cover the bodywork thoroughly. Gradually increase the thickness of paint with these thin coats so that the finish is even. Each layer should be allowed to dry partially—but it should still be slightly tacky—before the next coat is applied. The final coat is usually applied slightly

Candy colours (or as AMT used to have it, Kandy Kolors) are transparent dye paints that become progressively darker as more layers are applied. Testors still make some Candy-type paints, which come in very useful when sixties customs, such as Revell's model of Ed Roth's Road Agent, are reissued and need Candy Apple Red.

denser (or wetter) than the previous layers, which should leave the surface glossy—assuming a gloss finish—but not so thick that it will cause runs.

Then the spray can should be inverted immediately and a short burst sprayed—not at the model, obviously—to clear the nozzle of paint so that it will be ready for use again.

Items that have been painted must be left safely and securely to dry, and preferably somewhere warm. This is where the coat-hanger scores over the bottle stand. Not only does it have a built-in hook from which to hang it, but the model will also hang upside-down, which means that if any dust is floating around, it will tend to settle on surfaces that won't be seen. For my own use, I devised a drying cupboard built from melamine-faced chipboard and fitted out with three hanging rails—all from the local DIY store. In the bottom is an old tubular airing-cupboard heater, which keeps the air just on the warm side and speeds up the drying process. The parts are simply hung on the rails and left. A refinement would be to add doors, but to date I haven't done so, and the drying parts never seem to be affected significantly by any dust that may be floating around. However, it is still best to ensure that the atmosphere is as clean as possible, which brings me to the thorny problem of where to spray in the first place.

Any paint spraying requires more than adequate ventilation and, in an ideal world, anyone who needed to spray a model car would have an industrial spray booth with a moving curtain of water and thorough filtration. However, the world is not ideal, so most people will end up spraying their models in less-than-ideal surroundings. To improve the situation, commercially-made spray booths are available for model makers, and they range from simple open-sided structures in expanded polystyrene to more complex arrangements equipped with turntables and even filtration.

A spray booth should perform three tasks: prevent too much overspray from reaching the outside, stop anything outside from reaching the newly sprayed item, and—hopefully—catch and filter as much of the spray from the atmosphere as possible. However, day-to-day practicalities will probably dictate that, unless you can dedicate an area to such a booth, even the smallest may not be convenient.

Home-made alternatives can range from a large cardboard box to a wooden structure with built-in extraction (an old vacuum cleaner can be useful in this respect), which may be adequate to catch the overspray. It should not be beyond most competent modellers to build a spray booth that will suit their own circumstances, possibly with such refinements as extraction and filters. But whatever spraying facilities you end up with, good lighting is vital, and you will definitely still need adequate ventilation.

I suspect that most modellers—portable spray booth or not—will end up spraying outside, which at least solves the ventilation problem (as long as you don't mind the garden ending up some interesting shades). However, the weather will rarely be ideal: you really want it to be warm and slightly damp—but not in the form of falling rain, just enough to keep the dust down. Most of the time, however, it will be windy, raining or, frankly, too hot, which is just as bad. There is also the ever present problem of health hazards.

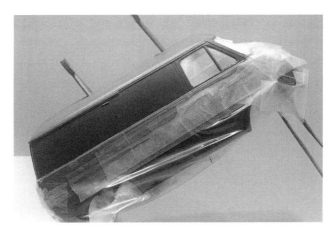

*Above* **When a two-tone finish is needed, some masking will be required. Here, the Monogram Chevy van is going two-tone, and with the first colour—dark blue—already applied and completely dry, it is masked for the next colour.**

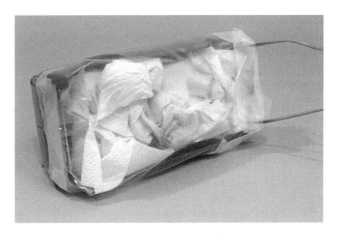

*Above* **When masking a body, include the inside. If this is not done properly, the paint will find its way under the edges, then back up and out of the windows. Kitchen towel has been used as packing, but it has been double sealed with masking tape, as it is very absorbent, and the paint could soak through.**

**With the second colour applied and the masking removed, it can be seen that the time spent on masking was worthwhile. Normally, the lighter colour is applied first, but with metallic paints—silver here—the darker is applied first.**

Of course, paint schemes need not be restricted to two colours: three or more can be applied using the normal masking techniques. On this AMT American Motors Matador, the white was applied first, then it was masked for the red and blue.

The contents of most aerosols are not that beneficial when wet, and some could be positively harmful. Consequently, it is always advisable to wear some form of mask to prevent inhalation of the paint particles, although there is some argument, even among the experts, as to which type is the most effective. In the end, you will have to decide just how much protection you want for yourself, and those around you, and take the relevant precautions.

As an alternative to aerosol sprays, there are devices that use air pressure (from a hand pump) as the propellant, and although they are not designed specifically for modelling paints, it should be possible to adapt them. They should also be able to spray acrylics, which are deemed to be slightly more environmentally friendly than enamels, lacquers and the like (although the exact meaning of 'slightly' depends on which expert you believe). To date, it has not been possible to formulate acrylics to work in a commercial spray can, although it would seem logical that this will occur at some point. However, they can be sprayed with an air-brush (see later in this chapter).

## DIFFERENT FINISHES

Gloss finishes are usually dense enough to cover the undercoat with relatively few coats, while retaining their shade and lustre. However, problems occur when spraying a light colour over red, or white over yellow, as normally you will find that the base colour will bleed through. This is another reason why priming is important. Not only will it provide the essential key for the paint, but it could also form an opaque barrier to the colour of the plastic. However, even some of the dense white primers have a job with red and yellow. In this situation, the only option is to use a grey primer first over, say, yellow, then use white on top of that. Ironically, it is probably easier to change a black plastic surface to white than to cover red or yellow. (This is also the reason why, today, most of the car kit companies use a neutral white or light grey as the moulding colour for the plastic.)

Besides a primer, some paints require a specific undercoat. The appearance of metallics, for example, will usually change depending on the shade underneath. A matt white undercoat produces a somewhat thin effect for the paint, while matt black gives it more depth, but makes the overall appearance darker.

Metalflakes, like metallics, can be affected by the colour of their undercoats, and usually it's best to use a shade that is similar to the top coat. If the top coat is metalflake red, use a matt red. However, as with all these tips, there are no hard and fast rules: metalflake red over, say, a matt blue base will give a different effect, which you may prefer.

Candy colours are transparent dyes, so the undercoat will show through, although this contributes to the effect. When AMT first made their Kandy Kolors, they supplied a gold base (which was also a self-etching primer) that gave the finish a warm effect. However, a silver base might be more appropriate for blues and greens. Other effects can be achieved by spraying candies — or Testor's range of transparent colours, which are much the same — over a base of the same colour, such as a metalflake finish. But all candies and transparents will change their effect as more layers are applied: a few layers for a light effect, more for a dark effect. Normally, it is best to make the layers of paint as thin as possible, as many model car bodies have fine details — emblems, lettering, etc — which you will not want to obliterate. However, there may be an occasion when you want a great many layers of paint for that special custom, and where other techniques have to come into play.

In this situation, you may wish to rub down the paint after each application, then add more layers on top. However, it is very important to ensure that each layer is completely dry first, otherwise the sanding and rubbing down will simply tear the surface. Paint formulated especially for models is rather soft — compared to car touch-up paint — and although it will appear dry to the touch after only a few hours, the full cure actually takes far longer. You will have to wait for at least a week, maybe longer, between applying a coat and rubbing it down, then applying more paint.

## TWO TONES AND MORE

It is perfectly easy to use two colours on a car body to match the full-size version. If you are dealing with race cars, they may run into three, four or even more colours.

Multi-tone paint schemes can range from those seen on

factory cars that were sold new with these sort of finishes (particularly during the fifties), through racing liveries in which the colours will be mixed with various decals, to custom arrangements of your own invention.

The first task is to apply the lighter, or lightest, of the colours required. This must be completely dry before any masking is attempted. The tape used for masking is very important. Specific tapes are made for models, and are the best to use if possible. The tape has to stick thoroughly so that paint doesn't creep beneath the edge, but as modelling paint can be soft, you don't want a tape that is too strong for the surface. Sometimes, you will find a convenient dividing line between the colours where the masking will be allowed a little latitude. This may take the form of a modern black bump strip along the side or, in a fifties car such as the '55 Chevy Bel Air, a convenient chrome strip (provided as a separate part in the recent Revell-Monogram kit). However,

most masking will be laid directly on top of a painted surface, with the second colour directly butting up to the first.

If the tape appears too sticky, the effect can be lessened by the seemingly odd action of holding a length of tape at each end and pulling the sticky side across your forehead! The oils in your skin will reduce the stickiness of the tape somewhat, although as with all techniques, a little experimentation is advisable. The tape should be cut by a sharp knife against a good straight edge, a steel rule being ideal. It can also be stuck on to a flat surface for cutting: a piece of glass is best, although clean Plasticard is also suitable.

With the masking tape in place to outline the edge of the second colour, the area of the body that will remain in the first colour must be covered as well. In this case, of course, the tape or covering does not have to be stuck down to the surface, as long as it is stuck to the masking tape. You can cut up something like a polythene bag to mask this area. However, be sure to cover the inside of the body as well. Paint is notorious for getting in around corners, and will creep under the body and back through the window openings if this area is not properly masked. Avoid using paper for this additional masking, unless it is very thick or waxed, as the paint will seep through most thin papers and bleed on to the masked surface.

Masks that are not straight lines can be made off the car body and applied with care, or the tape can be placed on the body in roughly the correct position, and the actual line carefully—very carefully, as you don't want to cut into the pre-painted surface—cut through the tape. Once the masking is in position, you should spray the second colour as soon as possible, as even with masking tape especially designed for

*Above* **Reference material—especially the excellent *Collectible Automobile*—is invaluable when it comes to choosing colour schemes. This AMT '53 Studebaker is going two-tone, with a tan roof. Overspray on to the area below does not matter, as there is a definite line between the roof and lower bodywork, which will separate the two colours. However, it is advisable not to let this build up too much, as the second colour may become uneven because of the layers of paint underneath.**

*Below* **The AMT '53 Stude finished in stock form (left) with the two other possible versions from the classic 3-in-1 kit. The competition version (centre) is a twin-blower Chrysler powered Bonneville racer. The third option, the custom version (right), features a chopped roof and custom rolled pans front and rear, all supplied with the kit. The competition version—Mr Speed—was built when the kit first appeared in the sixties, while the others were completed more recently.**

Decals will be found in the majority of car kits, and racing cars of all types will have very comprehensive decal sheets. A prime example is this Fujimi Mercedes in the Berlin 2000 scheme with all its signatures. Thankfully, all of them are decals.

models, glue residues can be left behind that are very difficult to remove. Try to avoid applying too many coats of the second colour, as this may cause a step between the finishes. After applying the top coat of the second colour—and before it is dry—very carefully remove the masking. This must be done at this stage, as it will be of considerable help in making the line between the finishes as inconspicuous as possible. With the paint still tacky, the edge will 'flow' ever so slightly, making the step between the two colours less obvious. It is also possible to polish out the step once all layers have dried completely.

If a feathered or misted effect is required between the colours, this can be achieved by not sticking down the very edge of the masking tape. By leaving a millimetre or so sticking up at an angle of around 45 degrees, you will allow the paint to mist underneath. A greater or lesser angle, or a greater or lesser amount of free tape, will change the amount of misting, although again it does require a certain amount of practice. A similar effect can be achieved without tape by cutting a mask of card and fixing this to the body with modelling clay or similar.

For special finishes, or when the colour you want simply isn't available in an aerosol, an air-brush will be useful. Air-brushes (and the simpler versions that generally tend to be called 'spray guns') work in various ways, but all apply a thin layer of paint to the surface in a very controlled manner. For example, a good air-brush can produce a line only a millimetre wide and, in the hands of an expert, can be used to achieve some of the most startling finishes on a model car.

For the simplest of tasks with an air-brush, that of applying a top coat of colour, the paint must be of the correct consistency. Many manufacturers make specific air-brushing paint, although usually in these circumstances you will want to mix your own. The normal procedure is to mix the actual shade you require, then thin it. This should be done with an appropriate thinner, not a general paint cleaner, the aim being to achieve the consistency of milk. The paint also has to be completely free of solids, and many devotees of air-brushing will strain the paint through mesh to ensure that it is clear of 'foreign bodies'.

Most paints can be air-brushed, and paints that are not normally found in aerosols—such as acrylics—can be thinned and sprayed, as well as enamels. Actual air-brushing techniques are an art in their own right, and there are many books on the subject. However, the spray produced by an air-brush is usually far thinner than that from an aerosol can, so the build-up of paint layers will take far longer, with the added danger that if you attempt to spray too much in one go, the paint may run.

Besides allowing you to apply your exact choice of paint and colour, an air-brush will also be extremely useful when it comes to creating weathering effects. More than any other technique, weathering—or, as it is more generally known, 'dirtying down'—makes a miniature look real. It is used all the time in the world of special effects miniatures (where it is also known as 'distressing'), but it is applicable to any field of modelling. It is particularly appropriate in car modelling if you wish to obtain the 'used' look that most cars suffer from. This can be purely from day-to-day use on the road, but it really comes into its own if you are dealing with an off-roader or a wreck in a junkyard.

Large amounts of mud and general debris can be reproduced with various plaster and sawdust mixes (see Chapter 10), which can be added to the chassis, wheels and tyres. However, general 'dirt' can be applied to any car, and an air-brush really is the only means of doing so. You need a thin mix of appropriate colours—browns, greys and red (rarely pure black)—which should be gently air-brushed over the relevant surfaces. Obviously, an off-roader will need more attention than a car used purely around town, and mostly it is a matter of degree—how much is applied and where. A detail such as the clear patch left by the wipers on the windscreen can be duplicated by cutting out wiper-sweep patterns from masking tape, applying them to the screen and spraying over the top. Removing the tape will reveal the 'clean' portion of the screen.

With the possible exception of the fully weathered finish, most cars do have a glossy appearance. Most gloss paints, candies and metalflakes do produce a shiny finish to one degree or another, but some of them may dry more matt

After-market suppliers abound, offering many styles of decal sheet for alternative versions of standard kits. Although race cars are by far the favourite, many companies also make decals for road cars. Fred Cady, located near Chicago in Illinois, offers a variety of alternative police car schemes for models such as the Revell Chevy Caprice. Among them are the Canadian RCMP markings illustrated here.

than others. Consequently, you may decide that a top coat of gloss varnish is required. This can also be vital when it comes to applying decals.

## DECALS

Most car kits come with at least some decals, if only for the licence plate and instrument dials. In the modelling sense, the term 'decals' almost always refers to the water-slide variety which, until recently, tended to be known as 'transfers' in British English. These days, the American terminology has been accepted almost universally. Regardless of the type of decals to be applied, however, one thing they all have in common is that they prefer to be applied to a gloss surface. This creates greater problems for aircraft and military vehicle modellers, as their subjects tend to have matt finishes. Applying decals over a matt finish invariably leaves that odd 'silvered' look, which is caused by air trapped under the decal because it cannot sit absolutely flush with the paint surface, as matt finishes are rougher than gloss paints. Consequently, the model has to be given a gloss finish, has to have its decals applied, then has to be sprayed with a matt varnish. This doesn't affect car modellers so much, as most cars are glossy (at least to begin with), so decals can usually be applied directly on to the top coat of paint.

Although most decal application is straightforward, and the sequence is obvious, race car schemes in particular are becoming extremely complex, and everything must be applied in the correct order. You may need to apply one layer first so that the next can overlap it. (At the time of writing, the record is held by a Hasegawa kit of a racing Porsche, which has four layers of decals at one point!)

Decals are printed on a paper backing, with a layer of glue sandwiched between the paper and design. The usual arrangement is that each decal has its own glue outline so, in effect, all you need do is cut roughly around the design. However, it is always advisable to cut as close to the printed outline as possible and, in some cases, the decals will be printed on an unbroken backing sheet, so there will be no separate decal outline anyway. Cutting close to the outline helps to remove any area of glue beyond the design, which

*Above* After-market decal sheets often need combining with special paints to create different NASCARs. Here, Slixx decals for the Hooters chain of US restaurants also need Hooters Orange paint from Tru-Match (top right on the pile).

*Below* Tamiya make a range of aerosols that are needed for many of their kits. For example, the Castrol Green, as used on their Honda Accord, is their own TS-35 Park Green.

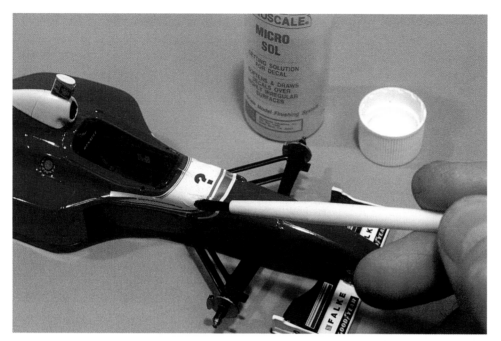

Some decals need decal softener to seat correctly. The best known of these products are Micro-Sol and Micro-Set. A few drops of 'Sol will break the surface tension and help the decals to float into place. Then Micro-Set can be used to stretch or shrink them to conform to shaped surfaces.

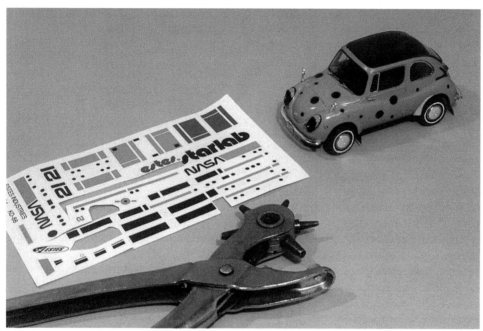

Fun can be had by taking a lateral approach to decals. The Subaru 360 Deluxe, by Hasegawa, is known as the Lady Bug in Japan, so why not add some spots? They can be cut from stock decal sheet, using a leather punch. However, in this case, suitable spots were found on an Estes rocket decal sheet.

can show up on the finished model, and can also assist in correctly seating the decal.

With the decal separated from the surrounding sheet, the universal practice is to soak it in some warm water for about 15 seconds. However, soaking times can vary, so do not be worried if this takes a little longer. Older decals will probably also need a longer soak.

You should be able simply to slide the decal off the backing into position and, with a slight dab of a cloth to remove any excess liquid, that should be it. However, other factors may come into play.

It's pretty easy to see that if a decal is applied to a flat surface, or a surface with a curve in one direction only, it should sit on the surface without too many problems. However, if the surface has a compound shape—curves in more than one direction—it may be difficult to seat the decal properly. Enter the decal solvents.

Firstly, there are liquids that assist in 'wetting' the surface, which helps prevent silvering, even if the surface has a gloss finish. Any liquid has a surface tension, and wetting agents reduce this, allowing the decals to seat better. Wetting agents (the best known world-wide is probably Krasel Industries' Micro-Sol) can be added as drops to the water, or brushed on to the surface of the model.

Dealing with surfaces that have compound curves is where another decal liquid—Micro-Set (or similar products)—comes into play. This actually stretches and shrinks the decal so that it conforms to the surface. Usually, the decal is slid into position, perhaps with the help of Micro-Sol, then a few drops of Micro-Set are applied directly on top of it. At this stage, the advice is 'don't panic', for the decal will start to wrinkle up and—the first time you use it—you'll think that the whole lot is ruined and lost forever. But whatever you do, *don't* touch the decal. Eventually, it will sort itself out and conform to the surface underneath. If you touch the decal too early, you are bound to tear it. About the only thing permissible is to tease the decal gently with a fine brush dipped in water, if you feel the decal is setting the wrong way. However, extreme care is needed, as decals in this state are extremely fragile.

Incidentally, wetting agents like Micro-Sol are very useful if you find you have a decal positioned in the wrong place and it has partially (or even completely) dried. Soaking the decal in Micro-Sol will usually loosen it enough to be able to slide a knife blade underneath an edge, allowing it to be carefully peeled away for repositioning. If you want to remove the decal completely for reuse, transfer it on to an old piece of backing paper and—assuming it's to be reused in the immediate future—keep it soaked in Micro-Sol. (Decals can be allowed to dry out and then be resoaked, but this process is not completely reliable.)

Note that some manufacturers have recently started to include a disclaimer that their decals are not decal solvent compatible. In reality, this is to protect themselves in case someone does make a mistake when using such solvents. Normally, however, all decals work perfectly well with commercial decal solvents. If you are in any doubt, the usual advice applies: test first.

Decals are an area where the garage and after-market industry offers a vast range of products. Many are made as options for NASCARs and other American racing machinery. This field is so popular, in fact, that AMT began to issue their Thunderbird and Monte Carlo sedans and Ford and Chevy Supertrucks as 'generic kits' without decals so that the after-market versions could be used.

The situation may arise where you cannot obtain the decals you actually want for your model. In this case, it is quite possible to make your own, and sheets of clear decal stock are sold by many manufacturers for this purpose. Depending on what you want to create, the pattern could be painted directly on to the clear stock, sealed with a clear varnish, then cut out and applied just like a normal decal.

In most cases, decal stock will also take photocopying and computer-type printing. With access to computers being so common, you may find that you can create your own design, then print it out, possibly directly on to the decal stock. This works with black and white and colour, and the only problems occur where a printer or photocopier has to pass the paper around rollers while printing. If the feed is straight through the machine, there should be no problems.

This facility also means that any reduction or enlargement of the image can also be incorporated and, in theory, any image could be transferred and reprinted from any source. (However, please note the copyright disclaimers that are usually printed on commercial photocopiers.)

## POLISHING

With the body finally finished as far as paint and decals are concerned, you can polish the result. There are specific polishes for model cars, but modellers have had many good results from materials as diverse as furniture and floor polish! However, that old axiom applies again: if you haven't used such compounds before, test first.

*Top* **If decals are not available, it is possible to make your own by copying on to clear decal stock. Some computer colour printers are suitable, as are colour photocopiers, provided they have a straight feed for the paper—decal stock does not like to be bent through 180 degrees, which can occur in some photocopiers. Here, the lettering has been generated on a computer in black, but the result will be in red.**

*Above* **By carefully placing the clear decal sheet, you need only use the amount required. Tape it carefully and firmly in position, using good quality thin clear tape, then pass it through the copier. The result may benefit from a top coat of clear varnish to protect the photocopied image, after which it can be cut up, soaked in water and applied in the normal manner. This model also demonstrates that it is possible to combine the apparently diverse model interests of automobiles and spacecraft!**

# Chapter Eight

# LIMITED-EDITION KITS

The model industry was not many years old when the modellers themselves began to hanker after products that the companies were not producing. Initially, and in the main, this desire was centred on aircraft, particularly for variants of existing subjects: 'Why are there so many Spitfire MkIVs when I want a MkXIV?' Not content with leaving it at that, some of these modellers began producing their own parts for the variants they wanted, using techniques that varied from vacuum forming plastic to casting in resin and white metal. Then a friend may have said, 'I wouldn't mind a set of those parts...', resulting in a short production run. Thus began what has generally become known as the 'cottage', 'garage' or 'after-market' industry.

Although the first additions of this type were for standard aircraft kits, the idea soon spread to many other subject areas, including cars, and a surprisingly large sub-industry was born. Currently, and world-wide, the mainstream model manufacturers comprise only about 5% of total companies in the industry; the remaining 95% come from the garage industry. Of course, this does not take into consideration the respective levels of production. Here, the percentages would be vastly different, for while the mainstream manufacturers are producing kits in the tens of thousands (if not more), most garage companies will be deliriously happy if they sell a hundred examples of a particular item.

Limited-edition production techniques usually involve a variety of moulding and forming processes, but not that of injection moulding styrene. That said, recently techniques have been developed that allow short runs of injection-styrene kits, the plastic being injected into hard resin moulds, not steel.

The first technique that the garage companies used was vacuuming forming. In this, a sheet of styrene plastic is heated until it is flexible, pulled over or into a mould, and the air rapidly drawn out from between the plastic and the mould. This causes the plastic to take on the shape of the mould. Once cool, it returns to its rigid form, and there is your new part. However, the process is quite time consuming (compared to the 30-second recycling time of an injection moulding machine) and very labour intensive. And even when the part has been removed from the vac-former, it will still be attached to the surrounding plastic sheet, which will have to be cut away before any more work can be done. However, it is a convenient process that is still used to produce many modelling items reasonably quickly and cheaply.

Many car bodies were produced in this way, especially during the sixties when slot racing was very popular, as they were very light. Although vacuum forming can still be used for producing individual parts—like hood scoops and the folded tops for convertibles—it is not really suitable for other parts of a car model. Consequently, it has dropped out of favour and been replaced by other techniques.

However, since you may come across vacuum formed parts, it is worth describing how they are used. First, they have to be removed from the surrounding material. The usual way of doing this is to carefully scribe a line around

*Left* **All white metal kits are limited editions, as nowhere near as many are produced as plastic kits. However, the approach is much the same. This South-Eastern Finecast MGA is a prime example, having a one-piece body, one-piece chassis and a wide selection of parts for engine, running gear and interior. It also has vinyl tyres.**

*Facing page, bottom* **The completed MGA. From the model's appearance, it is impossible to determine that the kit is made from white metal, and not plastic.**

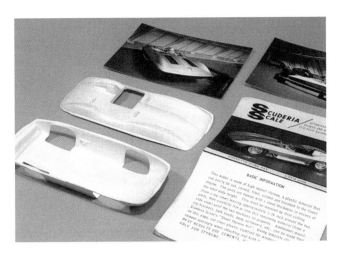

Complete vac-formed car kits are rare, but there have been a few, including this Corvette SS racing prototype. It is quite old and is a simple kit: two body halves plus a windshield. It requires a donor kit for all the other parts and a lot of work to complete. The reference photographs were taken by the author at the National Corvette Museum in Kentucky.

By far the majority of 'specialist' car kits are now moulded in polyurethane resin. Many are conversion kits for existing models, so you need a donor kit for the remainder of the parts. In this case, however — Mini Exotics' 1968 Mercury Cougar GT — you even get the body, so the AMT donor kit will only be required for the chassis, wheels and running gear.

the part, using one of the special cutting knives, or a special blade in a standard knife. The idea is not to cut through the plastic completely, rather to scribe a V-shaped groove. This will allow the part to be snapped away from the surround, leaving a clean(ish) edge, which can be tidied up by careful sanding on the same glass-paper board used for sanding tyres. Then the part can be glued into place. Being styrene, it will accept the usual plastic cements, and can be painted along with the rest of the kit.

Larger vac-formed sections will need extra attention, especially if they form two halves of an assembly and have to match. In this case, the two sections should be carefully sanded alternately, while checking constantly to make sure that you do not remove more plastic from one than the other. Once the fit is satisfactory, they can be glued together. However, since they will lack the locating pins of a standard

injection moulded kit, small scraps of Plasticard should be used inside the joint to ensure that everything stays in line and provide added strength.

One point to watch with vacuumed formed parts — large or small — is how they have actually been produced. The easiest way to make a vac-formed piece is to draw it down over the original shape — or a 'male' mould. This will result in a copy that is slightly larger than the original, by the thickness of the styrene sheet, and it will have any detail on the inside. This may not matter for some parts — hood scoops and the like — but for more complex parts, the detail needs to be on the outside. This means that a 'female' mould has to be made from an original, the styrene sheet being drawn into it. The result will be a copy that is not only the same size as the original, but also has all the detail on the outside. Both methods are still used, so if you come across vac-formed

*Top* **All American Models make a range of resin conversion kits for old and new machinery. The Cord Westchester sedan kit supplies the new body, interior and front seat, while the remainder must be sourced from the excellent 1:24 scale Monogram Cord 812. This has been available as several releases over the years, including one from Revell AG.**

*Above* **Once primed, the fact that the main body is resin, while the hood and fenders are plastic, is no longer apparent.**

parts, it is worth checking on which has been used. (See also Chapter 11 for details on making individual vac-formed parts at home.)

Although vac-forming methods have mostly been surpassed by other techniques, in one area they still reign supreme: that of producing clear window 'glass' for model cars. There really is no other limited-edition method that will work. Ironically, vac-formed glass is considerably closer to scale thickness than injection styrene, which is usually far too thick.

## MORE WAYS

If vacuum forming was not the most satisfactory answer to the problem of producing limited-edition components, a way had to be found that would duplicate the manner in which a standard injection kit was produced—as more or less finished parts. Although you need the massive pressures and high temperatures of a proprietary moulding machine to inject liquid styrene, other materials lend themselves to a similar process at much lower pressures and temperatures, the favourites being resin and white metal.

White metal is a low-melt alloy of tin and lead (lead being predominant, so the metal is fairly soft), which initially found favour with model soldier enthusiasts, who used it to mass-produce military figures. It can be centrifugally cast in a hard resin mould, the mould being spun while the liquid white metal is injected through the centre. Centrifugal force causes the metal to flow throughout the mould. After the metal has cooled, the mould can be opened to reveal an item that looks very much like a single plastic casting from a large injection machine (usually with a fair amount of flash). This technique can be used to produce any type of part, and even complete kits. It is one of the techniques favoured by the specialist companies who cater for the 1:43 kit market. Indeed, most companies who use white metal casting techniques do so purely for this smaller scale. However, some manufacturers do make larger-scale white metal kits, the

**All other assemblies for the Westchester Cord come from the Monogram kit. The only parts that really need adding are the windshield wipers— cut down examples from the spares box—which on the sedan pivot from the top, while the phaeton has them attached to the bottom of the windshield frame.**

most famous probably being the old Wills Finecast company in the UK, who produced a range of classic cars—mainly from the thirties—in 1:24 scale. These were made completely from white metal, although they had vinyl tyres and, in many instances, wind-your-own, very authentic looking wire wheels. Wills were taken over by South-Eastern Finecast, who added kits of their own. At the time, these included the only examples of the Jaguar MkII, MGB and Morgan in 1:24/5 scale, although now these are all available as standard plastic kits.

White metal is still a popular material for producing accessory parts. It has been included in kits such as Gunze Sangyo's High Tech range, where it was ideal for the chassis components. (However, many of these kits are now only available in their all-styrene form.)

White metal kits are similar to styrene examples in terms of assembly, but one item that will not be found is the runner. Although the white metal flows through the moulding channel into the mould cavity through a gate, like a steel tool for styrene, the alloy is too expensive to leave as scrap in the kit, so these parts are cut off and recycled. Consequently, although the parts break-down in a white metal kit is usually very similar to a plastic example, you will lack the convenient bits of runner that allow you to hold the parts while painting. This means that alternative methods have to be found.

Much of a white metal kit, like its styrene counterpart, can be sub-assembled first—engines still come in two halves with add-on goodies, whether they be in plastic or metal. Other parts may not be so straightforward to deal with, although the ingenious use of a drilled hole here and there—to accept a cocktail stick as a temporary hand-hold—can be employed. Alternatively, parts can be stuck to large clothes pegs, or pieces of wood, with modelling clay or double-sided tape. Bear in mind that white metal does contain lead, so washing your hands after handling the parts should become automatic.

Obviously white metal cannot be glued with standard polystyrene cement. When the kits were first introduced, methods of construction varied from soldering the parts together to using contact adhesive or—at that time—the new-fangled two-part resin mixes. It was some time before superglue became generally available, but now this has become the automatic choice for the assembly of white metal kits.

Being made in metal is advantageous for many parts of a model car kit. Items that are chromed or left in a natural metal state can really be chromed or finished as metal. Some kits supply parts of this type in pewter, which is another alloy of tin and lead. The tin is predominant, making the parts harder so that they can be polished to a suitable shine.

White metal kits can be painted in much the same way as plastic, although paints that would normally attack styrene without suitable primers can be used and applied directly to the metal. Consequently, virtually any normal car paints can be used, even cellulose. However, the body will still need the same preparation as a styrene body. White metal kits can suffer from a slight roughness over large areas, like the body, where the metal may have taken on a slight granular texture. Modelling putty, or car body filler for that matter, can be used to fill defects, then be rubbed down (wire wool is useful for metal car models). Finally, the body should be primed like a plastic model. The usual plastic detailing tips also apply, so white metal engines can be wired, fuel lines added and exhausts drilled out. Bodies can benefit from Bare-Metal Foil, or decals if required.

Once completed, an all-metal kit will not look any different to a plastic example, but if it is picked up, the difference will be apparent immediately—its weight!

Although white metal is a good material to work with, it may not be to everyone's taste. The material is still relatively expensive, and to anyone used to working with injection styrene parts, the change may come as a slight shock. Consequently, another material was sourced. This has found

**An example of a slush moulded body from Horizon's Batmobile range. The casting is solid, but as can be seen, the interior is built in and is full of detail, as is the underside. The completed kit can be seen in Chapter 13.**

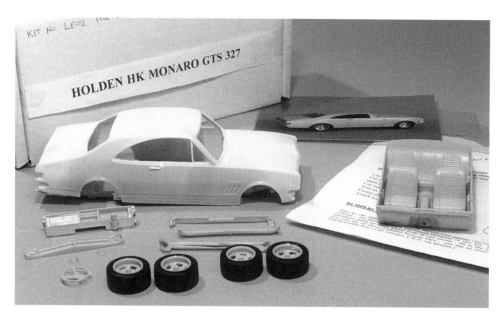

*Left* **An intriguing example of an Australian car, the Holden Monaro GTS 327. This is a resin kit from Cavalier, although at first glance, the parts look like injection styrene.**

*Facing page, top* **The completed Holden Monaro. Paint is Testors, while all the usual styrene detailing techniques, such as Bare-Metal Foil for the window surrounds, have been applied to this resin kit.**

*Above* **Testors have been specializing in resin 'slammer' kits—models without engines or interiors, hence the dark glass! They are moulded by Jimmy Flintstone and comprise a range of wild customs, such as this, the Mercster, which draws inspiration from the classic '49 Mercury Club Coupe, the AMT kit of which is shown in the background.**

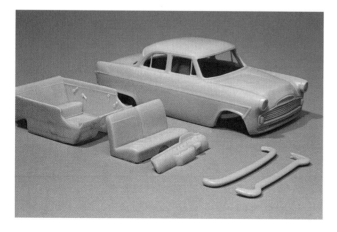

**Although most resin kits are of American subjects, others do appear occasionally. The Australian Holden shown at the top of the page is one, and this is a British Ford MkII Zodiac. The kit supplies most of the parts necessary to build a car that is unlikely to be produced as a kit by conventional methods.**

even more uses in the general model market, and the model car market in particular. It is resin.

Unlike styrene, resin does not require a high temperature to liquidize it for injecting. It is already liquid, requiring a catalyst to be added to cure it into a solid form. Consequently, resin does not need the steel moulds required for high pressures and temperatures. Instead, it can be injected into resin or hard rubber moulds. However, resin takes up detail just like styrene and, at first glance, a kit moulded in white resin will be difficult to tell from a similar kit in plastic. Resin is used for the production of many accessory parts for car models, and it is another favoured material for complete kits in 1:43 scale.

The popularity of resin has led to a surprisingly large number of companies (mostly in the USA) that make complete kits in resin, or kits that provide a large number of resin parts and may require a donor kit for the chassis and engine.

Small resin accessories were the first items to be turned out: for example, a new scoop for a NASCAR racer, a different hood for an up-market sedan, or a different grille for a GT version. However, it was not long before whole sections of bodywork were being made: a hardtop to convert a convertible, or a coupe body to replace a hardtop. Then, it was but a small step to produce complete bodies and interiors, which only required a donor kit for the chassis and engine. One more step saw the production of complete kits.

Individual resin car bodies, and complete kits, can vary considerably in style and quality. Early bodies were made by a process known as 'slush moulding', in which the resin was simply poured into a mould and left to cure. This produced a solid lump of resin, which meant, of course, that there was no space for an interior, an engine or any chassis detail.

Slush moulding has lost favour among modellers because of this, but it is still used occasionally. The new range of Testors/Jimmy Flintstone kits are solid mouldings, but in this case, they have been designed as 'slammers'. Whereas 'curbside' was invented as a term for car kits that did not have an engine, 'slammers' applies to kits that do not have an engine or interior, so they can be 'slammed' together very quickly. In fact, this situation does not apply to kits

in the Testors range, which need far more work, but the term has stuck.

The slush moulding technique is also used by Horizon for their Batmobiles. Created to fill gaps between the classic TV and movie cars, these are solid mouldings, but made to a very high standard. They have the interior and some chassis details already moulded in.

Most resin manufacturers, however, use moulding methods that produce parts in much the same style and thickness as normal styrene versions. Initially, many of these companies were set up to make alternative body parts for existing styrene kits, so the style of moulding had to match the kit moulding. There was no point in making a slush moulding of a new body if you had to fit it with a standard kit interior! The master patterns may well have been made using existing conventional kit parts, so the walls of the mouldings became thinner and thinner, until they matched those of the injection styrene kits.

With alternative parts being made, many adapted from existing kit parts, it wasn't that long before someone thought of re-creating a whole kit. Over the years, many kits have gone out of production, but they are still in demand by some modellers, and often when original examples are found they will have reached the lofty heights of collectability, making them too expensive to buy. The next best thing would be a resin copy. For this, all that is required is one original kit, from which the moulds can be made. Once you have these, they can be used to produce a similar set of parts to the original—but this time in resin.

Resin kits may include transparent red parts for rear lights, vinyl tyres and clear vac-formed glazing. They may even have the appropriate parts chromed (vacuum plating does not rely on the parts being metal, and resin will take vacuum plated 'chrome' as well as styrene). When such a kit is finished, it is very difficult—even for an expert—to tell it from the original, particularly from a visual examination alone. (In fact, if you are faced with a moulding of unknown origin, which may look like styrene, about the only way to determine which material has been used is to cautiously apply some liquid cement to a hidden area. If this dissolves

**Sometimes, a resin kit is the only way of obtaining a copy of a rare styrene kit. All American Models have taken some rare originals, such as this AMT 1961 Ford pickup, and reproduced them in resin. Note that the resin parts can be plated just as easily as styrene, and although you don't get an engine or wheels, these can usually be sourced from other kits.**

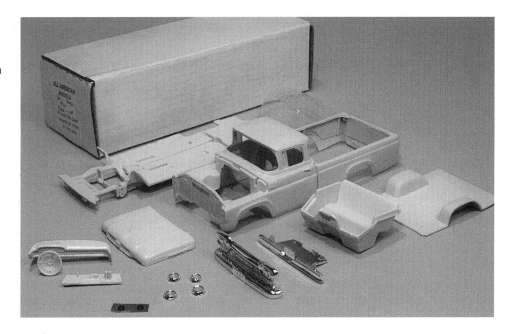

the surface, the moulding is styrene, or similar; if it doesn't, it's resin.)

## BUILDING A RESIN KIT

In many ways, the building of a complete resin kit can be approached in a very similar manner to a standard injection moulded kit. The parts will have been produced in a similar way, and you will probably find a resin runner attached to each part via the gate. Because of the lower pressures involved in resin moulding, invariably this gate will be a lot larger, so take extra care when cutting the part away from the runner. A razor saw is best for this, as snipping with nail clippers or side cutters could shatter the resin—it is more brittle than styrene.

Having freed the part, you should carefully file down the remains of the gate, sanding it smooth. Wet-or-dry abrasive paper works as well with resin as it does with standard plastic (see Chapter 9). As with styrene kits, you may find flash on some of the parts: it tends to be prevalent over window openings, although it is very easy to remove—most of the time, it simply snaps away, requiring the minimum of cleaning up.

Occasionally, a part may suffer from warping, but usually this is easily cured by immersing it in hot water and carefully bending it back into shape. When returned to room temperature, the part should stay in its intended shape.

The surface may also show slight faults, as with the white metal kits, but again standard modelling putty works well. However, this doesn't adhere to resin as well as it does to styrene, since resin is resistant to most solvents, so care

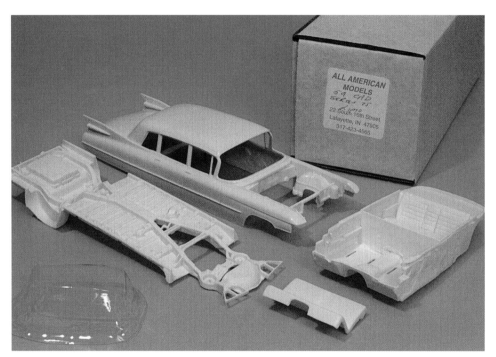

*Left* **Resin kits invariably rely on a donor kit for many of the parts. When the 1959 Cadillac first appeared in 1:25 scale, two standard kits were available: AMT's ambulance version—the Ghostbusters' ECTO-lA—and the Monogram stock Eldorado Biarritz. The latter is necessary when building the All American Models Cadillac limousine, the kit of which provides a new body, longer chassis and interior.**

*Below* **The completed 1959 Cadillac limousine with running gear and details from the Monogram kit.**

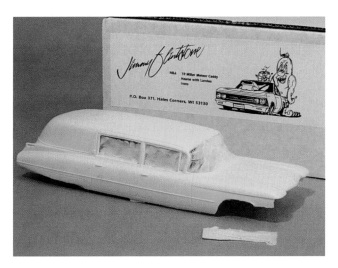

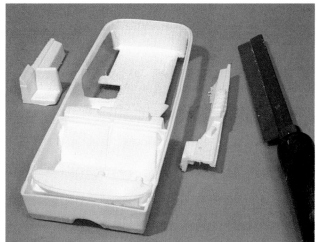

*Above* **To utilize AMT's Ghostbusters' Cadillac, Jimmy Flintstone produced a body for the Cadillac hearse, in this case, the 1959 Miller Meteor.**

*Above right* **Modifications to the ambulance interior are fairly extensive. The resulting holes can be filled with plastic sheet, and a new floor fitted.**

*Right* **The hearse body needs the ambulance fins. However, contrary to normal practice, they are best left off until the main paint has been applied, and any chrome strips, otherwise it is difficult to get behind them.**

*Below* **The completed Jimmy Flintstone/AMT Cadillac hearse, finished in funerial lilac and purple.**

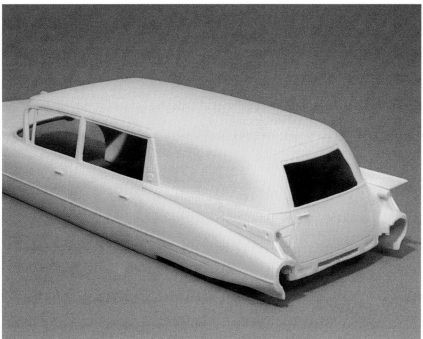

83

Another Jimmy Flintstone casting for Testors, the Divco truck in somewhat more 'street' form than its usual delivery colours. These kits are ideal for trying out different schemes, such as this two-tone design with decals from the spares box (probably from a recent Corvette kit).

should be taken if you are filling a shallow recess. In fact, it might be better to make such an area deeper, then rough sand it to provide a key.

Resin kits have also benefited from the introduction of superglue, which works extremely well with them. Therefore, it is doubly important to ensure that the parts fit together correctly when the glue is applied. Any attempt at removal later—even with debonder—will usually break the parts, not the joint.

Painting is also similar to a standard kit, with the proviso that the surface must be completely free of contaminants. To ensure easy removal of resin parts from the mould, the cavities of the mould must be treated with a release agent. This does tend to hang around on the parts and will prevent the paint from adhering to them. Consequently, it is even more important with resin parts than styrene to clean all parts thoroughly and decontaminate them before beginning any work.

Because resin is impervious to most solvents, paint sticks less well than with standard styrene. Even self-etching primers will not bond well. Consequently, light sanding is recommended for all resin parts to provide a key for the paint. You could even go over them with wire wool. (Some full-size cars that have resin—GRP—bodies, such as the Corvette, actually have the colour incorporated into the outer gel coat layers to get around this painting problem.)

Once applied, paint finishes work well on resin bodies, but there can be problems with a two-tone finish. For this, you will have to mask some areas of the body, but when you remove the tape, there is the danger of lifting the first layer of paint, no matter how dry. Consequently, some testing beforehand is recommended, together with the use of a tape that has the minimum of adhesive qualities.

All super-detailing tips apply equally to resin-bodied kits as to styrene versions (see Chapter 6). However, be careful when using Bare-Metal Foil, or similar products, which can lift the paint like masking tape. Bare-Metal Foil must be rubbed down first, then the excess peeled away. Provided the resin has been prepared to the highest possible standards

prior to painting, you should experience no problems. That said, it is always wise to be aware of the potential risk when removing excess foil, so that you don't remove a layer of paint as well.

## PHOTO-ETCHED PARTS

Besides vac-formed plastic, white metal and resin, a fourth material can also be found in limited-edition car kits and as accessories—photo-etched metal. In this case, original artwork is used to create a pattern that is normally etched photographically on to brass, but steel may also be treated. As far as car modelling is concerned, photo-etching has fewer uses than for, say, aircraft and armour, but it is particularly suitable for small items, such as seat belt buckles, scale grilles and name scripts.

Working with such small parts can be difficult. A clear work surface is vital, as are good lighting and a pair of small snips for cutting the parts. Usually, brass can be cut with scissors, but steel invariably needs snips. Be aware that these parts end up with very sharp edges, which will need filing down. Finally, superglue will hold them in place, although the very smallest of items—name scripts and the like—can often be secured with PVA glue or even gloss varnish.

## FROM MINOR TO MAJOR

Although the mainstream and garage companies work side by side, they have not combined as such. However, in some cases, the techniques and materials used by the garage industry to produce their limited-edition parts have been taken up by the major manufacturers. It is common to find photo-etched parts in aircraft and armour kits, and some car kits, while others include cast white metal components as well. Now, resin is finding its way into mainstream car kits, not to a great extent at present, but it's there. Gunze Sangyo, for example, have issued the Airfix/Heller kit of the Citroën 2CV for their Lupin III cartoon range. Most of the 2CV remains as per the standard kit in injection styrene, but the older style of bonnet necessary for this version is supplied as a moulded resin part.

# *Chapter Nine*

# CUSTOMIZING

Customizing, as a term, tends to be much maligned, but in fact, it simply means that an object has been tailored to suit an individual's personal preferences. It doesn't actually have to refer to a car, although it is with this subject that the word is usually associated. Even here, though, it tends to generate visions of a radical vehicle that bears no resemblance at all to anything produced by Detroit, and doesn't look as if it is capable of being driven on the roads—except that it has four wheels (and even this may not be the case).

This type of radical show car is one example of customizing, but really any modification that takes the vehicle even slightly away from what the original manufacturer intended comes under the term. It need be no more than a new set of wheels, a fancy paint job or a different grille.

What can be applied to the full-size car can be applied to the scale replica, making model cars arguably the most modified of all plastic kits. Ship, military and aircraft kits can all be altered to a certain extent, but nothing compares to what can be done to even the humblest car.

Like much of automobile terminology, the term 'customizing' originated in America, and while not all customized cars are of American manufacture, many of the customizing techniques work best on US automobiles.

*Right* **One of the oldest customizing techniques is to chop the top. At least one kit—the AMT 1953 Studebaker—actually provides the new top and chopped glass to start you off.**

*Below* **Compared to the stock height (left), the chopped top is immediately apparent. Dechroming and removing all the badges, as has been done to the custom Studebaker, also helps.**

When the first car kits appeared, especially those in 1:24/5 scale, from companies such as AMT, SMP and Jo-Han, custom parts were the first extras to be included. Among these were different wheels, hood scoops, louvres, spotlights, aerials, full body panels, new grilles and even complete bubble tops.

These early examples of customizing tended to be at the radical end of the market, and were so popular that the kit companies would use an artist's rendition of the custom version on the box, rather than the stock example. However, styles change in full-size cars, and this is reflected in the world of miniatures. Today, the type of full custom that was popular in the early sixties is more likely to be represented by the Pro-Street or Cal look. However, all types retain their devotees, and with the current resurgence (since the early nineties) of sixties-style cars, perhaps exemplified by the Californian lowriders, the kit manufacturers have followed

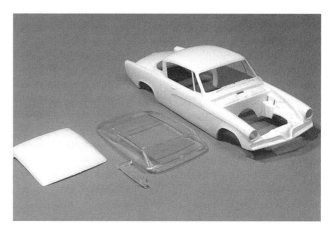

To lengthen a car to produce a stretched limo, you will need two identical kits. The slab-sided cars of the sixties and seventies tend to be easier to deal with than more modern 'jelly mould' shapes.

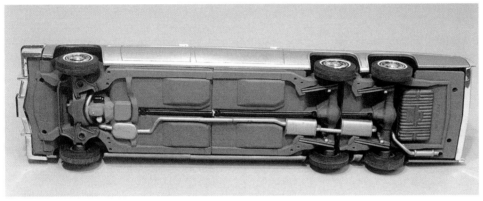

Besides the bodywork, the chassis also needs lengthening, but stagger the various joints to remove any potential weakness.

suit. First, they issued new kits of old cars from the fifties and sixties, then followed with lowrider versions of them.

What has altered, however, is the number of parts you will find in a kit. In the sixties, most manufacturers gave you a wide range of options for finishing your model, the 3-in-1 concept merely being the starting point. Some kits provided four options, while the record is held by MPC's kit of the 1932 Chevrolet, which gave you nine!

More recent times have seen a reduction in the number of parts supplied. You may only find an extra set of wheels or, perhaps, dress-up side skirts. But with the recent revival of interest in reissuing kits exactly as they were, many of these multi-part kit extravaganzas are being made again.

Before customizing methods are discussed in detail, one modelling technique that is likely to be required for even the simplest of modifications involves the use of modelling putty or filler. Often called body putty, it gained its name because originally it was developed for altering the bodies of model cars. These days, however, modelling putty will be found in the tool boxes of all model enthusiasts.

Modelling putty is a very fine compound that contains a similar base to polystyrene cement. This means that it will eat slightly into the surface of any styrene and create a strong bond. Most model companies, and the chemical companies associated with them, make their own versions of modelling putty, as do some accessory manufacturers. Always apply it in thin layers and, although modern putties

dry relatively quickly, allow adequate drying time between layers, otherwise a solid skin may form on top while the putty below remains soft.

The putty can be applied with some form of spatula or a scalpel blade. Try not to use your finger to shape wet putty: besides being difficult to remove from the skin, it contains harmful solvents. Brushing the putty with liquid cement will help in bonding it to the surrounding plastic, and also give the putty a relatively smooth surface. But no matter how smooth a surface you achieve, it will still need sanding.

Although putty can be sanded with any type of glass or emery paper, the best results will be achieved with wet-or-dry. This has a backing that is waterproof, so it can be used under water (which may be running or still) or simply wet. It can also be used dry, which may be appropriate in some situations. Check the surface by constantly running your finger over it, as this will reveal any imperfections. (Obviously, in the putty's dry state, the solvents will have evaporated, so it can be prodded safely with a finger.)

If you discover any imperfections, dry the surface thoroughly, apply more putty, and repeat the process. You may also find it helpful to apply a coat of primer, as this makes very tiny imperfections more apparent. On large areas, this process may have to be repeated several times to obtain a surface that is as smooth as glass, but it will be obvious when you've finally achieved this.

Body putty works very well, but don't expect it to fill

very deep areas or large gaps successfully. In this situation, build up the area concerned with scrap plastic until it is close to the finished surface. Then use the putty for final shaping.

Modelling putty is formulated to take modelling paints in the same way as styrene. Once it has dried, and been sanded and primed, there should not be any visible signs of the different materials under the top coats of paint.

The ideas for restyling automobile kits were adopted from the full-size counterparts. With these, the removal of all the trim, reshaping the front and rear pans, removing the bumpers and lowering the car all round became the norm, but some customizers even went to the extreme of radically altering the body shape. This could take any approach: new front and rear sections, removal of the roof (or replacement with a different style), different hood and trunk lids, and complete restyling of the interior. However, as far as the bodywork is concerned, customizing can—broadly—be divided into three methods: chopping, sectioning and channelling. These techniques can be applied to most car kits.

## CHOPPING

Chopping refers to cutting off the roof of the car, shortening the pillars and reattaching the roof so that it is lower. Note that all pillars on cars are referred to by letters of the alphabet, working back from the A pillar at the front, which holds the windshield. Most saloons, or sedans, will have three pillars—A, B and C—while estates, or station wagons, will have a D pillar as well. Some cars may have even more.

Any car with a roof can be chopped, but it is easiest to carry out on older cars with vertical pillars, such as those built before the mid-thirties. With these, any shortening of the pillars will not affect their position where they are reattached to the roof. Consequently, chopping a Deuce (1932 Ford) for a hot rod will be a relatively straightforward job, and this task is so common among hot rodders that full-size replica bodies can be purchased already chopped.

For a model car, it is very easy to decide how much to chop a roof, then mark the relevant pillars with a felt-tip pen and start cutting with a razor saw. It's best to remove the roof

by making the upper cuts first, then carefully cut each pillar down to size. Take care, however, as it is very easy to make the cuts not quite horizontal and also at slightly different levels. If necessary, make a template to keep the degree of cut the same for all the pillars.

Once the cuts have been made and you are happy that the roof will fit back into position, it's a simple matter to glue it in place. You can also add a couple of reinforcing strips inside if this seems necessary

To match the lower roof line, the window glass will have to be cut as well. This can be marked and cut in the same manner, but note that clear styrene is far more brittle than the opaque type, so there is a greater risk of cracking it. Even then, the cuts will not be as clean as on the pillars, although cutting very slowly helps, as does placing sticky tape over the glass first and cutting through both this and the plastic. If the glass is relatively flat, you may be able to replace it with clear acetate, held in position with clear contact glue. This will have a thickness that is closer to scale.

This style of chop is relatively straightforward, but it is quite obvious that if you cut the pillars of a modern car, particularly the backward-sloping A pillar and forward-sloping C pillar, they will not line up when the roof is reattached,

*Above right* **The interior of a stretched limo can be dressed up with a variety of fixtures and fittings, including a phone, computers, faxes and satellite communications from the dome-shaped object sitting on the trunk.**

*Right* **The stretched limo does look spectacular when completed. However, the opposite approach can also be taken, and vehicles can be shortened, as illustrated by the modified version of a Revell VW Microbus.**

**'Frenching' means recessing parts in the bodywork, such as these aerials on the rear fins of AMT's 1957 Ford Fairlane.**

and far more work will be entailed. If the B pillar—behind the front doors, and the only pillar that usually remains anywhere near vertical—is lined up, there will be a shortfall at front and rear. And if the A pillar is lined up, the B pillar may still be close, but the C pillar will be way out. The only solution is to do what the customizers of full-size cars do—extend the roof. If you have two examples of the same kit, the new roof can be made from the front half—or to be more accurate, just over half—of one kit and the back portion of the other. The joint can be strengthened by adding a strip of Plasticard underneath, while the top surface can be filled, then sanded with wet-or-dry. (The second kit can always be turned into a convertible if you are worried about wastage!)

If a second kit is not available, the only option will be to cut the roof in half, attach the two halves to the A and C pillars, and fill the gap between them. Most roofs do not have an identical cross-section along the length, so usually the best place to cut will be the centre-line running across the car, where the roof will probably be at its widest. Then, with the roof sections tacked into place on the pillars to ensure accurate dimensions, they can be joined by gluing strips of plastic to the underside. After this, the gap itself can be filled. This is best done by gluing thin Plasticard under the full length of the gap, then filling between the roof sections themselves. You could use a single solid piece of plastic for this, which will have to be sanded to the correct contour and have any gaps filled with putty, or several smaller pieces, which may make it easier to follow the roof contours. It is best to make the gaps between the new sections and the original roof slightly V-shaped so that the filler can be feathered and will blend the two pieces together invisibly.

There is one other slight problem that may occur when chopping a roof, which can apply to both the upright- and sloping-pillar versions. Both methods assume that the pillars are absolutely vertical when viewed from the front or rear of the body. However, they may slope inwards slightly towards the centre-line of the car. Again, this will produce a slight mismatch when the chopped roof is replaced, as they will be slightly too narrow at the top, the roof having retained its

original width. However, this is usually easy to overcome by carefully bending the relevant pillars outward. If necessary, strengthening pieces can be added to the inner surfaces.

Finally, all that will be required is a little filling and sanding (depending on the accuracy of your original cuts), after which the body can be finished in the normal manner.

Although chopping applies to cars with roofs, it is also possible to chop a convertible, although naturally only the windshield frame and glass are actually cut. The process is more straightforward, but due to the thin nature of most frames, much more care must be taken, while the advice already given applies to the glass.

## SECTIONING

In this process, a horizontal strip is removed from the sides of a car, making the whole body shallower and, consequently, lower. In theory, it can be done to any car, but it always seems to look best on American cars from the late forties and early fifties, the archetypal 1949 or 1950 Ford or '49 Mercury (all made as kits). Because these cars were so bulbous—especially when compared to modern machinery—the act of sectioning them made them far more streamlined. However, sectioning does involve much more planning than chopping a roof. You need to determine where to section the body, and by how much, for with the section removed, the parts may not necessarily line up. The basic idea is to remove a section from the widest point of the car body, so that when the halves are joined together again, they will more or less fit. However, car bodies usually have compound curves, so even if the major sections fit, it is more than likely that other parts will need filling and sanding.

Marking out is done in the same manner as for chopping, using a felt-tip pen and a straight edge to indicate the cutting lines. Note that it is doubly important to ensure that the lines are straight and parallel to one another. (Although it is possible to take a wedge out of a body for a really interesting effect.)

The usual problem that occurs when cutting around the body in this way is that the cuts are not made in the same plane, one side being lower than the other, so that the whole car is tipped to one side when put back together. Preventing this is really down to checking thoroughly before approaching the body with the saw. However, slight readjustments will probably be possible by sanding the two halves of the body on glass paper attached to a flat board (as for sanding tyres and vac-formed parts). That said, do not expect to adjust major misalignments in this way.

It may be necessary to clamp the body down in some manner—use double-sided tape or modelling clay, or even build a jig—so that the marking pen, then the saw, will follow the correct line around the body.

Even with all this care, when the two halves are joined, there will be gaps and areas where the two sections do not match up. Depending on the kit, some may need sections cutting away, packing with Plasticard and filling, while others may simply need working on with wet-or-dry paper.

Besides the body, other areas will need attention. Sectioning the body will probably mean that the grille needs sectioning as well—and if it is chromed, all the more atten-

Doors can be opened up when customizing a model. The AMT 1940 Ford panel truck has recently been rediscovered and reissued. In this kit, the rear door is separate and could be hinged. In fact, this is an earlier resin-bodied conversion, where the door has been hung on tiny hinges borrowed from a Revell early Ford station wagon kit.

A simple customizing project to make Face's car from *The A-Team* to go with the AMT GMC van. Apart from the appropriate colours, the red stripes were added from solid colour decal stock.

A popular customizing technique is to create a phantom—a version of a car or pickup that did not exist for real, but which could have. This is a conversion of the Monogram 1937 Ford sedan into a pickup, utilizing the same company's 1940 Ford pickup bed. The donor kit was not wasted, either: in this case, the '40 Ford has been given a scratchbuilt pickup bed, made from wood veneer. Note that the cab roof has been removed to turn it into a roadster.

tion. However, as sectioning the bodywork is usually carried out on a radical custom, the grille may very well have been replaced with a custom version, possibly a 'floating' grille (one that is attached without any visible means of support, so that it 'floats' in the grille opening).

Stock bumpers would also not normally be used on such a custom, and the manufacturers who make kits suitable for this sort of drastic surgery (like the '49 Ford and Mercury) invariably supply custom rolled pans, front and rear, to replace the stock items.

This radical work on the exterior will mean that the standard interior will be too high, so you will need to find a suitable place where it can also be sectioned. This might be along the top edge, purely cutting enough away so that it fits the new height of the bodyshell, or you may need to take a section from the interior itself. You may also find that the engine now sits too high in the frame, and is in danger of pushing through the hood. You can either build a massive hood scoop around it, or you can lower the block in the chassis by adapting the engine mounts. This type of car should also have lowered suspension so that it appears to be only (scale) inches off the ground. Again, most kits of cars from this era also have facilities for lowering the suspension to achieve the correct effect.

This type of custom—sectioned or not—invariably became known as a 'lead sled' because, before the days of polyester resin fillers, all the gaps were filled by working molten lead into them and quickly skimming it smooth. Today, the lead may have gone (both for health reasons and because it is extremely heavy), but the lead sled style remains as an eye-catching custom.

## CHANNELLING

Like sectioning, the purpose of channelling is to make the body of the car sit lower. However, instead of taking a section out of the body sides, the entire body is made to sit lower on the chassis. This technique relies on there being a separate chassis in the first place—most modern cars don't have one—and it works best on pre-war cars that have separate fender assemblies.

Channelling involves dropping the body lower through the fenders and trimming off the lower edge. In reality, it means cutting through the floor of the car to form channels that sit over the chassis rails.

With a suitable kit, try dropping the bodywork through the fenders to see how much of the lower edges can be cut away. Like sectioning, this will also involve reducing the height of the body and, because these parts were separate on early cars, the hood assembly and radiator shell, too.

The fenders can be omitted—a favourite for early hot rods. The interior either needs to be channelled—have slots cut in it—so that it will fit over the chassis rails, or simply reduced in height by removing the top edges. You will probably find that other parts of the body also need modifying. The rear wheel arches may need enlarging—radiusing—to accommodate the lower body and new larger tyres.

## LOWRIDERS

As mentioned previously, one of the most recent customiz-ing traits is the lowrider, which was born on the West Coast. Initially, these cars were made to sit really low and came with under-chassis neons to light up the suspension, and titanium bars that would scrape along the ground and produce a shower of sparks. Late fifties and early sixties cars were the favourite, as they still had the size and the expanse of chrome associated with archetypal American cars.

These vehicles could also be fitted with adjustable suspension that would make the car sit really low for 'show', but could be raised somewhat when it needed to 'go'. Then someone decided that raising and lowering the car could become part of the act, and the hoppin' car was born.

Lowriders use nitrogen powered rams to raise and lower their suspension, often to great extremes and at high speed, which can lift wheels off the ground, hence the hoppin'. Cars may literally bounce along with one wheel in the air, or pickup beds may take on a life of their own, whirling and dancing in a peculiar manner.

Hoppin' cars have come to the model car industry relatively recently and, to date, most have come from the garage industries. And in a hobby that is, to all intents and purposes, 'static', they have added a bit of movement. Garage kits are available that will convert a mere static bodyshell into something that can take on a life of its own. Most retain only the kit bodyshell, and sometimes the interior, but the latest examples are designed to keep the majority of the static kit intact, while the hoppin' features are mostly hidden. That said, wires will be needed to connect the motors to an external battery pack. And the first mainstream manufacturer has also come up with a hoppin' car, Lindberg having introduced a brand-new '64 Chevy Impala with hoppin' features.

## FULL STRETCH

Like any art form, customizing does not have hard and fast rules. For example, although many cars are sectioned by cutting out a horizontal strip, there is no reason why the cut cannot be made vertically to create a short or long car.

Long versions of full-size cars are common, as this is how most limousines are made. Perhaps surprisingly, there are no examples of these from the mainstream kit companies, and very few from the garage industry. This could be due to the fact that few suitable original kits are available. Limousines do tend to be based on the luxury end of the market anyway, and in the home of the 'stretched limo'—the USA—the idea of producing an 'annual' kit of the Chrysler Imperial or Lincoln Continental has all but passed. However, a few contenders are to be found: AMT reissued the 1966 Lincoln Continental in their Buyer's Choice series, while Jo-Han offered a suitable Cadillac in recent years; various large Mercedes are also available from Tamiya, Fujimi and Revell AG, as are the Celsior/Lexus (Tamiya, Aoshima, AMT) and the Volvo 760 (Italeri, Revell AG). All have been made in stretched full-size versions.

Obviously, if you want to make such a model, you will need two identical kits of the chosen subject. The procedure—at its very simplest—is a matter of combining the back half of one with the front half of another, the position of the cut dictating the length of the new version.

Limousines can vary considerably from a standard (if

Right **When Revell-Monogram reissued Monogram's Passenger Rocket, it prompted the idea of using it as a giant 'advertisement' on the roof of their Chevy van.**

Below right **The van had several modifications carried out (see Chapters 6 and 7), while holes had to be cut in the roof for the rocket supports. These came from the MPC Pilgrim Observer space station kit.**

Bottom right **The rear doors of the van were opened by carefully scribing around them, then sawing them free.**

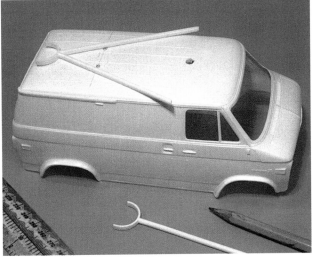

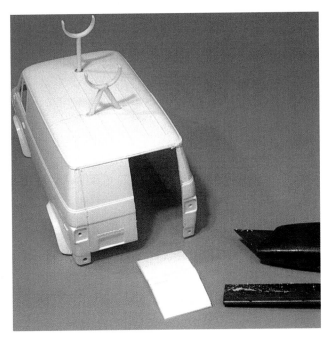

such a term is relevant) lengthening by about the width of a single door, which gives you the sort of limo suitable for weddings and funerals, to the more extravagant, as illustrated by the typical American stretched limo seen at airports and transporting rock stars. Some really take things to extremes with very impractical stretches that even have onboard jacuzzis. These are really designed for show rather than any practical purpose, as getting them around corners is a major manoeuvre.

The way in which the model is split and rejoined can follow the same basic route as the full-size equivalents, but it is worth remembering that a similar procedure that occurs with full-size cars—where the back half of a vehicle with frontal damage is joined to the front half of one with rear damage (known as 'ringing' if carried out illegally)—can result in the car splitting in half again! The major problem is that if a car is simply cut across the middle and welded to another, it will not be that strong, and although this is not dangerous in miniature, it does demonstrate that care should be taken when deciding on where to make the cut.

Three areas will need attention—the chassis, body and interior—and if the cuts in these areas are staggered so that they don't align, the result will be much stronger.

To create something approaching a standard limo, you will need to make it longer by about the width of one door. So first select a car that has a reasonably similar cross-section through the area that will be extended. This requirement does tend to make the slab-sided shape the best choice, hence the suitability of older Cadillacs, Lincolns and similar luxury cars.

The length of the body will dictate the rest, so modify the body first. Assuming the kit has an opening hood, and that you intend retaining this feature, it is best to utilize the rear door area for the conversion. If you cut at the front door line, you will risk weakening the structure even more, as it will be very close to the hood opening.

Cut behind the rear door of one body, and in front of the

rear door of the other. The roof will also need cutting, but if you stagger the position, making the cut further forward, and bear in mind the shape of the roof (see Chopping), this will add to the overall strength of the finished model.

The more slab-sided the kit, the more likely it will be that the joints will butt together, requiring very little extra work. You will need to add strengthening pieces behind the joint, such as strips of Plasticard, but that is probably all.

Then the interior can be held up to the body, and the amount of lengthening required marked off. Assuming that the kit has a separate front seat and the rear seat is moulded in, the cuts are probably best made immediately behind the instrument panel of one interior and forward of the rear seat of the other. This should provide enough extra length. If, however, the front seat is moulded in, you may have to make the cut immediately behind this seat, separate the two halves and fill the gaps with Plasticard or similar styrene sheet.

If you are lucky and the front seat is separate, the second example can be utilized in the rear of the stretched model, either facing forward or back towards the rear seat, making a sort of conference facility.

*Above left* **Early Batman comic strips seemed to suggest that the Batmobile was based on a '40 Ford sedan, so one was obtained and the roof lowered at the rear.**

*Left* **The obligatory Bat-fin was cut from sheet styrene, while the Bat-face at the front was shaped from a circular moulding. Note that the front wheels have covers similar to the rear—you are not supposed to ask how it steers!**

*Below* **The completed forties-style Batmobile, finished in a dark metallic blue. The windows are tinted dark red, and there is no interior. There is no engine, either, qualifying this model as a 'slammer'.**

With body and interior suitably lengthened, the chassis should be cut in yet another position to spread the load over the whole model. Many older kits had one-piece chassis, so lengthening them will simply be a matter of making straightforward cuts. You may find that moulded-in items—exhaust systems in particular—are out of alignment at this point, but if the model is intended only to be viewed from above, you may be content to paint it all black and leave it as is. Alternatively, the exhaust pipes can be rerouted using moulded plastic rod, or even the runners from the kit.

If the chassis is from a more modern kit, with separate suspension and the like, items such as the propshaft will certainly need attention, although it should be possible to join both examples from the two kits to make one longer drive shaft. The exhausts—assuming they, too, are separate—will also be easier to deal with: by combining the existing pipes, replacing sections with fresh pipes, or making up new systems completely. Normally, the suspension and the rear of the driveline will remain as before; there would be no purpose in altering these. However, some interesting variations can be attempted, such as giving the car six wheels, with two axles/four wheels at the rear. (Or, like Lady Penelope's Rolls-Royce, four wheels at the front!) Full-size cars that have such features as onboard jacuzzis need additional axles to take the extra weight, so the idea is not totally ludicrous.

Adding a second rear axle is not so straightforward as building a 'normal' stretched limo, as besides working out the installation of the axle itself, you will need to incorporate new wheel arches for the extra wheels. The appropriate parts should be available from the donor kit, but fitting them will involve more cutting and repositioning, while it is quite likely that the trunk area will have to be extended as well. The additional axle is unlikely to be driven on a full-size example—it's there purely to take the extra weight. However, with a simplified one-piece (or, by now, multi-

piece) chassis, this probably won't be a concern, and you can simply leave the axle and differential as is.

With the proliferation of mobile communications, such limos can be used as rolling offices or conference centres. If the layout suggested—seats facing each other—is followed, a table can be built from scrap plastic, and the interior decked out with various items of equipment that can be found in many kits. These range from mobile phones to faxes and even a computer. Modern police cars incorporate much of this high-tech equipment, so police car kits can often supply suitable pieces of hardware. The original MPC Dodge 440 police car came thus equipped, and the basic kit has been reissued several times: as Roscoe's car from the *Dukes of Hazzard*, as TV cop T. J. Hooker's mode of transport, and as the Gotham City Police Car from the first *Batman* movie. Although none of these is current, they can probably be unearthed from specialist dealers. Look also at the garage accessory manufacturers, as suitable pieces can be obtained from them, and at the EMA/Plastruct company who make, among their various offerings, office equipment in 1:25 scale (primarily for architectural model makers).

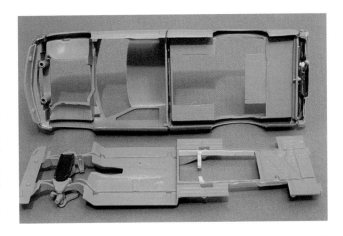

*Above right* **To convert an AMT/MPC Chevy Silverado truck into something fit for the drag strip, the engine needed relocating to the pickup bed.**

*Right* **The completed drag Silverado utilizes the twin-blower Chrysler hemi engine from the AMT 1953 Studebaker kit, and running gear from one of the Revell Pro-Street cars.**

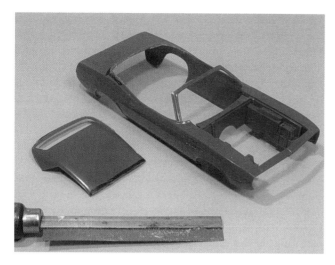

Wanting to build the special Plymouth Hemi 'Cuda driven by TV detective Nash Bridges, the first problem the author discovered was that there is no standard kit of the convertible version, only the hardtop. Consequently, the body from the Monogram kit was marked for the roof to be removed.

The completed Nash Bridges car, with scratchbuilt boot top and very thin wire added for the hood pins. After-market companies supply hood pin sets with photo-etched parts for the plates. The colour was changed from the original purple by priming it in grey, then white before applying the yellow.

Of course, you don't have to apply these stretching techniques to a luxury vehicle. Instead, you could create a fun custom by taking a car that would not normally be seen in limo form and stretching it. A good example would be a Mini which, due to its slab-sided design, would be quite simple to convert. In fact, full-size examples have been made.

The alternative, of course, is also possible, and the car can be shortened. This has been done with full-size custom cars, and there are examples of short (well, shorter than usual) Minis as well as stretched versions. It may be that if one model has been lengthened using the parts from two kits, there will be enough left to make a short example, too.

## OTHER POSSIBILITIES

Customizing techniques can also be used to produce a version of a car that otherwise is unobtainable. The simplest example is creating a convertible from a hardtop. Usually, all that is required is the careful removal of the roof, by cutting along the windshield and trunk lines. The window glass may also have to be cut if it is in one piece with the rest of the glazing. Then, the only necessary additions should be the sun visors (which, if they existed, will probably be moulded details in the roof) and the folded top. Sun visors can simply be cut from plastic sheet. If you want to super-detail them, you can add straps for sun-glasses, a vanity mirror on the passenger side, and—as found on most American car visors—a pocket for toll booth tickets.

The folded boot top may cause more of a problem, but a well stocked spares box should produce something that can be modified. Alternatively, it can be made from scratch by carving a thin sheet of balsa to shape and covering it with tissue soaked in glue. Also, many garage companies specifically make boot tops for conversions such as this. When you add the interior, you may find that there is a slight gap around the original rear pillars, as it may not fit snugly against the edge of the body. However, the folded top may cover this, or the gap can be filled with pieces of Plasticard.

More complex custom modifications could be employed to create a 'phantom'. This term applies to a stock vehicle that has been modified to turn it into another supposed stock version, but one that was not actually made by the manufacturer of the full-size vehicle. For example, it could be a van version of a car that actually only ever existed in sedan and coupe form or, as pickups have enjoyed a revival of interest in recent times, maybe a pickup version.

Phantoms seem to work best when based on older cars, notably those from the thirties, forties and early fifties. Creating a pickup version of, say, the Monogram 1937 Ford is possible, using the pickup bed from the '40 Ford or the more recent 1950 Ford. The back of the '37 Ford, and many other similar body shapes of this period, can be cut away to leave the front portion of the cab. Then, the back can be cut from the later model's cab and attached to the front part of the '37 Ford. Using the ubiquitous modelling putty to fill in the gaps, plus a deft touch with wet-or-dry, you will achieve the basic cab structure. With the chassis already assembled as a base, the body can be placed on top and marked where parts need to be cut, modified and filled. The pickup bed should also be placed in position to determine where it, too, may need modifying. The rear fenders are likely to need altering as well. This is the sort of customizing that allows you to utilize some of the custom parts that may be found in the kit—a modern engine and wheels, or fit the interior with a full-blooded stereo system (speakers and amplifiers are available from many after-market accessory companies).

You may be able to create a pickup cab by simply removing a vertical section of bodywork and gluing the back to the shortened front portion. Then, if you don't have a suitable pickup bed, you could try building a flat-bed type from sheet styrene, perhaps with wooden sides as a stake truck. In fact, the pickup bed can be covered with real wood, as many model stores stock very thin self-adhesive wood veneer. This can be stained or varnished, while 'metal' hold-down straps can be added with Bare-Metal Foil.

# Chapter Ten

# ACCESSORIES AND DIORAMAS

No sooner had the model car industry been born, than the companies began including a variety of bits and pieces with the kits. These were not additional parts for custom or competition options, but the sort of items that could be scattered around the finished model, as if it was on display at a car show and had won a trophy. Perhaps with this idea in mind, AMT introduced a new range of car kits in the early sixties. Until then, they had concentrated on 'annual' kits, developed from the promotional models. However, there were many other cars from earlier years that could be made, and to distinguish them, they called them the Trophy Series.

Each of these kits contained a miniature trophy, the sort of award that the owner of a full-size car would hope to take home from the local car show. And when you went to such a show, you would probably lay out the contents of the trunk, and maybe remove one of the custom wheels to display a finned and chromed brake drum. So if the customizers of full-size vehicles could do it, why not model builders, too? Thus, the accessory market was born; soon complete miniature scenes—dioramas—began to appear.

One idea that caught on pretty quickly was that, since pickup models were popular, they would be provided with something to carry in the pickup bed. Two of the earliest—again from AMT's Trophy Series—were the 1934 and 1953 Ford pickups. The '34 came with a host of goodies: tools and a toolbox, gas cans, a fire extinguisher and even a wrecker crane attachment, allowing the kit to be built as a tow truck. The '53 Ford came similarly equipped, but instead of the crane, it had oxy-acetylene welding equipment.

As two of the favourites of modellers, both kits have been available on and off over the years, and even in the nineties, both are still around. The '53 Ford is still an AMT product, although ironically—and probably from 'mislaid' tooling—the '34 Ford has most recently been offered as a Lindberg kit, but it is almost identical to the AMT issue.

These models were just the beginning, however. Trailers began to be included: from flat beds that doubled as display stands to box-type versions that came with the likes of AMT's Buick Special Station Wagon, which was also provided with a host of racing gear. Monogram entered the surfing scene with its Blue Beetle Custom 1929 Ford, complete with surf board and scuba gear. Revell added motor bikes, snowmobiles, wet bikes and off-road buggies as various trailer loads, while MPC even perched a canoe on the roof of its 1970 Pontiac Bonneville. AMT came up with camper tops and an outboard boat for Chevelle pickups, while Jo-Han and Aurora added suitcases to the trunks of their Rambler and Aston Martin DB4 respectively. Appropriately, Jo-Han also provided a stretcher with their Cadillac ambulance, and a casket with the Cadillac hearse!

**Accessories were included very early on in car kits. AMT, particularly, started providing a variety of extras, including a go-kart, the only drawback being that the various parts were spread through several kits, so you had to buy them all to complete the kart. (Although it was also available complete in at least one kit.) This shows an original go-kart as a load for the pickup bed of AMT's reissued 1961 Ford Ranchero.**

**Several modern kits have also been issued with accessories, among them Fujimi's Mitsubishi Pajero, which comes with a roof rack, cycle and two Thule roof-rack containers. You get the grass as well...**

And most interiors came with a wide variety of assorted equipment: reel-to-reel tape recorders (this was pre-CD, remember), TVs, telephones and even a stuffed toy animal for the parcel shelf! Many are still to be found in the various reissues, and even the odd brand-new kit will contain an interior accessory, but it must be said that these days it does tend to be a cell phone or the cover of a CD case, rather than a stuffed toy. One company, Fujimi, who seem to have taken the accessory kit to heart, have also produced a set of interior bits and pieces. They, too, went the modern route, offering such items as a skateboard and roller-blades, but they relented slightly, as one item was a teddy bear!

## GARAGE AND TOOLS
With the interior of the car satisfactorily full, something with

**And if accessories are not provided with a kit, a little lateral thinking will often work. Revell-Monogram's new '37 Ford delivery has the decals for Blony gum, but the bubble-gum machine is a doll's house accessory.**

which to perform repairs was also a natural for car kits, especially the commercial vehicles, although it was some time before a complete garage kit arrived. However, the various tools—screwdrivers, hammers and spanners (US, wrenches)—could be found in a range of kits, the '34 Ford included. In addition, these were the sort of items that the growing garage companies began to produce. R&D Unique still make a range of garage equipment and tools in white metal, from an individual screwdriver to a compressor and air tank.

However, when Fujimi came up with their Tools kit to go with their Garage kit (see below), they supplied the basis of any good workshop, all in one kit. This not only provides a hoist to raise the car (which is fully adjustable for most 1:24/5 scale cars), but also jacks, axle stands, an engine hoist and a crawler for the mechanic to slide under the car. Both electric and gas welders are supplied, complete with mask. Add to this a work bench, vice and shelving, which even comes with spare shocks, carbs, springs and the wooden crates in which they were delivered. The tools range from the usual selection of spanners and wrenches to an electric drill, and the whole lot is complemented by oil cans, batteries and even a funnel. Finally, for when the account has to be settled, there is a table, chair and phone!

## MAKING A SCENE...
It is a short step from adding accessories to creating a diorama, displaying the model in some sort of scene. This is not a new idea—model railway enthusiasts have been doing it for years, and few serious modellers in that field would be content with a locomotive and rolling stock running on plain track on a plain base. While car models (with the exception of slot and radio controlled cars) are not intended to move, one of the charms of model making lies in recreating miniature scenes that, to all intents and purposes, mirror reality.

However, there is no hard and fast rule about when a model with accessories becomes a diorama—not as far as

**The simplest accessory for any model car is a case. Many companies make these, including Revell-Monogram, Academy and Ertl. Here, cases protect two AMT Barris creations—the Surf Woody and its darker cousin, the Surf Hearse (top).**

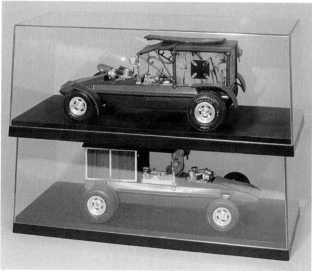

most modellers are concerned. And some very effective scenes can be created with the minimum of additions. (In fact, the only time it *does* seem to matter is during some model competitions, when it has been argued that a single figure added to a model has turned it from a solitary model into a full-blown diorama!)

The mainstream manufacturers have tried to offer dioramas of a sort in the past, but in the main, these have relied on that good old-fashioned material, card, to create a backdrop. No doubt, its use was influenced by the original shop displays, which were very prominent in the early sixties. With these, a manufacturer's assembled model was displayed on a suitable base with a backing extolling its virtues. This type of display has long been discontinued, but as with all things nostalgic, original examples have reached the stage of being extremely collectable.

## BACKDROP

AMT was probably to first company to include a card display with their kits, and they produced a whole range. Among them were a beach scene for the Meyers Manx Beach Buggy; a suitably ancient service station for the '34 Ford pickup; and a section of 'super highway' for their own futuristic design, the AMTronic (see Chapter 13). MPC extended this idea and, besides a pre-printed card back, for short while issued a series called Autoscape, which provided a pre-moulded vacuum formed section of 'ground' on which to sit the finished model. This also benefited from the fact that, although there was little point in repainting the pre-printed background, you could at least adapt the base to your own scene, and vac-formed styrene took enamel paints just as well as injection moulded styrene.

Although, in the main, these backgrounds disappeared from car kits, good ideas do travel in circles, and recently Revell-Monogram introduced a new range of American-style backdrops, based on an idea by modelling writer and collector Dean Milano.

In general, however, backdrops became the exception rather than the rule, and although the range of accessories continued to grow, no companies offered much in the way of other suitable diorama backgrounds. One item that would

have been a natural was some sort of garage scene, whether it be a domestic garage or a professional establishment, as all cars need servicing and repairs at some time in their life (some more than others...). In fact, and ironically, the only company to come close to this was Aurora, who were not exactly thought of as model car manufacturers. However, they did have a good track record with dioramas and, in the seventies, produced garage scenes in 1:16 scale.

Eventually, the 1:24/5 scale garage problem was solved, but not by one of the American manufacturers—this one came from Japan.

## GARAGES AND WORKSHOPS

Fujimi had been supplying an ever growing range of car kits, of both Japanese and European subjects, when they announced a series of Garage and Tools kits. The first—the garage—gave the modeller a basic kit that, in effect, was a box. The floor and two walls came with card inserts to represent suitable surfaces, while the other two walls and the ceiling were clear. If these were added, the whole lot became a dust-free display case. Additional kits could be added on— either in width or depth—and although Fujimi say that up to four kits can be used in this way, there is no reason why such a layout could not be extended indefinitely.

The kit is fairly flexible, allowing windows and doors to be fitted, and there is no reason why these cannot be adapted to other models with a scratchbuilt basic structure. Several materials can be employed here. Styrene sheet is the obvious choice, but for a backing, thin wood will make a more rigid structure. Thin ply and MDF (medium-density fibreboard) are the best, although thicker sheet materials, including blockboard, may be better for an actual base. Offcuts of wood can be obtained very cheaply from timber yards, while DIY stores invariably have a box of damaged oddments, which may contain something like a drawer front that has seen better days, but may be just right for the base of your next model.

## OTHER MATERIALS

Featherlight board is also very good as a structural material. This comprises two layers of card with foam sandwiched

**Figures are the most obvious accessories for a car display. A variety is produced, including these somewhat specialist examples from Jimmy Flintstone Productions, representing the builder of the Munster Koach and Drag-U-La, George Barris (centre), and their respective drivers (left and right).**

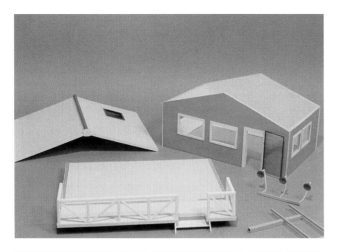

between them. Although it may not sound very strong, it can be, and it is very light. It cannot take the same knocks as wood, but it is very easily cut with a sharp knife and can be glued with contact adhesive or, better, a hot-glue gun. It takes paint very well; alternatively, sheets of Plasticard can be glued (spray glue works well) on to the surface.

Plasticard itself can be obtained with a wide variety of finishes as well as smooth, which suggests the possibility of exploring other sources for materials and ideas. There is no need for car modellers to stick purely to items specifically designed for car modelling. Most Plasticard sheets that are embossed with patterns were intended initially for railway modelling—they will have brick, stone, tiles and similar patterns. But even though the scales may not match, large tiles

*Above left* **Building a typical American drive-in—the Cadillac Cafe. The basic structure is made from thin MDF (medium-density fibreboard), covered in textured Plasticard. Strip styrene is used for window surrounds, hand rails and the like.**

*Left* **The building before painting. Note the etched brass screen door. The roof coping is an EMA half-round moulding.**

*Below* **The finished Cadillac Cafe. Cars are the Monogram '59 Cadillac (front), AMT '40 Ford delivery (far left) and AMT's Mustang built for Sonny Bono (far right), with its creator, George Barris, standing in front. Other figures come from Jimmy Flintstone, Rabbit Models and Tyresmoke Products/Miniature Autobits. The chairs are EMA, while the juke box and Coke machine are also from Jimmy Flintstone.**

in 1:76 scale can be small bricks in 1:25, and rough stonework tends to work in any scale.

Of course, you can always create your own patterns. If you paint some plain white Plasticard with a top coat of a suitable colour, once dry, it can be scribed with a pattern of individual bricks, for example. (A scribing blade is better than a pure cutting blade.) Where the pattern has been scribed, the white of the plastic will show up as the mortar joints between the bricks. For different coloured mortar, use a coloured Plasticard, or scribe first, then paint.

Exploring other modelling sources, the military field is a good one. Although the standard scale is smaller, at 1:35, many companies—such as Tamiya and Italeri—make items that can be adapted. A collapsed brick wall in 1:35 simply makes a slightly smaller collapsed brick wall in 1:25, and if you are working in the 1:32 car scale, it is better still. And even if no suitable ready-built item is available, you can scratchbuild something yourself.

## DOWN TO EARTH

When scratchbuilding a diorama, you can create a rough surface texture with that old standby, sawdust. This versatile material can be bought ready dyed in packs from hobby stores, or you can obtain it in bulk from a timber yard and dye it yourself. Frankly, however, if you have any power tools (such as a bandsaw or circular saw) in your workshop, you already have a handy source!

Sawdust can be mixed with emulsion paint, or thinned PVA wood glue, and applied to a suitable base. It can also be mixed with plaster for applying a rough surface in bulk. A slow drying plaster is best, as used for ceilings (Artex is one). Standard quick drying plasters—dental plaster or plaster of Paris—tend to be less suitable, as they dry too fast for most modelling work. However, quick drying plaster does have its uses, particularly in the form of the ubiquitous plaster bandage, this time adapted from the medical fraternity. Although plaster bandage is losing favour in TV hospital programmes, such as *ER* and *Casualty*, it is still available for modelling, one of the trade names being Mod-Roc. If you can source a bulk supplier, it'll be much cheaper.

Plaster bandage has the advantage that it can be moulded into any shape of landscape. The traditional method is to build a frame of chicken wire on a solid base. Then the bandage is soaked and quickly placed over the framework. Although the plaster cures quickly, it will allow sufficient time for any final prodding into shape, and more layers can be added on top if necessary. In fact, it isn't even necessary to go the chicken-wire route, as crumpled newspaper can work equally well as a 'frame'.

## BULK STYRENE

Another very useful material for creating a layered base is actually polystyrene itself, but in its expanded form. In bulk, this is known under various trade names, including Jabolite, but it will be familiar to most as the packing material for virtually any piece of electrical equipment you care to name. Whatever you may have bought—from computers to curling tongs—they are bound to have been packed in this light, white foamy material. It is also available in large sheets for insulation purposes. These are more useful if you want to build a large base, or a structure of some sort.

Expanded polystyrene has the advantage that it is light and, assuming it began life as packing, can be free. However, it doesn't glue together very easily. Although it is styrene, because it has been foamed, any of the usual styrene cements will melt the surface completely (although this can produce some interesting textures). Expanded polystyrene is best glued with either a specially formulated contact adhesive (available from home decorating stores and the like, as it can be used for gluing ceiling tiles), white PVA glue, or one of the plaster mixes, such as Artex.

You can cut expanded polystyrene very easily with a

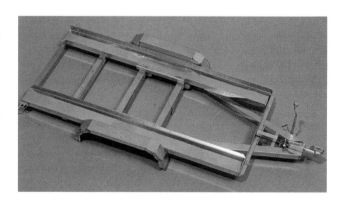

*Above right* **A trailer is an obvious addition to a car model, and over the years many have been provided in American kits. However, this one is of typical British design and comes from South-Eastern Finecast. It is built from brass sheet, which can be soldered together, plus some white metal parts.**

*Right* **AMT's Chevy stepside pulling the South-Eastern Finecast trailer, laden with Gunze Sangyo's Fiat 500.**

*Above* **Custom cars are invariably displayed at shows, often with the aid of lots of chrome and mirrors. A simple base can be made for a custom car, in this case Revell's Outlaw by Ed Roth, by applying chromed mylar or similar sheet to a wooden base. Alternatively, a small mirror could be built into the base to show off the underside of the car.**

*Below* **A simple diorama using Heller's Citroën B14 van, barrels from Monogram's beer wagon, and bottles from the Gangbuster accessories supplied with MPC's 1927 Lincoln. The table top is an EMA part with plastic strip legs, while the base is textured Plasticard.**

*Below right* **Vehicle courtesy of Airfix, palms courtesy of Britains, sand courtesy of the local builders' yard. Sandy scenes (desert or beach) can be created using the finest grade of sand, well dried. If you do not expect to move the model, it can be simply poured into place, otherwise glue it down with thinned PVA wood glue.**

sharp knife, and modellers who use it a lot will invariably have their own favourite tools for cutting, such as sharpened hacksaw blades and old kitchen knives—even an electric bread knife has been known to be employed, although it does tend to be useless for cutting bread afterwards... The material can also be cut with a hot-wire cutter, and several manufacturers make these commercially. However, be warned, in effect this burns the polystyrene which, although a safe and inert substance for most of the time, causes it to give off noxious fumes, so take appropriate action with filtration, ventilation and a mask.

Expanded polystyrene can also be sanded, and although this is safe as far as fumes are concerned, it does raise a cloud of polystyrene dust, which may not be good for the lungs. Because of static, the dust settles absolutely everywhere and will take forever to vacuum up!

## PAINTING

Expanded polystyrene can be used as a base for contouring materials, such as plaster bandage, Artex and sawdust, or it can be painted. However, although the surface is a foam, it is actually non-absorbent to water-based paints (hence its use as insulation and packing), and such paints will take far longer to dry on the surface. On the other hand, oil-based paints (enamels) will dry quicker, but check first that they will not eat away the surface.

In general, most scenic materials—plasters, sawdust, bandage and the like—take water-based paints very well. Domestic emulsions are the cheapest source for bulk paints, but they tend to be formulated in specific shades: do you want your desert scene Sunshine Yellow, or your muddy field Apple Green? However, creating a diorama could be a good reason to sort out all those part-used tins left over from decorating the house and stored at the back of the garden shed. You may be able to mix some interesting shades by adding a few darker colours.

In smaller quantities, the modelling acrylics also work extremely well on plaster and sawdust mixes, and don't for-

get poster paints, which are bought dry and can be mixed into anything else, even directly into the plaster and sawdust while still wet. Poster paint-type colours are also available in large quantities from DIY stores and builders' merchants for mixing into concrete and mortar. These may be a good source for duller shades.

## ON THE BEACH

You may be able to use genuine substances for dioramas. For example, if you are creating a beach scene with a beach buggy and bikini-clad sunbather, real sand can be used to represent, well, real sand. However, use the finest silver sand you can find (try aquarium suppliers as well as builders' merchants), otherwise the grains will be far too large. Ensure that the sand is quite dry before you use it. This may mean spreading it out on a tray and leaving it for several days.

The sand can be mixed with white glue and spread on the base, or the glue can be spread first and the sand sprinkled on top. When the glue has dried, tip the excess away and repeat if necessary. The final layer could be sprayed with a clear varnish, which will keep loose grains in place.

If your beach scene requires the sea as well—and this applies to any water feature—use a sheet of clear plastic over a suitably dark base, which will represent the bottom of the sea or pond. Acrylic sheet is best, as it is more rigid. The surface can be painted with transparent colours if necessary, rippled acrylic providing some interesting effects. If you want a rock—or a tree—protruding from the surface, don't cut the acrylic. Instead, cut the rock or tree in half and glue to each side of the clear sheet.

'Water' can also be made by pouring clear casting resin into a depression, after preparing a suitable bottom: sand, mud or whatever. The resin can be pre-tinted with colour, or painted with transparent colours after it has cured. If you want to suggest waves or ripples, they can be very carefully wiped on when the resin has nearly cured.

If your beach scene is to include a surfer and waves, the waves themselves can be formed by tipping the whole base while the resin dries and encouraging it to form the wave shapes. If you have used an acrylic sheet, you can pour resin on top of it to form waves. This will allow for a bit of practice, as it may not work the first time. The tips of the breakers can be added in white paint after everything has cured.

## GREENERY

Foliage can be obtained from a variety of sources. It might be easiest to buy several packs of pre-coloured model railway 'grass' and the like, then sprinkle it over the surface. These materials can be obtained in a wide variety of colours and textures, from almost dust to large lumps that could be used to represent mown grass, churned up earth, pieces of mud or stones.

You can also buy kits to make trees and bushes, although the cheapest means of obtaining the main structure of a tree is from the real thing. Small twigs can become the trunks and branches of trees in many scales. For a dead tree, this is all you need to use, perhaps with a bit of moss or lichen (green paint with a touch of sawdust) applied.

For living trees—and plants in general—some excellent etched brass sheets are available that provide foliage for an entire tree, individual leaves and ground based plants such as ferns. These can be assembled into some incredibly detailed miniature greenery. However, this takes time and quite a lot of skill. For a large expanse of greenery, it could also be expensive, as the brass sheets are not cheap.

Another option is to base the foliage on foam, which is also available from model shops for railway use. This can be chopped up finely (it may be already in this form) and sprinkled over glue applied to your twig. Alternatively, twisted wire can be used to form the trunk and branches of a tree, dipped in paint and the foliage applied in the same manner. Dyed lichen also makes good foliage for trees and bushes, as does teased out wire-wool, but do not paint this with water-based paints, as it will rust. That said, it may produce an interesting effect for an autumnal scene.

Check out large craft stores for other sources of wire,

**The theme of the car itself can often suggest a suitable scene. For Monogram's Macabremobile—the '59 Thunderbird of Elvira, Mistress of the Dark—a simple, but effective, diorama was built from a few Italeri military accessories (gates and pillars), some lichen and some real twigs for the branches. The 'moon' is a light behind translucent paper stretched over a cut-out in the black backing.**

Fujimi make a range of car servicing accessories, including this garage structure, equipment and mechanics. Here, the figures work on Monogram's Shelby Cobra. The only slight inaccuracy is that the whole scene is probably too clean!

Fujimi mechanics working on AMT's 1965 Chevelle station wagon. The tools and equipment are also Fujimi, except for the ramps, which come with the Chevelle.

Sometimes, you just need an 'ordinary' figure for your diorama. These characters originate from Preiser and are actually to 1:22.5 scale (to match LGB railways). However, where figures are concerned, exact scaling is not too crucial, and they fit perfectly well with 1:24 scale cars from Airfix/Heller (Citroën 2CV), Gunze Sangyo (Fiat 500) and Tamiya (Mini Cooper). The figures have also been available from EMA in their Plastruct range.

foam and dyed lichen. Some suitable materials may be available from aquarium suppliers.

## BUILDING BUILDINGS

Creating whole buildings for models is really beyond the scope of this book (for more details, see *Roy Porter's Model Buildings Masterclass*, also published by Windrow & Greene). However, using techniques already described, items such as featherlight board and embossed Plasticard can be used to form the main structures.

Brickwork can be scribed into the plastic, or adapted from embossed sheets, while even brick-effect wallpaper designed for dolls' houses can be used. The last may be too 'flat' and 'clean' in appearance, but there is no reason why it can't be weathered to a suitable shade. Doors and windows can be made from strips of wood or plastic, which is available in many pre-moulded shapes. Especially useful will be the vast range of items from EMA (Engineering Model Associates), also known as Plastruct in the hobby trade.

EMA has a vast catalogue containing a wide range of girders, beams, piping, railings, ladders and stairs, and even trees and furniture for all types of model making. Initially, these were designed for architectural model makers, but they have a much wider appeal to many other modellers. Most parts are moulded in ABS (acrylonitrile-butadiene-styrene), which is tougher than pure styrene, but can be glued with liquid cements. Girders are available in H, I, T and L sections, together with channels and square and rectangular beams, which are ideal for building structures. Tubing, domes and hemispheres can be adapted for a wider variety of purposes, from drainpipes to air tanks for a garage scene. However, once you have started using EMA parts, you will find that they offer an ever increasing range of possibilities.

In fact, the parts fit various architectural sizes, but as with many items, the scales are almost irrelevant. For example, girders are available in real sizes from approximately $\frac{1}{16}$ to 1in (EMA, being American, uses imperial dimensions, not metric), while tubing ranges from $\frac{1}{8}$ to 12in! And nothing need go to waste, as scrap lengths of girder can be used as a load for a pickup.

## ON THE TRACK

Cars can also find their way on to racing circuits, and various bases have been made to represent both American oval tracks and the more winding variety for Formula racing. Many are pre-printed card bases, which can be used as such, but of course, they will be completely flat. However, they could be useful as the basis for a more three-dimensional design: a slightly textured surface could be added to the track itself, while curbs could be raised slightly with Plasticard or plaster. Fences and crash barriers could be added, too. Use mesh intended for full-size car body repairs to represent the wire fencing that protects spectators from flying debris, and form crash barriers from strips of plastic sheet. Alternatively, EMA make half-round pipe, which can be used for strengthened crash barriers.

Over the years, racing equipment itself has been available from a variety of sources. One of the earliest was AMT's Drag Strip Accessories, which was a separate kit that

A mix of kits and accessories shown around AMT's Galles-Kraco March 88C car and the Kenworth T600A truck and transporter. The equipment is a mix of that supplied with the transporter—the pillar drill that can be seen inside the trailer for example—and Fujimi's Garage Accessories.

provided items you would find on the starting line. These included the starting lights, a loudspeaker, flags and even a broom to sweep the track. There was also a TV camera, but this dates the kit, as it was a huge multi-lens affair—it is all miniaturization and CCDs these days—but it would still be good for a vintage drag strip scene. This set was reissued in 1990, with the 1963 Corvette, in AMT's Prestige series, and in 1997 with other accessory packs as a Buyer's Choice.

AMT included race equipment with their race-rig trailers. These provided a basic workshop inside the trailer that carried the race car. Monogram offered pit accessories with their NASCARs for a while, too. The garage industry added to these with items such as stacks of tyres for tricky corners.

## THE POPULATION

Although strictly speaking accessories, figures have a special place in making a scene, no matter how simple.

Various card bases have been made over the years. Here, Revell-Monogram's 1955 Chevy Bel Air, in appropriate Pace Car colours, sits on Tyresmoke Products' banked circuit. The Chevy's two-tone finish is helped considerably by the fact that the dividing line between the colours is a chrome strip.

*Above* The famous scene from *Back to the Future II*, in which the time travelling DeLorean is pushed up to time travelling speed by a wood burning locomotive using suitably enhanced fuel! The raw material consists of the MPC/Airfix/AMT loco, The General, and the Aoshima/Halcyon/AMT DeLorean. The idea was to capture the spirit of the scene rather than be correct in every detail. (The loco is wrong, as it's a 4-4-0, whereas the movie version was a 4-6-0).

*Above left* The base for the scene is a piece of blockboard, with banking formed from expanded polystyrene and plaster bandage. Detailing was added with widened LGB track, model railway scenic lichen, tinted sawdust and real twigs. Water-based household paint was used for most of the colouring, and items were stuck down with PVA wood glue.

*Left* Although virtually invisible inside the completed model, the DeLorean does have a Marty McFly driver (a modified Fujimi figure) with a cape made from tissue soaked in wood glue. The temperature gauge sitting on the passenger seat was scratchbuilt.

Occasionally, they have been provided in kits, some from the very earliest days of Revell's multi-piece-body cars. Figures were included with all the 1:32 scale range, and many of the 1:25 series, including the '57 Ford station wagon, VW Microbus, Pontiac Club de Mer and Lincoln Futura. Later, it tended to be personalities, Aurora providing all three stars with their '49 Mercury Woody from The Mod Squad; AMT figures of Laurel and Hardy: and MPC all five members of the band Paul Revere and the Raiders, unusually moulded in polythene, not styrene (see Chapter 3).

In recent years, however, many companies have realized that figures, more than anything, will bring a scene to life, and a wide range has become available. Jimmy Flintstone, in the US, produces a series that even includes George Barris himself — useful to stand next to his own creations — and various scantily-clad girls for beach scenes. Rabbit Models, in the UK, now issue the older Freeway Design figures, which provide individuals suitable for diners, drive-ins or simply lolling around.

And the mainstream companies have also caught on. For many years, Tamiya produced their Campus Friends, a set of five students, one sitting on a scooter. Both Fujimi and Hasegawa have made sets of mechanics: the Fujimi examples to go with their garage; the Hasegawa figures specifically as Formula racing mechanics. Both also make sets of drivers: Hasegawa two sets of racing drivers, and Fujimi both racing and ordinary car drivers. Revell AG issued a truck drivers set, but as standing figures, they could be used anywhere, while Italeri made two Truck Accessory packs, which contained figures. Although the last were specifically for truck modellers, they could be used elsewhere.

Tamiya make a range of Formula figures and equipment, although as their Formula 1 scale is 1:20, this is the scale of the figures. Verlinden, best known for 1:35 military accessories, have made three 1:24/5 scale figures: two mechanics and a policeman. Police figures are also available from Rabbit Models, while Preiser offer a range of 'normal' (for want of a better term) figures that are pre-painted. These are also available unpainted in the EMA/Plastruct range.

And if you want animals as well as human figures, Tamiya have several as part of their 1:35 military range. One is a set of farm animals which, in larger scales, will simply represent smaller animals, while — oddly — a 1:35 scale cat is supplied with a German weapons loading crew, which makes a convenient 1:25 scale kitten!

Figures are made in all materials: styrene, resin and white metal. For painting, it is best to attach them at some convenient point (for example, a standing figure through a foot) to a rod that will act as a hand-hold.

Many of these figures are best primed overall first with something like Revell's Basic Color. This gives a good dense base coat on which to apply the rest of the finish. Publications are available that give detailed advice on painting figures, although this need not be as daunting as it may first appear. Usually, it is best to apply the basic colouring first, starting with the eyes (the most difficult part), then the rest of the flesh tones. After that, build up the clothing around them. Obviously, flat colours are the rule, with acrylics working particularly well, but this does not preclude

Smoke was formed from air-brushed cotton-wool. The airbrush also came in useful for providing the 'dust' on the DeLorean and — with the help of Sellotape cut-outs — the wiper pattern on the windshield. Pieces of real twig are scattered around the track.

the use of enamels. Some figure painters prefer other types of paint, even oil paints and tempera.

With the main colours in place, shading and edges can be added in darker or lighter tints as appropriate, using a very fine brush and a dry brushing technique: removing virtually all of the paint from the brush so that only a trace is wiped on to the model. Bold colours are rarely found on figures — even a black leather jacket won't be a true black — while wear will be found on the extremities of most clothing: elbows, knees and shoes. Little details can also help, so don't be afraid to modify a stance by changing the angle of an arm or the turn of a head. Touches such as adding a pair of glasses can also change a figure entirely. Tamiya's Campus Friends set even provided a length of wire and a rig to make a pair.

Some of the many accessory packs that have been available from the mainstream companies (there are many more from the garage industry).

# Chapter Eleven

# RENOVATING AN OLD KIT

Once completed, models can lead a perilous existence. Most do not benefit from purpose-made display cabinets and may find themselves exposed to dust, grime, everyday household hazards and constant touching with fingers. The model that once was your pride and joy may slowly deteriorate into something more fit for the junkyard. However, all is not lost, for old kits can be renovated and brought back to life.

Because styrene is so stable, little will have happened to the structure of the parts. About the only things that will damage styrene are some solvents and heat. As long as it hasn't been subjected to either, there is hope of recovering a model that may appear to be long past its 'sell-by date'.

There are pros and cons to renovation; with so many kits reappearing as limited editions or special reissues, you may ask, 'Why bother?' Often, however, a model may have a special meaning to the builder, yet may never be a candidate for reissue, particularly if the tooling no longer exists.

That said, renovation will only be worthwhile if a reasonable amount of the model still exists (regardless of condition). If you have a model that is reaching this stage, but you don't have the inclination to rebuild it immediately, the best advice is to ensure that all of the bits are kept together. If you can't store them in the original box, at least find another suitable container. The instruction sheet will also help, but if you are a collector, you'll have kept this anyway.

On the other hand, you may have acquired a model at a swap meet, or through a dealer, that you'd like to add to your own collection, but which perhaps is not built to the standard you would wish or, for that matter, may be missing various parts. Whatever the situation, the following may assist.

The actual restoration work will vary from model to model, depending on condition, but the first task is to discover just what has survived. This is where the instructions will prove very useful, for unless you have intimate knowledge of the kit concerned, you may have no idea what was intended by the manufacturer. Consequently, the instructions will be the main aid in establishing just what is there—and what may have to be re-created. If you haven't got the instructions, much will depend on guesswork and how the model is to be restored. If we assume that the kit dates from an issue in the sixties, most likely it will have the classic 3-in-1 options: stock, custom or competition. However, you can only build one version, so the fact that it may be missing the custom parts will hardly matter if you intend rebuilding it to stock configuration.

Factors that will apply to virtually every kit destined for rejuvenation are, first, disassembly and, second, paint. One usual reason for renovation is that the kit has started to disintegrate anyway—parts will have fallen off or been knocked off—and the actual disassembly may have occurred already. In this case, you will be faced with the task of separating the body from the chassis. The chassis of many old kits, particularly those from AMT, were held to their bodies by self-tapping screws, so this stage simply requires them to be unscrewed. This separates the chassis from the body, and

Sometimes, it's easier to wait until a favourite kit is reissued. My original Revell Stone Woods and Cook Willys, issued in 1963, was looking a little sorry for itself minus its back axle (background). However, the kit was reissued, and it was more straightforward to build it anew, using a Ford touch-up spray for the correct colour.

There will be occasions when a kit is extremely unlikely to see the light of day again, while to locate and buy an unbuilt original will be beyond the pocket. This is AMT's 1962 'annual' issue of the Chrysler Imperial, with its original box and instructions. However, it is minus a few parts and definitely needs new paint.

you will usually find that the interior and window glass can be removed at the same time, since they may be held in place by push-on plastic washers. Separating the body and chassis will also release the front and rear bumpers and grille, while the wheels will be pushed on to metal axles. Thus, it is relatively easy to reduce the kit to its main constituents.

Joints between parts will probably have been made with old-style tubed cement and may not be as strong as perhaps you thought when you first built the model. Consequently, it's very likely than many parts will simply snap away, leaving a (relatively) clean surface. You can also obtain solvents that are designed to break down these cement joints, so an application of one of these could be useful.

You will be extremely lucky if you do not discover that some parts are missing, and some thought will have to be given to how these will be replaced. But for starters, most renovation projects will involve a body that is covered in layers of paint of an indeterminate age and formulation, and the very next task is its removal.

Paint will dissolve in many solvents, but most will also dissolve the styrene, which defeats the object of the exercise somewhat. Therefore, a substance that will dissolve paint, but not styrene, must be found. Sanding the paint off is a possibility, but it is rather tedious and impractical, as it will also remove much, if not all, of the underlying detail.

The quest for a safe method of paint removal has occupied modellers for many years. In fact, it dates as far back as the sixties, when the two respected car modelling magazines of the day—*Car Model* and *Model Car Science* (both since long gone)—provided various tips on this thorny problem.

*Above right* **The major problem with the bodywork is that the windshield frame is broken and the parts are missing. The paint also needs removing, so it's Modelstrip to the rescue.**

*Right* **The parts needed to be stripped of paint are liberally plastered with the Modelstrip paste, then sealed in a polythene bag so that it will not dry out, and left somewhere warm for at least 24 hours.**

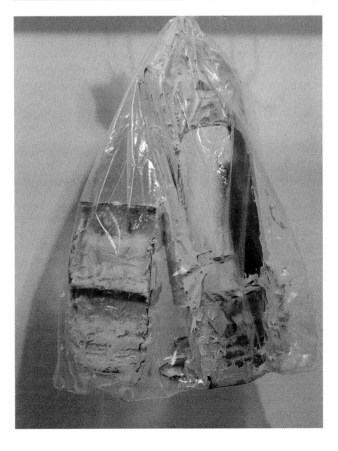

A lot of newspaper will be needed to protect everything when the parts are removed from their bag and washed in clean water. Then you will—should—be left with the plastic in its original state, albeit dulled and sometimes with a brown tint.

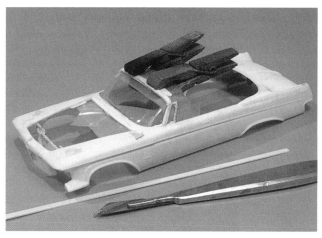

The windshield surround was built up from styrene strip, clamped into place using the glass as a template. One sun visor had to be scratchbuilt. Various holes in the body were filled and sanded with wet-or-dry abrasive paper when dry.

In those days, two favourites emerged: one was glow fuel, developed for glow-plug engines in flying model aeroplanes; the other was ordinary automotive brake fluid. Both worked to a degree, and immersing the various parts in the liquids would usually cause the paint to float off. But it tended to take ages, was extremely messy and (particularly in the case of glow fuel) was not cheap. (The cost of brake fluid could be reduced by employing used fluid.) However, it was always advisable to check that the substance would dissolve the paint, and not the parts themselves.

In more recent years, other substances have been tried, including many commercial domestic cleaners. Oven cleaner is invariably quoted as a favourite, and it usually works quite well, but again, it is vital to ensure that only the paint is being dissolved. If you have kept all the original parts of the kit under renovation in their box, you can try the proposed paint remover on spare parts that you will not need. Otherwise, if you have any doubt, you will have to experiment on an area of the kit that will not be seen—the upper surface of the chassis, say, or the underside of the body.

This problem of paint removal has also been explored by commercial companies. Revell AG, for example, issued their own Color Ex for some time. Personally, I have found a substance called Modelstrip to work the best on virtually all finishes. This is an alkali-based paste, manufactured in the UK, that is liberally brushed on to the painted surface and sealed in a polythene bag (so that it does not dry out). Then it should be left somewhere warm for at least 24 hours, such as an airing cupboard. (As Modelstrip is very sticky and tends to get everywhere, it is a wise precaution to place the polythene bag inside another cleaner bag, otherwise the contents of the cupboard may be 'stripped' as well...)

After a day or so, the parts will resemble something that has escaped from a particularly bad science-fiction movie. But don't worry. Carefully remove them from the bags and wash them in water to reveal the plastic surface again. It may be slightly discoloured, and high-gloss plastic may have lost its shine, but as the object of the exercise is to rebuild the kit, this should hardly matter. Stubborn areas of paint should be

attacked with an old toothbrush, and may need a reapplication of the paste. You may find it worthwhile to leave the whole body in the bag for longer than 24 hours. Once, by accident, I left a set of parts for over two weeks, but this did not seem to affect anything drastically. Certainly, it had no greater detrimental effect on the plastic surfaces.

Modelstrip works on all normal modelling paints, except cellulose (which should not have been used on styrene anyway), polyurethane (used in some varnishes) and some factory finishes. Also, it does not like candy colours, although extra scrubbing with a toothbrush seems to work. Currently, the oldest paint I've had experience of removing with Modelstrip was 35 years old, and the stripper removed it all in one go after about three days of soaking.

One slight problem with Modelstrip is that it cannot be sent by ordinary post, and its availability can vary in the UK, let alone world-wide. Check the References section for details of availability and the US equivalent.

All paint removers need careful handling. Always read the instructions completely, use disposable gloves and protect work surfaces.

After the paint has been removed, wash all the parts thoroughly in soapy water to remove any final traces of the stripper, particularly before applying any new paint. Having revealed the original surface of the body, you can examine it for any flaws hidden by the paint. It may be cracked, in which case, it should be a simple matter to tape or clamp the sides of the crack together and run a line of liquid cement along the back. Holes may have been drilled for aerials and the like, which are no longer required. There may have been custom fins, louvres or scoops that are no longer needed, but which will have left their mark.

Holes can be concealed with body putty, but larger ones may need to be filled with a piece of plastic first, then finished with putty. Any items removed from the main parts will have left marks where they were glued in place. These areas will need rubbing down and possibly filling as well. In addition, some areas may be damaged with edges broken or such pieces as fin tips missing. Very small areas can be built up with putty and blended in, although anything larger will probably need some additional scrap plastic adding first. The replacement of the missing tip of a rear fin, so common on American cars of the fifties and sixties, may need a small hole to be drilled in what remains and plugged with plastic rod. This can be either sanded to shape or built up with filler.

On convertibles, one area that is extremely vulnerable to damage is the windshield surround, as it does not enjoy the support afforded by a sedan's roof. If this frame is broken, or missing, it can be built up from plastic strip, carefully cemented in place, then sanded to shape. Use the windshield glass as a template, but take care not to allow any glue to mar its surface. If necessary, cover both sides of the glass with tape, then tape it temporarily in place.

While on the subject of 'glass', clear plastic parts may be the most difficult to deal with when it comes to damage. You may be able to polish out small marks, using one of the modelling polishes, or possibly toothpaste, metal polish or kitchen cleaner. Larger blemishes may have to be sanded lightly first: use very fine wet-or-dry, aiming to remove all the blemish, then polish as described.

Clear styrene is brittle, and the most difficult faults to correct are cracks or, worse, where pieces have broken off. It may be possible to repair a crack by gluing, followed by careful sanding and polishing, which should remove most of the line. However, if bits are missing, the only solution will be to make new parts.

If you are very fortunate, you may be able to source a new screen from a similar kit that has been reissued. If the damaged piece is flat, or curved in one plane only, any glass can be replaced with acetate, or similar, gluing it in place with contact adhesive or—taking extreme care—with the tiniest amount of superglue. However, if the piece has compound curves, as have many windscreens, the only option will be to make a new one, and the only practical method of doing this is by vacuum forming.

Small vacuum forming machines are available and, for

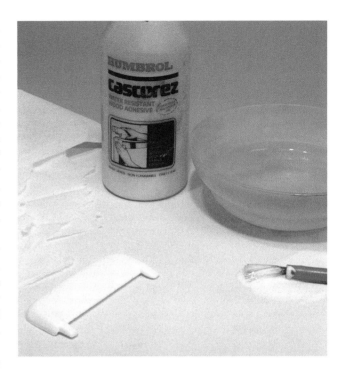

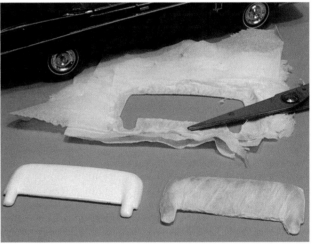

*Top right* **The folded boot had been lost, so a similar example was found and copied, using tissue paper soaked in PVA wood glue.**

*Above right* **When dry, the copy was cut from the surrounding tissue and peeled from the original.**

*Right* **The renovated kit, resplendent in Testors Burgundy Red Metallic. Bare-Metal Foil supplied the chrome and—in recognition of the fact that many old kits included a cuddly toy—the back seat features a giant teddy bear from a doll's house set.**

a time, Mattel sold home vac-form machines that still turn up in sales occasionally. Most modellers, however, will lack access to a proper vac-former. Fortunately, it is possible to make parts of this type by makeshift methods that are suitable for one-offs. You will need a heat source—a hot-air gun is best, but a large hair drier or an electric heater may also work—some plastic sheet and a master to mould over.

A piece of clear styrene sheet should be held in some sort of frame, perhaps cut from a piece of plywood. For one-offs, attaching the styrene to the frame with double-sided tape should work well enough.

If enough of the original part survives, it can be used as the master pattern. Any gaps can be filled with body putty and sanded smooth, being backed with plastic sheet if necessary. Of course, the fact that it is not clear does not matter. Back the whole piece with modelling clay for strength.

Heat the clear sheet, keeping the source moving to spread the heat evenly. Take care, for styrene will burn! Check the flexibility of the sheet by carefully tapping it with a finger—it will rebound when about right, although some experimentation may be required. Then, when the sheet

appears to be flexible enough, quickly pull it down over the master, and hold it there until the plastic has cooled. A proper vac-form machine will draw the air from beneath the plastic, pulling the sheet tightly on to the master, but for simple shapes this manual technique usually works well. Once cool, the sheet can be lifted from the master, and the excess trimmed off. Then, the new part can be cemented in place. Note that because the sheet was pulled over the master, the new part will be fractionally larger than the original, but for items such as windscreens, this may be of no consequence.

This technique need not be restricted to clear parts only; you can make other replacement parts in the same manner, using ordinary white polystyrene sheet. Just remember that a new part will always be slightly larger than the original.

To make a part that is identical in size to the master, you will need a female mould. If we assume that you already have one part, but need another, and that the shape is fairly simple without any undercuts, a female mould can be made quite easily. Push the original part into a block of suitable modelling material of the type that can be oven dried. Remove the part (hence the need for no undercuts, otherwise it would be difficult to remove the part cleanly) and dry the clay. To make a new piece, pour two-part resin, car body filler or similar into the mould. When this has cured, remove it and clean it up as necessary. The result will be a piece that is virtually identical to the original. When it has been super-glued into place and painted along with the rest of the body, you should not be able to tell the difference.

Chrome plated parts can cause another headache during reconstruction, as the plating—not being real chrome—will be very thin and may have worn off or, at the very least, lost its shine. The chrome strips around windows and along the sides of bodies can be finished with Bare-Metal Foil. This can also be used to repair other plated areas, such as bumpers, although sometimes it is less effective on very large areas. While paint straight from a bottle or aerosol is nowhere near as shiny as proper chrome—or foil—Humbrol

*Above left* **One of IMC's most famous kits is Bill 'Maverick' Golden's Little Red Wagon. Lindberg have reissued the kit, but this provided an excuse to renovate one of the original IMC versions, using Fred Cady's new set of LRW decals. Also to be included was Jimmy Flintstone's white metal figure of 'Maverick' himself.**

*Left* **The completed duo, the newer Lindberg version being on the left and the rebuilt IMC original—with Cady decals—on the right. 'Maverick' salutes both.**

silver from a newly opened tin does tend to be at its shiniest and can be used for small details. Also, Testors Chrome spray is about the shiniest straight from a spray can.

Parts can be rechromed, and companies in many countries offer this service. Your parts will go in with other items to be bulk plated. It is not that cheap, or convenient, but you may consider this a worthwhile option, particularly if you have a lot of items to be recovered.

However, most renovations will rely on the remains of the original finish, which will mean recovering as much of the surface as possible. Whatever you do, *don't* polish the plated parts—this is the quickest way of removing the very thin surface. In fact, any rubbing will do more damage than good. If the chrome is excessively dirty, gently wash it in warm soapy water, but keep any rubbing to the minimum.

Of course, many areas of a model where chrome is used need not be completely chrome. Grilles for example have a substantial amount of black in the recesses, so the tip about using a thin wash of matt black (see Chapter 6) can also apply to a rebuild. Sixties kits tended to have headlamp lenses moulded into the bumper and grille assembly, so they were chrome, too, but they need not be. They can be painted as described in Chapter 6, and there may be turn signals to paint, and a grille badge. So by the time all these details have been added in their correct colours, you may find that there is not much tarnished chrome left to worry about.

Other missing items could be wheels or tyres, although it is usually easy to source these from other kits or the garage companies. Accessory wheel packs are available and, provided you don't want genuine stock items, a set of aftermarket mags will probably suffice for a rebuild.

Engines can also be found from alternative sources, but this is one area where the problem can be solved simply by keeping the hood closed.

Interior renovation can be approached in much the same way as the body. Paint applied by hand comes off just as well (usually) as sprayed paint when you use a paint remover, and with the parts clean again, they can be rebuilt. Some early kits may have had upholstery material applied, which can cause problems depending on how it was held in place. If it was glued with contact adhesive, usually the glue will have dried up long ago and the material fallen off anyway. However, if something was used that has eaten into the seat's surface, this may need more cleaning up, and possibly even seat patterns rescribing. Alternatively, apply some new upholstery material.

The instruments should be clear again, having had any paint removed, and can either be carefully repainted or detailed with suitable decals of the dials. The steering wheel may be one item that is missing, but many kits contain two, or more, steering wheels and—if you are not worried about the rebuild being completely stock—the spare can be borrowed from another kit.

Overall, renovating an old kit requires a lot of effort, being far more arduous than building a new one straight from the box. But there will always be a special place in your collection for such a rebuild—especially if the original tooling has long departed to that great scrap-heap in the sky!

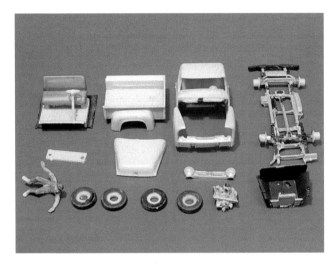

*Above right* **Renovation need not be restricted to larger scales. Here, Revell's 1:48 scale Ford pickup, which has seen better days, has been stripped down to its main sections. (This was done before the kit was reissued in the Selected Subjects Program.)**

*Right* **The Revell Ford pickup rebuilt as a USAF vehicle to transport the pilot of Collect-Aire's X-20 DynaSoar (a purely fictional craft, as the X-20 never got further than a wood and metal mock-up!).**

# Chapter Twelve

# THE COLLECTING PHENOMENON

When modern construction kits were first introduced, having built number one in a series, the modeller then wanted number two, three and so on. He, or she, didn't want number one again, it had to be something new. This process continued for many years, during which the model companies were constantly being encouraged to produce more new items. The concept of collecting model kits for their own sake, and the somewhat perverse notion that you went totally against their primary purpose—to be built—wasn't even contemplated. That notion was some way in the future.

But the world in general, and the West in particular, began to see a growth in the markets for nostalgic and collectable items and, frankly, anything and everything became collectable to someone. Even an item that, only a few years ago, you wouldn't have given house room may now have a value, so you can't afford to throw it away. Someone, somewhere, is bound to want it.

In the general toy market (where the model kit seems to have been placed, albeit reluctantly and somewhat inappropriately), first it was teddy bears and tin-plates, then trains and jigsaws, followed by die-casts and slot cars. The model kit could not be ignored, however, so these also joined the

ranks of the collectables. But there is a strange difference with kits. Toys came ready-made, and provided you didn't lose any parts of your original Corgi James Bond Aston Martin DB5, throw away the box or, heaven forbid, repaint it, it didn't lose any intrinsic value it might have acquired. But this does not apply to the Airfix version of the same car. In this case, you have to leave everything intact inside the box—and 007 has to take the bus instead!

As far as model kits are concerned, there was only one reason for manufacture, and that was for them to be built. Now, however, to be collectable, a model must remain unbuilt and intact, so a kit's entire *raison d'être* has been lost—it is doomed forever to remain in bits.

This phenomenon probably only started to rear its head in the late seventies. Until then, everyone was quite happy to buy a model, build it, buy another and so on. The idea of purposefully keeping a model unbuilt was not even contemplated. Yes, models did remain unbuilt, but this was usually a matter of practicality: you had bought more than you could possibly deal with at the time, but all would be assembled at some time in the future—well, that was the idea. It would be impossible to say exactly when model kits joined the ranks of collectables, but the interest became apparent when the prices of second-hand kits began to soar (even kits that were not deemed collectable). Suddenly, the models that one had amassed, and which provided convenient and cheap loft insulation, became expensive loft insulation! When you read that someone had just paid $200 for a kit that cost you 9/6d in 1964, and you still had that kit stored away, you had to think long and hard before deciding to dig it out and build it.

There may be another aspect to this hankering after the older style of kit, concerned more with the fact that we like to think of 'old' equating to 'different'. Older models, like their full-size equivalents, do tend to look more individual when compared with their modern counterparts, which look as though they've all been designed by a computer in a wind-tunnel (which, of course, they have). Never mind that older cars were less reliable, had the drag coefficient of a brick and the fuel consumption of a 747. These old kits represent styles of cars that are no longer made and rarely seen, so they have come to be sought after. In the past, each country's cars did tend to look as if they belonged to that country. A Mini would not be mistaken for a Beetle, or a Citroën 2CV, or a Fiat 500, and certainly not for a Cadillac Eldorado

**There are many aspects of collecting. You might, for example, want to collect all the models of a particular vehicle, such as all the issues of AMT's Bigfoot monster truck. Here, all the 'Bigfeet' are shown together.**

Biarritz. In the main, even multi-nationals kept to particular products for specific countries. Ford of Britain's cars were different to those produced by Ford of America, or Ford of Germany for that matter. When the company released the Probe for the British market not long ago, it was the first American-built Ford sold in the UK since the Model T!

Admittedly, for many years it was the notion of car manufacturers to build a 'world car', but this never seemed practical. A car designed to potter around the winding country lanes of rural Britain would not necessarily be suitable for the interstates of the American mid-west. Now, however, cars around the world are becoming indistinguishable from one another, being set apart by only relatively minor idiosyncrasies that individual nations still demand. Japan has manufacturing plants in many countries; BMW and Mercedes build in the US; and General Motors are selling right-hand-drive Cadillacs for the UK market. Perhaps the 'world car' has arrived, but it may be of less interest to modellers than the Mini and '59 Eldorado.

The kit companies themselves were relatively slow to react to the new collecting phenomenon, or maybe they saw it and chose not to acknowledge it. After all, they were in the business of supplying new kits. In fact, tooling was regularly modified for new releases, especially 'annual' car kits, which were changed to match their full-scale counterparts. When the natural lifetime of one subject was considered exhausted, companies would reuse parts of the moulds for an entirely different model, or drastically modify the original into something completely different. (And the idea that, once deleted, a kit was gone forever was even reflected by the kit numbering system, old numbers being issued to completely new kits. Aurora commonly followed this practice, particularly in the early years.)

But that's not to say that kits were not reissued at all; many were, often with a few updated parts or a change of decals. The use of kit tooling has to be maximized in an attempt to keep ever spiralling costs to a reasonable level.

**Star Cars**—vehicles featured in films and TV programmes— are popular with collectors, and with old kits invariably the price will be higher than for a standard version of the car— should it exist—even if the 'star' connection is purely the box. The Ghostbusters' Cadillac ambulance, however, came as anything but stock, although the parts could be used to build something approaching the stock vehicle (see Chapter 8).

However, in the early eighties, Revell were the first to acknowledge that there was a market for nostalgic, if not exactly collectable, kits: they introduced the History Makers. These ran as two series in 1982 and 1983, comprising a range of old kits, many of them dating back to the late fifties, which had not seen the light of day since then.

The kits were issued in new History Makers boxes, not in reproductions of the original boxes, with new layouts for the instructions. However, they gave builders and the new breed of model enthusiasts—the collectors—an opportunity to acquire kits that they had probably never seen before, only glimpsed in old catalogues or read about in magazine articles. They also allowed those who *did* have original unbuilt kits, still in their boxes, a chance to build kits that had gone from loft insulation to investment.

Although many cars are among the most sought after kits in the collectable market, it is surprising that none was included in either History Makers range. Initially, two were advertised in early editions of the History Makers Series I catalogue—the multi-piece-bodied Porsche Carrera in competition form and the 1960 Corvette—but neither actually appeared. (Ironically, the History Makers and similar ranges are themselves collectable these days.)

Following Revell's lead, Monogram (at that time, still independent from Revell) produced their own range—the Heritage Edition—but it, too, was surprisingly bereft of anything automotive. Modellers had to wait until the nineties, when Revell-Monogram (by then, one company) introduced the Selected Subjects Program—followed by Ertl's similar

*Above* **Box art is one of the key features that determine the collectability of a kit. These examples for Monogram's Li'l Coffin show car range from the original issue (top) to the most recent (bottom), which was released to celebrate the company's 50th anniversary. In the long term, it will probably be the first and latest issues that become the most collectable.**

*Below* **Monogram's Li'l Coffin show car, subject of several reissues over the years.**

Buyer's Choice—for old car kits to reappear in force. Moreover, this time, they were issued in more or less original-style boxes.

These models really were aimed at the collector as well as the builder, so much so that there were great protests when the first SSPs arrived, as they still bore their original copyright dates, addresses and any other text related to the first issue. Those who had held on to original kits saw the prices dropping, especially as, to the uninitiated, the new versions looked exactly like the old kits. There were even isolated cases of unscrupulous individuals passing them off as such.

Consequently, later SSPs began to include new copyright dates, any new addresses and the licensing logos from the full-size car manufacturers that were becoming obligatory. This time, it was—relatively—straightforward to identify these kits from the originals. The kit companies seemed to have achieved the correct balance: they were close enough to the originals to satisfy most builders, but had sufficient detail changes to pacify the collectors.

In reality, though, none has matched an original completely, and the most reliable means of checking is to look at the decal sheet of any kit under dispute. Even if the model appears to be a genuine original, but could be a first-run SSP, the decals will have the current wording on the back.

In addition, many of the boxes have a different depth to the originals, and many more have completely different dimensions, the original size no longer being manufactured. Usually, the printing will not appear the same, either. In the main, the original artwork will have vanished long ago, so the artwork for an SSP has to be scanned from an original box. Any changes are made in the computer, using a graphics package, and the modified artwork printed out. However, this invariably makes the new box look slightly different to the old: if anything, the image may appear sharper, more 'electronic', while the colours may be more intense. Plus, the box itself may be assembled in a completely different manner, which applies to many Revell kits, particularly from the late fifties and early sixties

These days, virtually all boxes, from all manufacturers, are designed to fold flat for ease of transport and storage.

The old kits from Revell—and many others, including Aurora, Lindberg and Monogram—were issued in rigid boxes, while the artwork was printed separately on paper and glued around the box. The paper was slightly glossy, as well, and gave the image a particular look, which you do not get when the artwork is printed directly on to the box. The former method is far too costly today (although there are exceptions), so this difference is an immediate give-away when it comes to distinguishing new from old.

Overall, however, the Selected Subjects Program has worked extremely well and, at one point, Revell and Monogram were reissuing 48 kits a year between them. Not all were cars, and some may not have been as desirable as others, but the scheme was well received by builders and collectors alike. More recently, the yearly total has dropped slightly, and the reissues have combined both names. Even some Aurora kits have also reappeared, as Monogram bought most of the Aurora tooling in the late seventies. However, they did not buy the name, so the Aurora logo cannot be used on the boxes. Instead, there is original Aurora artwork with the Revell-Monogram logo.

It is even more ironic that the items forming the main part of the kit—the plastic parts—are, in many ways, the least important in the collectors' market. AMT's ever popular 1953 Ford F100 pickup has been offered in a variety of styles of box and forms of kit over the years, and has almost always been available. But even though the parts have remained more or less the same, it is the older box styles that are more valuable, the original Trophy Series box not having reappeared to date as a Buyer's Choice.

However, examples of the very first issue of a kit may not necessarily be worth the most. A more recent issue may have had a far shorter run, or be linked to a specific series, and can acquire a greater value. AMT, particularly, issued kits in many forms, and their 1950 Ford in its Tournament of Thrills guise, for example, is arguably worth more than the original Trophy Series version. Even more up to date examples, where a specific series has been formed, can create their own devotees. AMT reissued many kits in their Customizing Series as late as the eighties. The '49 and '50 Fords were available in this way, as was the '49 Mercury, and these kits still contained all (or most—a few items did change) of the parts from the original 3-in-1 Trophy Series. This particular series also contained a set of modelling tools for those who wished to go in for complete restyling.

This type of reissue was continued with the introduction of the Prestige range, another set of classic cars—Trophy Series and some 'annuals'—being reissued in Prestige boxes. This time, each kit offered the bonus of a desk-top pen holder display base.

Ertl, who had owned AMT since 1982 and MPC since 1986, had already offered some limited reissues through their subscription magazine, *The Blueprinter*. Individual 'collectable' kits were made available, although only to those who subscribed to the magazine. They also came in plain boxes bearing *The Blueprinter* name, not reproductions of the originals. However, in this way, builders at least managed to obtain reissues of such kits as the Monkeemobile, the Munster Koach, Drag-U-La and the

*Top* **Revell and Monogram started the recent craze for reissuing old kits with their Selected Subjects Program.**

*Above* **Many subjects attract collectors, such as anything to do with James Bond. The original Airfix kit (top right) and its US version (top left) are both worth a great deal in mint, unbuilt condition, as is the Aurora lookalike (bottom right). The Doyusha version (bottom left) is a new kit, but when discontinued, it will probably join the ranks of collectables.**

1964 Ford Galaxie. Ertl then introduced their own version of the SSP series, calling it Buyer's Choice.

As with the SSPs, kits in the Buyer's Choice series have also reintroduced boxes with the original artwork, and most include reproductions of the original instructions (complete with intriguing details, such as references to AMT aerosol paints, which haven't been made for many years). AMT-, MPC- and Ertl-labelled kits have been reissued (no Esci so far), at least one of which dates back to 1961.

Currently, the concept of reissuing car kits in this manner has remained almost the sole prerogative of the American companies. This aspect of the hobby originated there, and other companies around the world are much younger when it comes to car kits. However, Tamiya are reissuing some of their original 1:12 scale Formula 1 cars, in more or less original-style boxes, while Airfix have reissued many of their 1:32 scale 'modern' cars. However, none of

Items from within the model industry are also becoming collectable, such as this type of assembled display model, which was intended for shops. These were very common in the early sixties, but they haven't existed for many years. Because they are card, they tend not to survive particularly well, although they do have the advantage that if one good original can be found, others can be colour photocopied. Their popularity has also prompted Revell-Monogram to produce their recent range of card dioramas of typical American subjects—diners, motels and gas stations.

the latter has appeared in its original style of packaging—a polythene bag with a header—probably because it is not the most practical method these days.

Products from companies that are no longer in existence are also sought by collectors, as a finite number of kits will have been made. As far as cars are concerned, IMC (the Industro-Motive Corp.) have their particular enthusiasts. Although they never produced that many kits, the majority were cars, and most of those were in 1:25 scale. Currently, Testors own the IMC name and some of the tooling, but other moulds went to Union in Japan. That company produced their own boxes for the kits, which included the VW Beetle, Chaparral and MkII Ford GT. However, no one appears to have seen the tooling since, and although Testors leased some of the IMC tooling that remained to Lindberg— the Little Red Wagon, Cougar II and Mustang II—these other kits remain obstinately absent. IMC is also collectable by dint of distribution—or lack of it. IMC kits were never officially distributed in the UK when they were current, so they are probably more collectable in Britain than in the US. With others, such as the Airfix 1:32 scale car range, the opposite may apply for similar reasons.

Of the names no longer in existence, Aurora is a collectable favourite world-wide, perhaps *the* favourite, although they covered far more subjects than simply cars. Much Aurora tooling was destroyed, either because it was damaged accidentally and deemed not worth repairing, or simply due to that early phenomenon when new kits were always wanted to replace the old ones that had had their day. Monogram acquired much of the Aurora tooling that remained when the company ceased trading, and although they have reissued some of Aurora's 1:25 scale cars (no 1:32 to date), the originals in Aurora boxes will obviously be more valuable than the Monogram reissues. (The more so because, as mentioned, when Revell-Monogram do issue Aurora originals in Aurora-style boxes, they cannot use the Aurora logo.)

To date, perhaps the oddest aspect of this whole business has come about through the arrival of a new company, Playing Mantis. In the main, they specialize in toys (interestingly, many based on designs that started as kits), but they have also taken a completely new approach to the collectable kit market, having identified the desirability of old Aurora kits that can never be reissued (even by R-M), as the tooling no longer exists. What Playing Mantis have done, under their Polar Lights name (note the play on 'Aurora'!), is to make completely new tools for styrene copies of old Aurora kits, something no one has done before. Resin copies are regularly made of old kits, but no one had thought about making completely new steel tooling—mostly, it must be said, because of the cost. However, with the soaring values of old Aurora kits, obviously it appeared worth the risk.

These new kits are based on genuine originals, from which the tooling will have been copied. They may not necessarily be absolutely identical, most being subjected to minor changes here and there to benefit the detailing or assembly, but to all intents and purposes, they are originals. This even applies to the box art, following the lead of the SSP and Buyer's Choice series. The Aurora box art is reproduced almost as per the original, in this case even to the use of semi-glossy paper, although the boxes are of the fold-flat type, not rigid. Currently, the Polar Lights series concentrates on horror subjects, but the vehicle caricatures— Mummy's Chariot, Frankenstein Flivver and the like—have been retooled, as has Carl Casper's The Undertaker dragster, one of the very few Aurora originals of show cars.

To date, Polar Lights are the only company to completely retool collectable kits, although Revell-Monogram have had to make some new tooling for their SSPs. The clear windshield parts for the Futura and Club de Mer had to be retooled, as the original mould could not be located.

Collecting, by its very nature, can also involve specific subjects, which may span manufacturers' boundaries. One very specific collectable subject is Star Cars, vehicles that have featured in movies or television series, or that are associated with a star's name. These are approaching several hundred in total, if you include everything that has a vague connection with the subject, and some kits have a very tenuous connection, simply borrowing a name. Many of these kits have become highly desirable in their own right, and a kit with a star connection—even though this may only be in the box art—is usually worth substantially more than an identical kit with identical parts, but packaged in a 'non-star' box. Although the kits may still be relatively recent, once they go out of production, they tend to increase in value out of all proportion. When MPC first produced their *Dukes of Hazzard* kits, they sold in the hundreds of thousands, but as soon as they were deleted, the price of the General Lee skyrocketed (even though it was not particularly accurate!).

The Star Car connection also seems to work in retrospect. Although, in recent years, Batman has been associated with the Big Screen, many people remember the TV series and the 'original' Batmobile. This was built by George Barris, who converted the Lincoln Futura show car. This Batmobile was never offered as a 1:25 scale kit (by mainstream companies at least), only in 1:32 by Aurora (together with some Japanese copies). However, a Lincoln Futura kit was made by Revell, being one of their earliest in 1:25 scale and still, at that stage, using a multi-piece body. At the same time, they also made a General Motors show car, the Pontiac Club de Mer. Of the two, however, the Futura was the more collectable, much of the interest being because of the Batman connection. Resin copies of the Futura were around for some years, together with a resin version of the Batmobile based on the Futura kit, but not the Pontiac. However, luckily for all of us (except the producers of the resin kits—and those with stashes of original Futura kits!), both the Futura and Pontiac were reissued in Revell's SSP series and, at last, could be built as intended.

The availability of the Futura kit also allowed the somewhat bizarre possibility of being able to build the replica Futura, as well. Since the original had been converted into the Batmobile, one enthusiast re-created the full-size car in fibreglass. This, in turn, became a Star Car, as it was featured in the pilot episode of the TV series *Viper!* It is such oddities that make the hobby even more interesting.

The original Futura and Pontiac also introduced another area of collectability, as a sub-division of Revell products—the S-type kits. These carried an advertising device on the sides of their boxes to indicate that they were moulded in the new-fangled plastic, styrene, and not acetate, so you needed Revell's new—Type 'S'—styrene cement. (It may not be too surprising to learn that acetate kits had the letter 'A' on the sides of their boxes—see Chapter 1.) There were never that many cars in the S-range, but an enthusiast will tend to collect all S-type kits—planes, spacecraft, ships, the lot, along with the cars. In this case, however, you definitely must have the original boxes, as this is one box-art feature that is usually removed from SSP reissues.

Of course, 'collecting' can be a slight misnomer when it comes to the kit industry. It automatically conjures up a vision of all those kits that will remain forever unbuilt, but it really means no more than you 'collect' something!

*Above* **Revell-Monogram have recently issued older kits in collector tins. Not all the kits may be collectable in their own right, but the tins have given them a new lease of life.**

*Above* **Of course, one aspect of collecting is to obtain some sort of association with a person or place. Here, Ed Roth himself has signed the box for his new Beatnik Bandit II kit.**

**Reissued kits in collector series are not absolutely identical to the originals, so much of the value attached to the latter should not be affected. Although AMT's '64 Mercury Marauder kit seems identical (the Buyer's Choice label is on the cellophane wrapper), close inspection reveals AMT's address on the original upper box, but not on the new version.**

## Chapter Thirteen

# THE GALLERY

Previous chapters have dealt with specific aspects of building model cars. This chapter is an opportunity for me to show off some special models that are personal favourites, either as individual models or in scenes using the models. Some came from my own ideas, others were inspired by a variety of sources. Perhaps they will give you some ideas of your own. Each is accompanied by an explanation of how that particular set-up came about together with any other points of interest.

Many of the models shown here have been included in dioramas, which in amateur model making tend to be built as permanent arrangements—the materials are glued down and the cars and figures fixed in place. (This is the case with the *Back to the Future* diorama described in Chapter 10.) However, when building miniature scenes for special effects purposes, which forms a large part of my professional work,

I rarely make them in that way. Instead, they are built 'soft': materials are scattered over the base—rocks, vegetation, buildings and structures simply being placed in position without fixing. This allows them to be repositioned for alternative shots. When the set-up is finished with (and the rushes viewed to check that all is okay!), the diorama is broken up and stored for future use. Although the pictures in this chapter were set up for still photographs rather than the moving image, most were produced using the special-effects technique, and if you look closely you will see that many figures, and some equipment, reappear in different scenes.

I would also point out that these scenes are meant to be viewed as models, not as accurate representations of reality. Therefore, many of them lack backgrounds, or have simplified backgrounds, although even these can be effective in the right setting.

**Combining kits is a favourite for model companies, as it can give older models a new lease of life. AMT have done this many times over the years, but one of their most popular was titled Diamond in the Rough. It combined one of AMT's best selling kits, the 1953 Ford F-100 pickup, with a trailer that had been included in several other kits over the years. To this was added the 'Diamond', a car that had lain abandoned in the corner of some field, but which—to the expert eye—had definite restoration potential. For this, the tooling for AMT's 1940 Ford sedan was altered slightly to include dented panels and broken glass. (Later, the tooling was returned to pristine**

**condition.) With this kit there was a great opportunity to do precisely the opposite of what is usually done with car models—this time make it as dirty and grubby as possible. There are various ways of producing a rusty finish, but one of the simplest is to paint the car first in rust red, then cover it with a thin top colour that can be rubbed away to reveal areas of 'rust'. Alternatively, rust can be dry brushed on to appropriate areas afterwards. Fillers, such as talc or French chalk, can be added to paint to make large areas of really crumbly rust. No figures were included in the kit, but I added two Fujimi mechanics to the scene.**

*Right* A favourite whenever it's taken to model shows, this set-up utilizes models from three different manufacturers. The tow vehicle is the Revell (just pre-Revell-Monogram) Dodge Ram VTS; the trailer comes from the Revell Chevy Van and Race Rig (where the van was actually a Monogram original); and the Viper GTS on the trailer is an AMT kit (Revell also make a version).

*Left* Normally, models are made of full-size originals, but occasionally the reverse applies. Tom Daniel designed the Red Baron show car for Monogram, who made it as a kit in two scales—1:24 and 1:12. The latter also included the miniature Fokker Triplane and 'Red Baron' skull, which also turned up in later issues of the smaller model. However, the design was then built as a full-size car, using a Pontiac OHC straight-six instead of the Mercedes aircraft engine of the model.

*Below* Combining my two personal modelling interests—cars and space—is not always easy. This scene was based on a photograph taken in 1931 of a vehicle used by Robert Goddard, who launched the world's first liquid fuelled rocket in 1926. After the initial flights in Auburn, Massachusetts, the test site was moved to Roswell, New Mexico. To transport the rockets from the workshop to the launch tower, Goddard used a converted Model T Ford, nicknamed 'The Hearse'. The model is based on an AMT Model T pickup: the bed became the trailer, while a van-type body was built on to the chassis. It is displayed with a background representing the launch site (to 1:48 scale, approximately half that of the kit, to give the scene some depth). The figures were converted from Hasegawa aircraft maintenance personnel, while the gas tanker was modified from a 1:43 scale die-cast.

*Above* Emergency vehicles have formed a small, but important, part of car and truck modelling. In recent years, Jo-Han's kit production has tailed off, but in the past, they have made some excellent kits in this area, including the

Cadillac ambulance. This has been available in two stock forms: one run by a fire service (left), the other hospital based. A third utilized the bodywork for the twin-engine drag strip monster, the RRRRoarin RRRRambulance!

*Below* Two subjects that go naturally together—especially on the US West Coast, and in many a Beach Boys track—are cars and surfing. In this beach scene, we are looking away from the sea (which avoided creating the surf itself!), the sand dunes having been created by carving expanded polystyrene into natural shapes. Some of the colouring was ordinary household emulsion, peat being used to fill gaps. Then various

coloured flocks and sawdust were sprinkled over the top before adding suitable vehicles and figures. Clockwise, from top left: Revell VW van, which came with the surfboards in the centre of the picture; a VW Beetle with a surfboard from Hasegawa; AMT's Surf Woody; and Ed Roth's Mini powered Surfite (Revell), which came with the Tiki Surf Club hut. Figures are a mix of Tamiya, Rabbit Models and Hasegawa.

*Right* Unfortunately, the body of this Revell Porsche 928 melted while being dried too close to a heat source, so the whole lot was consigned to the spares box. However, when AMT started releasing the famous 'Bigfeet', it seemed too good an opportunity to waste, so the Porsche was flattened slightly more and the glass crazed with liquid cement.

*Below* A specific modelling interest of mine are Star Cars— vehicles that have appeared in movies and TV programmes, or are associated with stars' names. This scene depicts a show where some Star Cars have been put on display. Anti-clockwise, from left: *The Beverly Hillbillies* truck, based on a 1921 Olds (MPC); Dan Tanner's 1957 Ford Thunderbird from *Vega$* (AMT); the car from UNCLE, as used in *The Man from UNCLE* (AMT); KITT from *Knight Rider* (MPC/Airfix); the Panthermobile, as used in the titles for *The Pink Panther* cartoon series (Eldon/Doyusha); and Ian Fleming's other movie creation, Chitty Chitty Bang Bang (Aurora).

*Right* This, I admit, is not a new idea. It was inspired by the ZZ Top album *Afterburner* and the accompanying videos, which show their '33 Ford turned into a space shuttle. This conversion, seen next to the standard Monogram ZZ Top Ford kit, used one of the car kits and a Tamiya 1:100 scale Orbiter. The front half of the Ford was combined with the back half of the Orbiter, and a great deal of filling and sanding was required before the top coats of colour could be applied. These consist of Testors transparent Hot Rod Red over Guards Red.

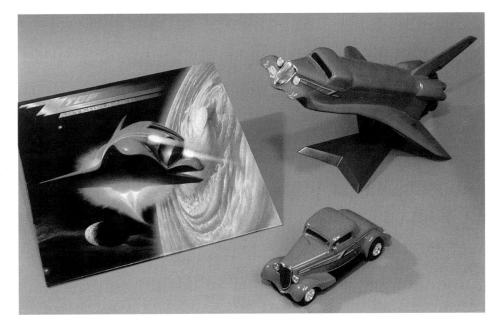

*Right* Building models can be informative as well as pleasurable. These three kits show how the dragster has developed over the years. In front is the generic slingshot design of the sixties (AMT); in the centre, an early rear-engined type, developed by Don Garlits, from the late seventies (Revell); and at the rear, one of the most recent monsters, with a far longer body, giant wing and small front wheels (Revell).

*Left* One of the strangest 1:25 scale car kits ever produced was the AMTronic. Although many kit companies have produced futuristic vehicles, usually based on factory show cars, AMT went to great lengths to produce a model of what a 'visitor from the 21st century'—as the adverts proclaimed—could actually look like. The AMTronic was two cars in one. When combined, it was an interstate cruiser that ran on wheels initially, but on appropriate roads, could use a hovercraft effect and magnetic guidance rails for control—the passengers could sit back and watch the video screen in the rear compartment. For city use, the front section could be detached and driven like a conventional car. The kit also included a cardboard diorama display base.

*Right* The future as it should have been. Another simple way to combine two unrelated subjects, and two different scales. The connection is the era, as Revell's Lincoln Futura (1:25 scale) nicely complements the Werner von Braun 3-Stage Rocket (1:288 scale), made originally by Strombecker and reissued by Glencoe Models. Both date from the fifties, when there was great enthusiasm for technology in general, and the future in particular. Incidentally, while only one original Futura was built, it was variously painted in pearlescent greenish-blue and bright red. However, the black exterior with red interior had been contemplated and, of course, is very similar to the Batmobile scheme.

*Above* Although, in 1:24/5 scales, American—and increasingly Japanese and German—machinery dominates, the British car industry (as was) hasn't done too badly. Here, we see enthusiasts gathered at a car meet where British sports and sporty cars are being celebrated. From the left, they are: Sunbeam Tiger (AMT), 1930 Bentley 4.5 Litre (Heller), Lotus Esprit (Monogram), MG TC (Monogram), Morgan 4+4 (Tamiya), Triumph TR3A (Gunze Sangyo); Jaguar XK120 (Monogram); racing Mini Cooper (Tamiya); Austin-Healey 100-Six (Revell), MGB (Aoshima/Revell AG), Ford Capri (Doyusha). In the centre is the E-Type Jaguar (Revell). Figures come from Rabbit Models, Tamiya's Campus Friends and Tyresmoke Products, (although the last are no longer available, as the company has gone out of business.)

*Below* Rush hour in Gotham City. Some Star Cars have been produced in greater numbers than others, and—in recent years at least— Batman's mode of transport has proved very popular. This street scene shows Batmobiles from: (back row, left to right) the third movie, *Batman Forever* (Revell); the TV series, a 1:22 slush moulded resin kit (Lunar Models), *Batman—the Movie* (AMT); (front row, left to right) the fourth movie, *Batman and Robin* (Revell-Monogram); and fifties-era comic strips (Horizon). The background was produced from roughly cut featherlight board—the idea was to create the mood rather than precise straight lines—fixed together with a glue gun. A few girders and ladder sections were added, then everything was sprayed matt black, after which vague patterns were sprayed in grey through a mask.

*Left* Rally cars have been popular over the years with many kit companies. They have ranged from the famous Monte Carlo Mini to recent four-wheel-drive Subarus. However, this Mercedes Unimog was the winner of the truck class in the 1985 Paris-Dakar Rally, one the most gruelling in the world. Revell AG produced the Unimog in 1:24 scale from new, and the basic kit has since been offered in a wide variety of other forms: from fire tender, through military vehicle, to snow plough. The base for this scene was borrowed from a diorama featured in Chapter 10, while the figures are from Fujimi.

*Left* This scene is another that allows the combination of kit subjects. Polar Lights have re-created many of the original Aurora kits by literally retooling them, the original moulds having been destroyed long ago. Here, their new model of the classic *The Addam's Family* house overlooks the reissue of Carl Casper's The Undertaker custom dragster.

*Facing page, bottom* Dioramas can be created with very little background material. Here, a wooden base has hoardings that came as pre-printed cards (from Tyresmoke—unfortunately no longer available). To this, a variety of cars, vans and figures has been added, together with a few other accessories. The vehicles are the Hasegawa VW delivery van, Monogram's Chevy 20 van (as featured in Chapters 6 and 7) and Tamiya's Mini Cooper. The figures are from Tamiya's Campus Friends, which includes the scooter and rider, and Rabbit Models. One enthusiast looks over a go-kart (centre), an old AMT accessory, while downstage left are two pedal cars, both resin kits from Grandpa's Toys. The Flyer cart and tool box (foreground, far left) came with AMT's Meister Brau Puller Tractor.

*Below* **Until the Tamiya model of the classic Jaguar MkII came along (left), the only example in 1:24 scale was the Small Wheels kit (right) which, unfortunately, is no longer made. This was in white metal and included disc wheels (the Tamiya kit has wire wheels). The metal kit was acquired for conversion into the personal transport of one Chief Inspector Morse, for which it only needed the correct maroon finish, vinyl roof, wing mirrors and radio aerial plus, of course, the appropriate number plate.**

*Above* **The starting point for these two Star Cars, from the cult movie *Two-Lane Blacktop*, was actually the license plates. These—produced as photo-etched parts by Tyresmoke Products—simply needed the Pontiac GTO and '55 Chevy to complete them. The Chevy was heavily modified from stock and, consequently, needed the most work. The conversion used a Revell kit as a basis and also featured such items as the two drag slicks in the trunk, the internal gas cap (just visible on the left) and a tool kit, courtesy of the Fujimi Garage and Tools set. The Pontiac (Monogram) required far less conversion work, but it did need hand-made decals. (Details of the full conversion appeared in the November 1998 issue of *Scale Models International*.)**

# REFERENCES

You can build a model car kit 'straight from the box'. However, there may come a time when you require some additional features, extra materials, special parts or a specific reference to further a modelling topic. The range of references world-wide is vast, and there are many starting points for achieving such aims, from magazines and books to the local library. You can examine full-size vehicles at car shows and in museums, many of which specialize in partic-ular subjects. And, of course, the ever increasing scope of the Internet allows information on virtually any subject you want to be called up with a few clicks of a mouse and a local telephone call.

The information provided here is a jumping-off point for following up references, whether it be to the companies themselves, the vast after-market sector, specialist dealers in collectable kits or the World-Wide Web.

THE MAINSTREAM COMPANIES

This section lists the world's mainstream manufacturers of car kits. Note that some have free 'hotline' phone numbers, but at present these only work within that country. In the main, these companies do not sell directly to the public; the addresses are given for enquiries only.

**Academy Model Co. Ltd,** Seoul, South Korea
UK distributor, Toyway Ltd; US distributor, Minicraft
**Accurate Miniatures Inc.,** 100 Center Street, Charlotte, NC 28216-4064, USA; tel. (704) 391-1176, fax. (704) 391-0975
UK distributor, Amerang Ltd
**Airfix,** Humbrol Ltd, Marfleet, Hull HU9 5NE, UK; tel. 01482 701191, fax. 01482 712908, hotline 0800 132379
**AMT,** The Ertl Co. Inc., Highways 136 & 20, PO Box 500, Dyersville, IA 52040-0500, USA; tel. (319) 875-2000, fax. (319) 875-8263, hotline (1-800) 553-4886
Ertl Europe Ltd, Falcon Road, Sowton Industrial Estate, Exeter EX2 7LB, UK; tel. 01392 445434, fax 01392 445933
**Aoshima Bunka Kyozai Co. Ltd,** 12-3 Ryutsu Center, Shizuoka City, Japan; tel. 54-263-9198, fax. 54-263-2521, URL http://www.aoshima_bk.co.jp
UK distributor, Amerang Ltd; US distributor, SATCO
**Dapol Railways Ltd,** Lower Dee Exhibition Centre, Mill Street, Llangollen, Denbighshire LL20 5RX, UK; tel. 01978 860584, fax. 01978 861928, e-mail <dapol.drwho@btinternet.com>
**Dragon Models Ltd (DML, Shanghai Dragon and Kirin),** Kong Nam Industrial Building, 10/Fl, B1 603-609 Castle Peak Road, Tsuen Wan NT, Hong Kong; tel. 2493-0215, fax. 2411-0587
UK distributor, RIKO International; US distributor, Marco Polo
**Doyusha,** 21-27-4, Arakawa, Arakawa-ku, Tokyo, Japan
UK distributor, Amerang Ltd
**Esci,** The Ertl Co. Inc., Highways 136 & 20, PO Box 500, Dyersville, IA 52040-0500, USA; tel. (319) 875-2000, fax. (319) 875-8263
Ertl Europe Ltd, Falcon Road, Sowton Industrial Estate, Exeter EX2 7LB, UK; tel. 01392 445434, fax. 01392 445933
**Fujimi Corp.,** 4-21-1, Toro, Shizuoka City, Japan 422
UK distributor, Amerang Ltd; US distributor, MRC
**Glencoe Models,** PO Box 846, Northboro, MA 01532, USA; tel. (508) 869-6877, fax. (508) 869-2462
UK distributor (some), Pocketbond Ltd
**Gunze Sangyo Inc.,** 1-8-1, Yanagibashi, Taito-ku, Tokyo 111, Japan; tel. (03) 3863-1300, fax. (03) 3863-1310
UK distributor, Amerang Ltd; US distributor, Marco Polo
**Hasegawa Seisakusho Co. Ltd,** 3-1-2, Yagusu Yaizu Shizuoka, 425-8711, Japan; tel. (054) 628-8241, fax. (054) 627-8046
UK distributor, Amerang Ltd; US distributor, Marco Polo
**Heller SA,** Chemin de la Porte BP5, 61160 Trun, France; tel. 02.33.67.72.84, fax. 02.33.36.57.07, e-mail <73674.131@compuserve.com>
UK distributor, Humbrol Ltd
**Italeri,** via Pradazzo 6, 1-40012 Calderara di Roma, Bologna, Italy; tel. 39-51-726037, URL http://www.italeri.it
UK distributor, RIKO International; US distributor, Testors
**Jo-Han,** SeVille Enterprises, 17255 Moran Avenue, Detroit, MI 48212, USA; tel. (313) 366-2230, fax. (313) 366-2230

**Lindberg,** Craft House Corporation, 328 N. Westwood Avenue, Toledo OH 43607; tel. (419) 536-8351, fax. (419) 536-4159
UK distributor, Richard Kohnstam Ltd
**Matchbox** *see* Revell AG
**Minicraft Models Inc.,** PO Box 3577, Torrance, CA 90501, USA; tel. (310) 325-8383, fax. (310) 539-2018
UK distributor, Toyway Ltd
**Monogram** *see* Revell-Monogram
**Pocher,** Rivarossi s.p.a., via Pio XI 157-159, 22100 Como, Italy; tel. 031-541-541, fax. 031-540-752
UK distributor, Richard Kohnstam Ltd
**Polar Lights,** Playing Mantis, PO Box 3688, South Bend, IN 46619-3688, USA; tel. (219) 232-0300, fax. (219) 232-0500, hotline (1-800) MANTIS-8, e-mail <sales@playingmantis.com>, URL http://www.playingmantis.com
UK distributor, Amerang Ltd
**Promodeler** *see* Revell-Monogram
**Protar snc,** via Fucini 1, 40033 Casalecchio di Reno, Bologna, Italy; tel. (051)-57-54-92, fax. (051)-57-53-59
UK distributor, Models of Distinction
**Revell AG,** Henschelstrasse 20-30, D-32257, Bunde, Germany; tel. 0-52-23-965-0, fax. 0-52-23-965-488, URL http://www.revell.de
UK distributor, Binney & Smith (Europe) Ltd; US distributor, Revell-Monogram Inc.
**Revell-Monogram Inc.,** 8601 Waukegan Road, Morton Grove, IL 60053-2295, USA; tel. (847) 966-3500, fax. (847) 967-5857, hotline (1-800) 833-3570, URL http://www.revell-monogram.com
**Scale Models,** 301 5th Street NW, PO Box 327, Dyersville, IA 52040-0327, USA; tel. (319) 875-2436, fax. (319) 875-2753
**South-Eastern Finecast,** Glenn House, Hartfield Road, Forest Row, East Sussex RH18 5DZ, UK; tel. 01342 824711, fax. 01342 822270
**Tamiya Plastic Model Co.,** 3-7 Ondawara, Shizuoka City, Japan; URL http://www.tamiya.com
UK distributor, Richard Kohnstam Ltd; US distributor, Tamiya America Inc.
**The Testor Corp.,** 620 Buckbee Street, Rockford, IL 61104, USA; tel. (815) 962-6654, fax. (815) 962-7401, URL http://www.testors.com
UK distributors, RipMax Plc (some), Pocketbond Ltd (some)

**Importers and distributors**

UK
**Amerang Ltd,** Commerce Way, Lancing, West Sussex BN15 8TE; tel. 01903 752866, fax. 012903 765178
(Accurate Miniatures, Doyusha, Fujimi, Gunze Sangyo, Hasegawa, Imai, Polar Lights)
**Binney & Smith (Europe) Ltd,** Ampthill Road, Bedford MK42 9RS; tel. 01234 360201, fax. 01234 342110
(Revell AG, Revell-Monogram, Matchbox)
**Models of Distinction,** 23 The Woolmead, East Street, Farnham, Surrey GU 7TT; tel. 01252 716981, fax. 01252 718374
(Protar)
**Pocketbond Ltd,** PO Box 80, Welwyn, Herts AL6 OND; tel. 01707 391509, fax. 01707.327466, URL http://www.btinternet.com/~pocketbond
(Glencoe Models—some, Testors—some)

**RIKO International/Richard Kohnstam Ltd,** 13A-15 High Street, Hemel Hempstead, Herts HP1 3AD; tel. 01442 261721, fax. 01442 240647 (Dragon, Italeri, Lindberg, Tamiya)
**RipMax Plc,** Ripmax Corner, Green Street, Enfield EN3 7SJ; tel. 0181 804.8272, fax. 0181 804.1217, e-mail <ripmax@compuserve.com>, URL http://ourworld.compuserve.com/homepages/ripmax (Testors—some)
**Toyway Ltd,** PO Box 55, Letchworth, Herts SG6 lSG; tel. 01462 672509, fax. 01462 672132
(Academy, Minicraft)

USA
**Marco Polo Import Inc.,** 532 S. Coralridge Place, City of Industry, CA 91746; tel. (818) 333-2328, fax. (818) 333-7870, URL http://www.marcopoloimport.com
(DML/Dragon, Gunze Sangyo, Hasegawa)
**MRC,** 200 Carter Drive, Edison, NJ 08817; tel. (908) 248-0400, fax. (908) 248-0970
(Fujimi)
**SATCO,** PO Box 38, 11426 10th Street, PO Box 38, Stanley, IA 50671-0038; tel. (319) 634-3999, fax. (319) 634-3998, hotline (1-800) 700-2826
(Aoshima)
**Tamiya America Inc.,** 2 Orion, Aliso Viejo, CA 92656-4200; tel. (714) 362-2240, fax. (714) 362-2250
(Tamiya)

WHO OWNS WHAT?
Sometimes, it is useful to know where original tooling has gone, as this, at least, will give you a starting point. However, the following list is by no means definitive. Although a manufacturer may have access to tooling, this does not mean that a kit will be reissued.

**Aurora** Most tooling is owned by Revell-Monogram. Some kits have been reissued under the Monogram and Monogram-Europe names, while others have been offered with original Aurora box art (bearing the R-M logo) in the Selected Subjects Program. Some tooling was destroyed in Aurora's early days, leading to Polar Lights making new tools for many classic Aurora kits.
**Frog** Most tooling went to the Soviet Union (as was—actually the Ukraine), the kits being reissued under the Novo label. Revell AG have access to much of the aircraft range, and have released many, but none of the cars. The name Frog was recently acquired by the Anglo-Singapore group Amaquest.
**Gakken** Much of the car tooling is with Academy and Minicraft.
**Gowland & Gowland** The Highway Pioneers are currently with Dapol, who have been reissuing them during 1998.
**Hawk** The tooling is with Testors.
**Hubley** Many of the 1:20 scale metal kits are issued by Scale Models (as Hubley). Some of the tooling for the 1:24 scale kits is with Minicraft.
**IMC** Much is owned by Testors, and some kits have been issued by Lindberg. However, some tools went to Union in Japan and, apparently, never returned.
**ITC** Glencoe Models own the rights to ITC tooling, but the only cars to have been issued are some of the Precision Miniatures.
**Merit** Some tooling is with SMER (Czech Republic); the whereabouts of the rest is unknown.
**MPC** Most tooling is with Ertl. The kits continue to be issued under the AMT name and, occasionally, under MPC in the Buyer's Choice series.
**Renwal** Most tooling is owned by Revell-Monogram, although some (apparently no automotive subjects) has been sold to Skilcraft (part of the Craft House Corp., with Lindberg).
**SMP** The SMP range of cars was incorporated into the AMT line when AMT bought the company.
**Strombecker** Glencoe Models have the rights to much of the Strombecker tooling, but to date no cars have been reissued.

THE SPECIALIST GARAGE COMPANIES
Although it is relatively simple to list the mainstream model kit companies, the same cannot be said for the garage companies. Those specializing in automotive subjects run into the hundreds, so only a selection can be listed. However, see ORGANIZATIONS AND MAGAZINES for a publication that contains a listing of over 400 suppliers of car modelling products.

Most supply by mail-order, and where they take the usual credit cards this is noted by (C) after the entry. UK distributors are only listed where they deal with one company only. However, many of the items will be available from other specialist importers.

Many of these companies are one-man operations, so it is advisable to send either a stamped addressed envelope (SAE) inland, or adequate

International Reply Coupons (IRCs)—available at Post Offices worldwide—if you are in a different country, for replies.

**All American Models,** 22 South 16th, Lafayette, IN 47905, USA; tel. (317) 423-4565, e-mail <aamresin@aol.com>
Resin parts, bodies and kits. List available for large SAE (C).
**Bare-Metal Foil Co.,** PO Box 82, Farmington, MI 48332, USA; tel. (248) 477-0813, fax. (248) 476-3343, e-mail <72314.3322@compuserve.com>, URL http://www.bare-metal.com
Bare-Metal Foil.
**Detail Master,** PO Box 1465-D, Sterling, VA 20167, USA; tel. (703) 404-3630, fax. (703) 404-3631, order hotline (1-888) 338-5798, e-mail <detlmastr@aol.com>, URL http://www.detailmaster.com
**Fred Cady Decals,** PO Box 576, Mount Prospect, Il 60056, USA
Special decals. List available for SAE/IRCs.
**Grandpa's Toys,** PO Box 255, Jackson Center, OH 45334, USA
1:25 scale resin pedal cars and other accessories.
**Jimmy Flintstone,** PO Box 371, Hales Corners, WI 53130, USA; tel. (414) 425-9592, fax. (414) 425-4828
Resin figures and car bodies. Catalogue available (C).
**Mad Dog Models,** Ron Bolton, 3693 Hackett Avenue, Long Beach, CA 90808-2415, USA
Resin bodies. Catalogue available for SAE/IRCs.
**Mini Exotics,** 936 Peace Portal Drive, PO Box 8014, Blaine, WA 93251, USA; tel./fax. (604) 585-4146
Resin bodies and conversion kits. Catalogue available for large SAE.
**The Modelhaus,** Don Holthaus, 5480 Traughber Road, Decatur, IL 62521, USA; tel. (217) 864-4402
Resin bodies. List available for SAE/IRCs.
**Parts By Parks,** 501 North 2nd Avenue, Marshalltown, IA 50158, USA; tel. (515) 752-3866
Turned aluminium parts.
**Rabbit Models,** 1 St Peter's Close, Eastcote, Ruislip, Middx HA4 9JT, UK; tel. 0181 429 3761
White metal figures, mostly in 1:24/5 scale.
**SATCO,** American SATCO, PO Box 38, 11426 10th Street, Stanley, IA 50671-0038, USA; tel. (319) 634-3999, fax. (319) 634-3998, hotline (1-800) 700-2826
Tyres. Also supplier of US versions of Aoshima kits with left-hand drive. Catalogue available (C).
**Slixx Decals,** 13075 Springdale Street, Suite 456, Westminster, CA 92683, USA; tel./fax. (714) 891-4212
Special decals, notably for US race cars. Catalogue available (C).
UK distributor, Hannants
**Tru-Match,** Realistic Racing Colors Inc., 1811 Ruffin Mill Circle, Colonial Heights, VA 23834, USA; tel. (804) 526-5074, fax. (804) 526-4547
Special paints, providing exact colours for race cars.

**Paint removal**
Two specific products are made for removing old paint from models. If you cannot locate either product in your usual model shop, contact the company direct for a local supplier.

**Modelstrip,** Oakwood Lodge, Aylmerton, Norwich NR11 8RA, UK
**Strip-A-Kit,** Hanger 3 Arlee, PO Box 361, Arlee, MT 59821-0361, USA; e-mail <doghaus@montana.com>

(Please note that the UK company Tyresmoke Products, whose products are mentioned in the text, are no longer trading.)

SPECIALIST DEALERS AND SUPPLIERS
With the rapid increase in the collectability of plastic kits, there has also been a growth in companies that specialize in obtaining hard-to-find models. The following companies deal exclusively in car models, include them in their lists, or cover a particular aspect of car modelling, such as supplying accessories. Most issue catalogues, lists or brochures. All offer a mail-order service and, mostly, take credit cards—indicated by (C) after the entry.

**Car Kits,** 101 Kensington Road, Southend-on-Sea, Essex SS1 2SY, UK; tel. 01702 615397, fax. 01702 615397
Specialist car kit dealer. Catalogue available (C).
**Collect-Aire Models,** 186 Granville Lane, North Andover, MA 01845, USA; tel. (508) 688-7283, fax. (508) 685-0220
General collectable kits, including a few cars. Catalogue available (C).
**Collectakit,** 35 Chapel Avenue, Addlestone, Surrey KT15 lUH, UK; tel. 01932 840766
General collectable kits, including automotive. Publisher of *The Enthusiast's Guide to Airfix Models.*

# REFERENCES

**Comet Miniatures,** 44-48 Lavender Hill, Battersea, London SW11 5RH, UK; tel. 0171 228 3702, fax. 0171 924 1005
Wholesale and retail, mostly science fiction, but many Star Cars. Catalogue available (C).

**Four Star Collectibles,** PO Box 658, Dracut, MA 01826, USA; tel. (603) 635-7639, e-mail <abfgl4a@prodigy.com>, URL http://pages.prodigy.com/4star
General collectable kits, including cars. Catalogue available.

**H.G.Hannant Ltd,** Harbour Road, Oulton Broad, Lowestoft, Suffolk NR32 3LR, UK; tel. 01502 517444, fax. 01502 500521, e-mail <sales@hannants.co.uk>, URL http://www.hannants.co.uk
London retail shop: 157-159 Colindale Avenue, London NW9 5HR; tel. 0181 205 6697
Wholesale and retail, mainly aircraft and military, but also cars. Catalogue available (C).

**Hobby Bounties,** 865 Mountbatten Road, #02-91/92, Katong Shopping Centre, Singapore 1543, Singapore; tel. 4401890, fax. 3441782, e-mail <amaquest@pacific.net.sg>
Wholesale and retail, mainly science fiction, but some cars, especially from Far Eastern companies. Catalogue available (C).

**Hobby Heaven,** PO Box 3229, Grand Rapids, MI 49501, USA; tel. (616) 453-1094, fax. (616) 791-9295
The major specialist collectable car kit dealer in the USA. Also supplier of new kits. Catalogue produced three times a year (C).

**John F. Green Inc.,** PO Box 55787, Riverside, CA 92517, USA; tel. (909) 684-5300, fax. (909) 684-8819, e-mail <info@greenmodels.com>, URL www.greenmodels.com
Collectable kits, mostly science fiction, but some cars. Catalogue available (C).

**King Kit,** Springhill Trading Estate, Shifnal, Shropshire TF11 8DR, UK; tel. 01952 405020, fax. 01952 405030, e-mail <1060554.1147@compuserve.com>
General collectable kits, including cars. Catalogue available (C).

**Marshall Auto Supplies,** 19 Prestwood Road West, Wolverhampton, West Midlands WV11 IRJ, UK; tel. 01902 861422, fax. 01902 688869, e-mail <106456.1162@compuserve.com>
Supplier of, mostly, US accessories. Catalogue available.

**Samone Hobbies,** PO Box 42, Darlington, DL1 2XP, UK; tel./fax. 01325 358991
General collectable kits. Catalogue available.

**Scale Auto Parts (UK),** Fingy Nest, Dunmow Road, Takeley, Herts CM22 6SP, UK; tel. 01279 871615
Supplier of, mostly, US accessories. Catalogue and newsletter available.

## ORGANIZATIONS AND MAGAZINES

For builders and collectors of all kit subjects, *the* organization is the Kit Collector's Clearinghouse. It is run by John Burns, and the subscription includes a bi-monthly magazine, the *KCC*, which contains articles and classified ads. John Burns also compiles and publishes the *Collectors Value Guides*, which list values for collectable kits. Contact John Burns, KCC, 3213 Hardy Drive, Edmond, OK 73013, USA; e-mail <cheersjwb@aol.com>.

**International Plastic Modellers' Society** (IPMS) was formed in the UK, but now has groups world-wide. There are many local societies and special interest groups (SIGs), including some for cars and other vehicles.
UK enquiries: IPMS, Neil Wharton, 35 Lea Close, Broughton Astley, Leicestershire LE9 6NW; e-mail <nick@ipmsuk.globalnet.co.uk>
US enquiries: *IPMS Journal*, PO Box 6138, Warner Robins, GA 31095-6138; tel./fax. (912) 922-3918
**Model Car Buyer's Guide,** PO Box 1465-C, Sterling, VA 20167, USA; tel. (703) 404-3630, fax. (703) 404-3631
Lists over 400 US and foreign model car companies—mainstream and specialist. Price $4.95, plus p&p (C).

### Modelling magazines
*Collectible Automobile* 7373 N. Cicero Avenue, Lincolnwood, IL 60646-1613, USA
*Car Modeler* Set up as a companion magazine to *SAE*, now under the Kalmbach Publishing banner.
Kalmbach Publishing Co., 21027 Crossroads Circle, PO Box 1612, Waukesha, WI 53187-1612, USA; tel. (414) 796-8776, fax. (414) 796-1383, e-mail <editor@carmodeler.com> and <customerservice@kalmbach.com>, URL http://www.carmodeler.com
*Fine Scale Modeler* Premier American general modelling magazine.
Kalmbach Publishing Co., 21027 Crossroads Circle, PO Box 1612, Waukesha, WI 53187-1612, USA; tel. (414) 796-8776, fax. (414) 796-1383, e-mail <customerservice@kalmbach.com>, URL http://www.finescale.com

*International Tamiya Magazine* Features some car modelling articles, many as full-colour spreads.
Nexus Specialist Interests, Nexus House, Boundary Way, Hemel Hempstead, Herts HP2 7ST, UK; tel. 01442 266551, fax. 01442 266998
*Model Car Journal* For many years run directly by the editor, Dennis Doty. However, from issue 124, the name has been incorporated into *Toy Cars & Vehicles*.
*Toy Cars & Vehicles*, Krause Publications, 700 East State Street, Iola, WI 54900-0001, USA; tel. (715) 445-2214, fax. (715) 445-4087, e-mail <kpinfo@krause.com>, URL http://www.krause.com
*Plastic Fanatic Magazine* Specialist car modelling magazine.
Plastic Fanatic Inc., PO Box 15308, Honolulu, HI 96830-5308, USA; tel. (808) 220-4734, fax. (808) 737-0454
*Scale Auto Enthusiast* One of the oldest American model car magazines.
Kalmbach Publishing Co., 21027 Crossroads Circle, PO Box 1612, Waukesha, WI 53187-1612, USA; tel. (414) 796-8776, fax. (414) 796-1383, e-mail <editor@scaleautomag.com> and <customerservice@kalmbach.com>, URL http://www.scaleautomag.com
*Scale Models International* The premier British general modelling magazine, incorporating Freewheelin', written by the author.
Nexus Specialist Interests, Nexus House, Boundary Way, Hemel Hempstead, Herts HP2 7ST, UK; tel. 01442 266551, fax. 01442 266998

## THE INTERNET

If you are already on-line, you will need no explanation as to what the Internet is all about. However, if you are one of those who wonders if it is all worth it, firstly understand that it is still all so incredibly new. Although elements associated with it, such as electronic mail, have been around for a while longer, the Internet, as it exists today, dates from the mid-nineties, and it is growing, without exaggeration, every second.

This is not meant to be a primer on the Internet—many books and magazines are available for that purpose—but it is an attempt to explain how this electronic medium can assist model making.

Basically, the 'net can be split into three sections (although there are many sub-sections). First, there is e-mail—electronic mail—which considerably speeds up communications world-wide, and is really a cross between sending a postcard and a telex, although additional files (which can be a separate list, a graphic, or a photograph) can usually be attached. So if you want to send a picture of your recently completed model of an E-Type Jag electronically to a friend in Australia, it can be done.

As an extension to e-mail came the newsgroups, where most of the interactive correspondence goes on. You select (termed 'subscribe') the newsgroups you want and the next time you are connected to the system it will download them. The idea is that initially you just 'lurk'—read, but don't reply—for a period of time to get the feel of the group, then you can post your own comments and queries. Most newsgroups also contain an FAQ (frequently asked questions) section, which helps to define what is deemed appropriate behaviour for that group.

The specific newsgroup for model kits is <rec.models.scale> where currently 99% of the model orientated chat goes on. Currently, there are over 26,000 newsgroups, and many Internet service providers (ISPs) do not allow access to them all for various reasons, ranging from the time it takes them to access the material to some not being deemed suitable for a broad audience. Some model related newsgroups are in the <alt> section, which not all ISPs supply, as it is totally unregulated. Thus, if you want, say, <alt.binaries.models.scale>, you will have to choose an appropriate ISP.

The third main section associated with the Internet is the World-Wide Web itself, which is where all the Internet sites are situated and which can bring you details of—virtually—any subject you require. Once you subscribe to an ISP, you will obtain access to the 'net and, along with it, one of the browsers, the two most popular being Netscape and Explorer. These, in turn, give you access to the search engines—Yahoo, Lycos, Excite, Alta Vista and the rest—which perform the task of searching for your topic.

As an example, I wanted details of the Plymouth Hemi 'Cuda, used by Nash Bridges in the TV series of the same name. A simple "Nash Bridges" placed in a search engine window produced a number of sites, including the official TV company site, one of which featured photographs of the car.

Many model companies are already on-line with both e-mail and web sites, and the URLs (uniform resource locators), or addresses, for the sites have been given where relevant. Note that although most include the usual <www>, this is not always the case, Compuserve, for example, may use <ourworld> instead, so although the rules are usually straightforward, if the system doesn't appear to be working, it can often be worthwhile trying different combinations. More model companies—large and small—are coming on-line all the time, so any listing will be immediately out of date. However, if you are uncertain as to whether or not a company has a web site, besides trying the search engines, you can simply try putting in <www.*company name*.com>, which will often bring up the appropriate site.